D1104859

AVID

READER

PRESS

Gambler

Secrets from a Life at Risk

Billy Walters

with Armen Keteyian

Avid Reader Press

NEW YORK LONDON TORONTO
SYDNEY NEW DELHI

AVID READER PRESS
An Imprint of Simon & Schuster, Inc.
1230 Avenue of the Americas
New York, NY 10020

First Avid Reader Press hardcover edition August 2023

AVID READER PRESS and colophon are trademarks of Simon & Schuster, Inc.

For information about special discounts for bulk purchases, please contact Simon & Schuster Special Sales at 1-866-506-1949 or business@simonandschuster.com.

The Simon & Schuster Speakers Bureau can bring authors to your live event. For more information or to book an event contact the Simon & Schuster Speakers Bureau at 1-866-248-3049 or visit our website at www.simonspeakers.com.

Interior design by

Manufactured in the United States of America

10 9 8 7 6 5 4 3 2 1

Library of Congress Cataloging-in-Publication Data

ISBN 978-1-6680-3285-5
ISBN 978-1-6680-3287-9 (ebook)

For Susan, for believing in me and always being there

For Grandmother, for raising me the right way

Contents

Contents

Prologue

October 11, 2017.

It's two in the morning and sleep is nothing but a memory. I'm flat on my back on a three-inch mattress eyes wide open, staring at the sagging bottom of a top bunk. The air reeks like a truck stop toilet.

Ten of us are crammed into a tiny room (eighteen by twenty-two feet) built to house four Navy airmen. It's my first night inside Federal Prison Camp (FPC) Pensacola. A fellow inmate would later describe the look on my face that day as "shell-shocked." I had officially entered another dimension of time and space. A single thought was running on a continuous loop through my head:

I am seventy-one years old. How in the hell did I get here?

Logistically, the answer was simple. After my felony convictions on ten counts of insider trading, a private prison consultant I had hired to advise me on a number of matters recommended two prisons—Taft Correctional Institution near Bakersfield, California, or FPC Pensacola in the Florida Panhandle.

I dismissed Taft because of the poor air quality in the Central Valley. Pensacola provided a far shorter commute for my wife, Susan, from our Louisville home. The facility also offered a Residential Drug Abuse Program, which I certainly qualified for given my history with alcohol. If I successfully completed the nine-month program, it could cut a full year off my five-year sentence. I also believed that Pensacola would provide a more temperate climate and soothing gulf breezes.

Big mistake.

As I prepared to report to prison, fast-moving Hurricane Nate was bearing down on the Gulf Coast. I worried that, if Susan and I waited too long to leave Kentucky, I'd miss my Tuesday morning reporting time.

We arrived on Saturday and checked into a Pensacola hotel. As Nate hit with a fury that night, Susan and I huddled in our room while the wind whistled outside. On Tuesday morning we woke up in a daze.

Susan couldn't bear to say goodbye at the prison gate. Instead, we hugged and kissed in private. My parting words were meant to ease her fear.

"I can handle this as long as you're okay," I said.

"I'll be okay," she replied. "Don't worry about me."

Shortly after 6:00 a.m., I walked into the administrative office at FPC Pensacola, a single bag of belongings in hand.

"William Walters, reporting," I said.

The intake office was called Control. I got the point when a corrections officer greeted me with a bark: "Stand right there!" I stood diligently until another officer appeared.

"Stand outside," he ordered.

As I would soon discover, the serene exterior of FPC Pensacola was a mirage. The cozy church chapel and campus-like setting were cruel illusions that masked the conditions inside. The admission process is designed to dehumanize and deliver a single, stark message:

We own you.

I stood alone outside until 7:30 a.m., when a corrections officer named Green approached to begin the intake process—or tried. Officer Green proved incapable of operating a new electronic fingerprinting machine and left me holed up in a tiny cell, air-conditioning blasting away. I sat alone, waiting, waiting, and more waiting. He finally showed up again around two in the afternoon with an old-fashioned fingerprint pad.

I was then passed on to another officer, Ms. Gamble, who would be my cheerful counselor for the next thirty-one months. She warmly inquired if I had eaten. I told her no, so she went to the cafeteria and returned with something I did not recognize. My appetite disappeared with my introduction to prison food.

Next came a visit to Laundry, where I was outfitted by an inmate named Rock in five sets of polyester prison "greens"—shirts, pants, T-shirts, etc.—along with an ill-fitting pair of steel-toed shoes. The shoes were so tight that I lost a toenail the first day, my sock soaked in blood.

After the Laundry visit, I was returned to Ms. Gamble. We walked up three flights of stairs to Dorm C, the top floor of a crumbling red-brick building. Two hundred men lived on my floor when it was fully occupied, ten or twelve to a room. Another two hundred or so were housed in Dorm B, one floor below. The administrative offices were on the ground floor. A separate "A" dorm, with a different layout, could hold as many as 275 more inmates.

The rooms in "B" and "C" dorms were identical. Each was crammed with five or six bunk beds and small lockers for storing personal belongings. A single community table was bolted to the floor. Black mold stained the walls. Down the hall were two main bathrooms with a half-dozen stalls and curtained showers. A river of urine ran through the bathrooms. The smell of farts and rancid food further fouled the air.

If you research FPC Pensacola, it's listed as a minimum-security federal prison located on Saufley Field, an auxiliary area of the local naval air station, the home of the Blue Angels, the famed U.S. Navy Flight Demonstration Squadron. Pensacola is about 175 miles from the state capital in Tallahassee and sixty miles east of Mobile, Alabama. Tourists come to Pensacola for the sandy beaches, waterfront restaurants and bars—charms that were no longer available to me.

Dig a little deeper and you'll find the area is home to jet-fuel-soaked air, bone-chilling winters, unremitting rain, and some of the worst drinking water in the United States.

In 2009, *Forbes* magazine ranked FPC Pensacola as the second "cushiest prison" in the country—a country club for white-collar criminals who enjoyed swimming and golfing at the taxpayers' expense. If that was ever true, the place had changed dramatically by the time I arrived.

The ramshackle dorms, built in the 1940s, were falling apart. Air chillers ran at arctic levels except in summer, when you needed them most. During North Florida winters, temperatures could dip into the twenties at night. To keep from freezing, my fellow convicts and I had to purchase sweatpants, sweatshirts, and T-shirts, as well as winter gloves, while smothering ourselves in blankets at night.

Day two brought more bad news. Dr. Luis Berrios examined the short list of drugs prescribed by my longtime physician and promptly eliminated two of them. He replaced an anti-inflammatory drug to ease the pain of three shoulder operations with a different prescription that tore up my stomach.

Dr. Berrios was kinder to my feet than my stomach. He took one look at my lost toenail and issued me a pair of softer shoes.

When I walked into the cafeteria, I took a seat away from everyone else. As I stared at a lump of something I could not identify on my plate, an inmate from a nearby table spoke up.

"William, come over and sit with me."

His name was Luis Duluc, better known as Louie. The son of two physicians, Louie came from a wealthy family in the Dominican Republic. In December 2014 he had been sentenced to eleven years in prison for his role in a massive scheme perpetrated by the physical therapy rehabilitation company he owned.

By that point, I was on prison overload and didn't want to step on any toes, bloodied or not. But Louie seemed to have a handle on things. So I started asking questions.

"What do you do here?"

"How do you get a good job?"

"How's the commissary?"

Louie had all the answers and knew all the angles. He'd been inside Pensacola for nearly three years.

The next time I bumped into Louie, word had spread that the new guy, William, went by another name. And had something of a reputation.

"So, William," Louie said, "do people call you Billy?"

I gave Louie a sheepish grin and said, "My friends do."

My life ran off the rails when I was just eighteen months old. After my father died at age forty-one, my twenty-five-year-old mother hightailed it out of town, leaving three young children in the care of separate relatives.

It took me decades to get back on track. You see, from my teenage years to my early forties, I lived on the edge and flaunted it. I was a heavy drinker, a chain-smoker, and a gambling addict with a capital *A*. I hung out with all sorts of questionable characters while hustling pool, cards, golf, and every other game of chance. I risked life and limb practically every day of my boom-and-bust existence.

I married for the first time as a seventeen-year-old. Within a year, I became a father. By age twenty-three, I was twice married with three kids I loved but hardly knew.

Back in my wildest gambling days, I was tossed into a car trunk at gunpoint and beaten beyond recognition. One day, I woke up lucky to be alive and, finally, a light flickered in my muddled brain.

This is not working. I'm a dead man if I don't change my ways.

I quit drinking and smoking cold turkey at the age of forty-two. But without a doubt, my smartest move was marrying my third wife. During our forty-six years together, Susan Walters has been unflinching in her loyalty, even when I screwed up badly. We met during the darkest of times—I was a bankrupt, divorced alcoholic whose young son had just been diagnosed with a terminal brain tumor.

Susan inspired me to be better. She is my best friend and helped make me the man I am today.

By age thirty, I finally had matured enough to be a loving husband and father. My transformation didn't happen overnight. I slipped and slid backward a dozen times or two. But I beat my addictions and overcame my worst vices to become a successful gambler, entrepreneur, businessman, investor, philanthropist, father, and husband.

I still gamble, but I approach it strictly as business. I stay out of casinos (mostly) and wager on football, golf, and a few other sports. News organizations ranging from ESPN to *60 Minutes* have called me the most successful sports bettor in history. I don't place bets on whims or team loyalties or tips overheard in the barbershop. My research is far more sophisticated than most (as you will see), and I have a small army of experts behind me.

However, I'm not just a bettor. I've made hundreds of millions in the stock market and business as well as sports gambling. With my earnings, I built a legitimate group of businesses from scratch that included residential and commercial real estate, thirteen golf courses, and twenty-two car dealerships.

Now for the ironic part: when I was indicted for the sixth time, having beaten all but the only one I was guilty of—a bookmaking charge in Kentucky—I was in my seventies and enjoying as clean and righteous an existence as I had known in my lifetime.

All hell broke loose in 2011 after I took a shot at the U.S. Securities and Exchange Commission in the final minute of an otherwise flattering profile on *60 Minutes*.

My brief tirade at the tail end of a terrific interview no doubt ticked off the powerful forces that control Wall Street, including federal prosecutors who had pursued me for twenty-seven years. I was sued by the SEC, investigated by the FBI, indicted by the U.S. Department of Justice, and audited by the Global High Wealth Industry Group, the so-called "Wealth Squad" of the IRS—all at the same time.

You could say that I was hounded and harassed by people who were desperate not just to put me in prison but bury me.

The Justice Department did not take me down when I was gambling and drinking and scrambling day-to-day while surrounded by mobsters, hustlers, and shysters. I wasn't busted because I'd run afoul of mob enforcer Tony "the Ant" Spilotro or other nefarious types from my more reckless days.

No, I was nailed because of my stock trading and association with Wall Street legend Carl Icahn, professional golfer Phil Mickelson, and Dallas community leader Tom Davis, then on the board of Dean Foods.

Carl is the only one of the three I still respect. As for Mickelson, well, I will have a few things to say about him. Bottom line, if he had simply taken the stand in my trial and told the truth about the public information I had provided him, I believe that I never would have stepped foot inside a rat-infested Pensacola prison.

The truth is, Phil liked to gamble as much as anyone I've met. And I've known some of the biggest gamblers in the world. To give you an idea of how much Phil liked to gamble, he called me in September 2012 from the Medinah Country Club outside Chicago with an astounding request. He asked me to place a $400,000 wager for him on his own United States team to beat the Europeans in the 39th Ryder Cup.

I'll be the first to admit that I'm wired differently. My brain never rests. I am impatient and can be intimidating when my temper gets triggered. That volatility has done me more harm than good. Like many people, I've made a few enemies because of it.

I was not a good bet to even graduate high school, but I made it thanks to an advanced degree in street smarts. Then again, how smart could I be to go broke so many times in my life?

I turned seventy-six years old while chronicling my story in these pages. The characters you will meet include a Scorsesean cast with nicknames like Jim Dandy, Puggy, Sarge, Treetop, Cabbage, and Texas Dolly, along with famous and infamous folks both worldly and underworldly, such as my mortal enemy, the disgraced former casino czar Steve Wynn.

I will share some tales that I hope will enlighten, entertain, and educate you. I'd also like to get a few things off my chest, to share some information you haven't seen before. And I'll say things that probably will make some folks unhappy.

And you know what I say to that?

Exactly what Muhammad Ali, the pride of my native Kentucky, wrote in his autobiography, *The Greatest*.

I'm a fighter
I believe in the eye-for-an-eye business
I'm no cheek turner
I got no respect for a man who won't hit back
You kill my dog you better hide your cat

But let's be clear about one thing: My motivation is not to extract revenge. No, I have devoted years to writing this book for three reasons:

First, to inspire those who struggle with addiction to lead better lives. I truly believe that my story will help people. Maybe you have given up hope. Maybe you grew up under tough circumstances. Maybe you were raised without a parent. I want you to understand how and why you can overcome adversity and succeed.

Second, to expose the full truth about the felony convictions that landed me in a federal prison for thirty-one months. To explain how federal prosecutors colluded with senior agents at the FBI to bring charges of insider trading after decades of investigating me on phony allegations of illegal bookmaking. How they broke the law in their pursuit of me, covered up their wrongdoing, lied and then admitted their crimes only after getting caught.

And third, to share my secrets on sports gambling. To reveal for the first time the details of a handicapping, betting, and money management system that made me a successful gambler. Secrets that will help casual, recreational, and professional bettors tip the odds a bit in their favor.

My philosophy on life is simple: You come into this world with nothing, and you leave with nothing. So seize every opportunity to leave a legacy that might inspire others to make the most of their time on earth. At the end of the day, there are two people you can't bullshit—yourself and your maker. You will be judged by the way you've lived and by whether you've followed your servant's heart.

For the longest time, I was anything but a shining example. But I firmly believe that we can benefit more from studying the lives of sinners than saints.

After reading my life story, I hope you feel the same way.

1

Chicken or Feathers

It's five thirty in the morning West Coast time on a jam-packed college football Saturday. I'm in my home office in front of three computer screens pulsing with colors, squares, and numbers that only the most sophisticated sports bettors and handicappers understand.

White squares. Red squares. Black squares. Pluses. Minuses. Cities and states masquerading as teams. Baltimore. Detroit. Dallas. Kentucky. Michigan. Minnesota. Texas. The battle lines drawn over the point spread—the posted number that bookmakers believe to be the difference between two competing teams.

I've been up since 4:30 a.m. double-checking games and adjusting *my* predicted numbers developed in concert with my brain trust, a collection of some of the smartest minds and most sophisticated numbers guys on earth.

The games with odds to my liking are listed on a legal pad to my right along with the corresponding power ratings. The greater the difference between my rating and the point spread (also known as the "posted line"), the more I'm going to bet.

My wagers could vary from as little as $8,000 on an early-season college basketball game to more than $3 million on an NFL playoff game.

Now and then, I look up from a desk cluttered with pens, pads, tiny candies, and breath mints to the array of computer screens positioned in front of me. There, I see the latest barrage of ever-shifting information from more than four dozen sportsbooks around the world.

The data include the latest figures on point spreads, moneylines, first- and second-half totals, weather conditions, player injuries, starting times, and more. All of it is fluctuating in real time with white boxes turning red then black as the line adjusts.

The computer to my left lists the day's college football games. My middle screen reflects a similar list of college basketball contests. The screen on my right offers information on tonight's NBA games and tomorrow's NFL schedule.

For the next eighteen hours, the only times I'll get up from my chair will be to eat and go to the bathroom. I'm in the zone, orchestrating bets on about 150 games and tapping into more than 1,600 betting accounts worldwide through an intricate network of proxies—"beards," "runners," and "partners." To hide my identity and maintain an edge against our competitors, my team deploys tactics and equipment not unlike an undercover spy operation, including disguises and voice-altering devices.

Why?

Because today I will have $20 million in play.

And tomorrow I'll wake up and do the same thing.

I'm a gambler. But not just any gambler.

My wagering has run the spectrum—pitching pennies in dingy racetrack bathrooms, hustling pool in back-road shanties, betting thousands of dollars on a single putt on golf courses, and losing millions in Las Vegas casinos. And that doesn't include betting billions of dollars collectively on nearly every American sport.

For nearly twenty-five years, I was an addict. I could not control the craving, the need to be in on the action, especially when drinking—dual dependencies that wreaked havoc on my life and the lives of those around me.

They say smart people learn from their mistakes, but it took me a long time to figure that out. Fortunately, I am extremely hardheaded and driven. It's also possible that I simply outlasted my mistakes.

Today, sports betting is Big Business and getting bigger and bigger year after year. Maybe I was just ahead of my time.

This transition began in 2018, when the U.S. Supreme Court struck down the 1992 Professional and Amateur Sports Protection Act (PASPA), which had made it illegal to bet on sports in any state but Nevada.

In doing so, the Supreme Court allowed states to determine whether to legalize sports gambling. As I write, betting is legal in sportsbooks and on mobile apps in thirty-eight states, the District of Columbia, and Puerto Rico. According to the American Gaming Association, a record $100 billion was wagered in 2022 with commercial sportsbooks in the U.S. alone.

The rapid growth of this new industry has been fueled by full-throated endorsements from major sports leagues that for many years opposed any form of legalized betting. Their past position is epitomized by this quote from NFL commissioner Pete Rozelle: "I have frequently expressed my opinion that legalized gambling on sporting events are destructive to the sports themselves and in the long run injurious to the public."

Rozelle is long gone (RIP Pete) and so is the NFL's anti-gambling stance. With an eye on their bottom lines, professional football and its heavy-breathing brethren—MLB, NBA, NHL, and the PGA Tour—have joyfully jumped into bed with the likes of DraftKings, FanDuel, Caesars Entertainment, BetMGM, and Fanatics. In 2023, NFL owners officially welcomed gambling, voting to allow sportsbooks in stadiums to operate on game days.

The leaders of these sports now acknowledge what they've known for years—Americans love to bet on games. By making it legal and lawful for people to participate in sports gambling, online and otherwise, the government is creating jobs, generating tax revenues, and cleaning up the criminal element.

Gambling websites are now taking wagers on everything from football to boxing to tennis to UFC and fantasy sports. I wouldn't be surprised if they started accepting bets on whether it will rain before dinner tomorrow night. The bet-takers and bookmakers promote their services with a blizzard of ads featuring star athletes and celebrities including Peyton, Eli, and Archie Manning, Jerry Rice, Barry Sanders, Kevin Garnett, Jamie Foxx, Kevin Hart, and J. B. Smoove.

How fierce is the fight over this booming market? In November 2021, the New York State Gaming Commission granted mobile sports-betting licenses in their state for the next ten years to a pair of entities representing the biggest names in the gaming industry. One of the groups included Caesars Sportsbook, Wynn Interactive, and Resorts World; the other consortium included FanDuel, Draft-Kings, BetMGM, and Bally's Interactive.

The collective price they paid to host New York's betting operations for the next decade was $250 million—a one-time fee of $25 million each—and a 51 percent state tax on gross gaming revenue. In January 2022, the first month that online sports betting was available in New York, the state set a national record for the highest total handle in a single month—$1.67 *billion*. In the fiscal year ending in March 2023 New York took in more than $16 billion in handle.

My greatest successes as a gambler came only after I got serious about wagering as a business. I've kept my methods to myself over the years even as other gamblers tried all sorts of ways to figure them out or steal them. They have hacked my phones, cloned our beepers, rifled through my trash, and offered bribes to my employees.

I've fended them off and refused to share my secrets—until now. Truths that I will explore and share in this book are aimed at recreational and professional bettors looking for an edge.

Truth No. 1: My bets are based on extensive research, a vast network of experts and insiders across the country, and my own finely honed instincts.

Even avid bettors often do not grasp all of the factors and variables that go into a professional making an informed wager. I've eaten, slept, and breathed sports betting 365 days a year for more than five decades, driven by my obsession to grind out an advantage against bookmakers and other gamblers.

Truth No. 2: Betting sports is about one thing and one thing only: *value*. Which means your prediction needs to be better than the bookmaker's and you need to get the right number at the right price. Nothing else counts. And that leads me to:

Truth No. 3: The percentage of gamblers who are successful enough to earn a living is less than 1 percent. Frankly, I think most people would make more money washing cars. Why? The professional term is "eleven to ten odds." A sports gambler must lay down $11 to win $10 and pay $11 for a loss.

Warning: The following example may cause a short in the wiring of your brain if you do not share my enthusiasm for gambling calculations.

If Gambler A bets Team A in a contest and Gambler B bets Team B, each man puts up the requisite $11 and a bookmaker ends up holding a total of $22 from both bettors. If Gambler A wins, he gets his original $11 back plus $10 more, a payoff of $21. In the same scenario, Gambler B loses $11. If the book is properly balanced, the house keeps the extra dollar, the so-called vigorish, also known as "the vig" or "juice."

This mathematical formula means that gamblers need to win 52.38 percent of their bets just to break even. For the average bettor, that's like trying to swim the English Channel at night, doing the backstroke, without a wetsuit. Surrounded by sharks.

Truth No. 4: There are a very small number of gamblers who gain an edge by specializing in one sport and betting as soon as the line comes out. Those guys make a living, but not what I would consider serious money. Most of them last fewer than five years. The problem with this approach is that their betting limits are very small and the lines move very fast.

What separated me from the rest of the pack is that I beat all major sports for thirty-six straight years. I should mention that I quit betting baseball in 1995. Not because I wasn't winning. No, I quit because my team had to work virtually 365 days a year betting every facet of every major sport—sides, totals, halves, and futures. And it was killing us.

My approach to sports betting is militaristic.

If your average Joe thinks of himself as G.I. Joe—meaning one man with one gun and no backup—then, in my heyday, I was more like a Navy SEAL or a CIA special ops warrior. During my thirty-six-year winning streak, I had an armory of sophisticated weapons and a vast array of intelligence at my disposal.

My wagering decisions were based on weather patterns, field conditions, team morale, injury updates, and historical records, to name but a few factors. My expert analysts gathered a thousand points of data and fed them into a computer programmed with pro-prietary algorithms and probability theories.

Armed with a headset, speed dialer, and the betting equivalent of a Tomahawk missile—an almost endless supply of cash—I struck a wide array of targets from every direction through a clandestine network of accounts based in Las Vegas, Costa Rica, British Virgin Islands, Europe, Panama, Gibraltar, and everywhere in between.

If you were able to breach my many levels of security and listen in to my war room, this is the language you would hear:

Alabama minus 10. Up to fifty thousand.
Detroit plus seven. Up to sixty thousand.
Loyola Marymount as low as 8, open order. No limit.
Cleveland Browns, we're looking for as low as 1½. Bet all you
    can bet.

My special forces made hundreds of surgical hits in a single weekend, including one Super Bowl bet of $3.5 million alone. At times, I was overseeing more than $1 billion a year in gross wagers.

I've been around gamblers since I was six years old. I've seen it all: smart money, stupid money, sharps, half-sharps, suckers, and squares. I've run into every sort of hustler, scuffler, con man, and bullshit artist you can imagine. I've dealt with killers, drug dealers, celebrities, billionaires, and a thug-fest of would-be tough guys.

For the longest time, I could not resist that sweet voice called Action whispering in my ear, drawing me in, pulling me down. For years, I lived what gamblers in the South like to call a "chicken or feathers" existence; flush one day, dead broke the next. I've lost cars, houses, businesses, and marriages. I gambled until I had all your money, or you had all of mine.

There was no middle ground. I'd flip you a nickel for every quarter I had. My goal was to win every dollar you had, to drain you dry before you drained me. I bet without fear.

It's safe to say I was on a suicide mission at one point in my life. Not happy until I lost every penny I had—only to wake up and try to win it all back. Chicken or feathers. Time and time and time again.

2

Kentucky Home

I was born into rural poverty in Munfordville, Kentucky, a place where even today time crawls and potluck dinners and front porch gatherings remain local pastimes. My hometown is a farming community of some 1,600, not counting dogs and cows. It's a notch in the Bible Belt surrounded by soybean, hay, and alfalfa fields as far as the eye can see.

Located halfway between Louisville and Bowling Green, Munfordville, the county seat of Hart County, sits on the banks of the slow-flowing and serpentine Green River celebrated in the song "Paradise." John Prine's 1971 coal country classic includes the lyric "Down by the Green River where Paradise lay." (Prine was not referring to my hometown as a paradise, but to Paradise, Kentucky, about eighty-five miles to the west.)

Everywhere you turn in Munfordville, there's one church or another. Most are some form of Southern Baptist. Local billboards preach the Word, proclaiming "Thou Shall Not Commit Adultery" and "The Holy Bible. Truth. Wisdom. Hope." I don't remember seeing any that condemned gambling, but then again, my fellow Kentuckians had a higher tolerance for certain vices.

Like most Walters men, my father burned at a hard and fast rate. Thurman Walters had an abiding taste for liquor, which was exceeded only by his passion for games of chance. He was a month shy of forty years old by the time I showed up.

I was named after my uncle, Roscoe "Bill" Walters, who was known as Bill Luke. He was a hustler, gambler, and serious card player, so my namesake was well chosen. Uncle Bill bought, sold, and traded farms for a living. Later, he ran a highway rest stop for the state. When he wasn't working or keeping a casual eye on his six children (five boys and a girl), odds were that Uncle Bill was off playing cards.

Back then, Kentucky folks adopted an early version of Airbnb, but it was more like Pokerbnb. They opened their homes—beds and all—to card players who cut them in on the pot in exchange for hosting seven-card stud games. These roaming games often lasted for days, even weeks. Losers moved on. Winners took naps until the next challengers arrived. The wealthier farmers and businessmen were known to play for thousands of dollars.

Uncle Bill nicknamed two of his sons Garland "Big Maverick" Walters and Jimmy "Little Maverick" Walters after the poker-playing rounder in the popular television show *Maverick*. Prematurely gray and handsome, Garland even resembled the star of that show, actor James Garner.

Big Maverick was like a big brother to me and long regarded as one of the best poker players in the country. He eventually moved to Vegas, where he made a good living playing cards, including some deep runs with the big boys in the World Series of Poker. He passed away in 2023 at the age of eighty-five. His little brother, Jimmy, was a great seven-card stud player. Sadly, he died in a car wreck while coming home from an all-night card game in Kentucky on July 13, 1979.

My father died on January 26, 1948, at Kentucky Baptist Hospital. The death certificate blamed his demise on a rare form of bowel ulcer that wasn't alcohol related. When he passed at the age of forty-one, I was six months shy of my second birthday.

As such, I never knew my father. I have no memories of him, only a faded photograph of me standing at the edge of his grave holding my mother's hand. Yet, somehow, I grew up with a strong desire to honor his memory and to make him proud.

I was the third of three children born to Aileen "Dale" Quesenberry Walters, a sweet though troubled young woman cursed with bad luck, including an auto accident that left part of her face disfigured. My mother was fourteen years old, less than half my father's age, when they married in 1937. Her education ended in the sixth grade.

My oldest sister, Barbara Ann, was born the year after my parents tied the knot. She was followed three years later by Martha Dale. Public records reveal my mother twice tried to divorce my dad—in '43 and '44—before my arrival on July 15, 1946.

Since most folks in rural Kentucky were called by their first and middle names, I was known as "Billy Thurman" from that day forward. My early childhood was not the sort that stirs fond memories. My mom was ill-equipped to care for three young children. At twenty-five, she couldn't cope, so she drank out of anger and frustration.

One day, shortly after my father died, she picked up and fled north on Highway 65 to the big city of Louisville. Her children were not invited along. One sister was left with an aunt, the other with our paternal grandmother. By the grace of God, I was entrusted to my mom's mother, which proved to be my salvation. I knew her simply as "Grandmother."

Lucy Quesenberry was fifty-seven years old when she took me into her care. A plus-size woman widely hailed as "Mama Lucy," she lived on a gravel road across from the meticulously maintained Munfordville Municipal Cemetery. From her front porch, I could see my father's headstone.

By the time I moved in with her, Grandmother was no longer living with Clarence Marion Quesenberry, whom she married in 1909. My mother was one of their six children. Papa Cush was living in his own place in Kessinger, a hamlet just off Route 88. He died there at the age of ninety-two in 1977.

Papa Cush was country through and through, a slow-moving man with thick bushy eyebrows. He enjoyed idle time, suspenders, white straw hats, chewing tobacco, and the Cincinnati Reds on the radio. I suspect that late nights and amiable women were also on his list of favorite activities. I base this on a family story about how one of his sons, my uncle Harry, went off to war and left behind a teenage girlfriend. Upon returning home, poor Harry discovered that she was dating Papa Cush.

Welcome to Kentucky.

My grandmother's home, long since torn down, was a one-bedroom rental for ten dollars a month—no running water, no bathroom—with an outhouse and cistern out back. Night after night, we shared the only bedroom.

I can still smell apple pies baking in the oven and homemade pancake syrup bubbling on the stove. And I see Grandmother on her hands and knees scrubbing the linoleum kitchen floor or tending to a front yard full of flowers.

A devout Baptist and fiercely independent woman, Grandmother raised me like she had raised her own children, with a loving heart and a firm hand. She was blessed with integrity and strong character. The first words she taught me were *Yes, ma'am*, *No, ma'am*, *Yes, sir*, and *No, sir*. Grandmother instilled in me good manners, commitment, cleanliness, and religion. She was simply the nicest, sweetest human being I have ever met.

Church was her life. No matter how little money we had, she never let a collection plate pass without an offering. By the time I was four years old, Munfordville Baptist Church, founded in 1914, was the center of my universe. Grandmother would take my hand as we strolled a few blocks to the Lord's house for three services on Sunday, a Wednesday night prayer meeting, and a Saturday fun night hosted by the Royal Ambassadors, a Christian youth organization.

Our youth group played baseball and basketball, and went on fishing trips, too. I loved my days as a churchgoing boy. Baptized in first grade, I still remember the words I sang every Sunday to hymns like "The Old Rugged Cross."

On a hill far away stood an old rugged cross
The emblem of suffering and shame
And I love that old cross where the dearest and best
For a world of lost sinners was slain.

To make ends meet, Grandmother held down two jobs. After fixing me an early-morning breakfast each day, she cleaned homes before walking to her lunch shift in the kitchen of a local restaurant. She dropped me off with Uncle Harry, who provided a form of adult supervision as my male role model and father figure.

At six foot one and 220 pounds, Uncle Harry was the strong, silent type, a rugged World War II and Korean War vet who loved guns, hunting, and stock car racing. Folks said I picked up some of Harry's looks and friendly manners, which I took as a compliment. Uncle Harry and Grandmother gave a young boy without roots a sense of family and belonging.

Uncle Harry was the proud owner of the Q&R pool hall, a simple place with a lunch counter, jukebox, soft-drink dispenser, and a couple of pinball machines. It was a lively local hangout, especially on weekends, when farmers and their families came to town. The smell of hot dogs, hamburgers, and pickled pigs' feet perfumed the air amid other musty odors. The main attraction, of course, was the four pool tables that stood between the lunch counter and the urinal in back.

It's safe to say Uncle Harry was not the world's most attentive babysitter, especially during business hours. On my first visit as a four-year-old, he led me to a pool table in the back, stacked a couple of wooden Coke boxes for me to stand on, and stuck a pool cue in my hands.

Uncle Harry didn't even bother to flip on the lights. No need. I felt instantly at home, a Kentucky kid with gambling in his blood. In no time at all, I was cracking the cue ball against the break and scattering colored balls across the green felt.

As a child in search of stability and a sense of belonging, I couldn't have asked for a better hangout. I learned many a life lesson in my uncle's poolroom, though not the sort they taught in Bible class or grade school.

I learned that pool tables may look the same, but there are subtle differences. One pool table may be tilted a half degree to one side, another may have pockets that are tighter than others.

I also learned the importance of matchups and the ways of hustlers, including partners inclined to double-cross you and dump a game. I learned that certain players can shoot the hell out of a four-by-eight-foot table, but can't play a lick on a larger tournament table.

I learned who craved competition and who crapped their pants in crunch time. How a pool cue slides easily for most players when there is nothing but pride on the line and how hands turn twitchy when there's a week's worth of grocery money at stake. How to assess what gamblers call the "choke point" and exploit it.

That knowledge made me dangerous from a young age.

So did the fact that I played without fear. Call it instinct. Call it a curse. Call it the Walters Way. I wasn't happy until I was playing balls-out, with every last dollar I owned at risk.

At six years old, I was racking balls and hustling pool for a penny a game. By age ten, I was a star at the Q&R. Locals got to calling me "the Kid."

My little legend only grew after I played a simple game of nine-ball for twenty bucks against a hotshot out-of-towner. The pool hall's railbirds, who could smell a fish a mile away, had set the hook. They talked me up, knowing they were in for some solid side action.

Near the end of our game, all the hotshot had left was the nine—a little corner pocket shot any good player makes 95 percent of the time. As he eyed the angle, I reached into my pocket and grabbed a wad of bills from my paper route held together by a thick rubber band.

I sensed the guy's choke point was a hundred bucks. I knew I had more than that in my hand. Just before he was ready to take his shot, I tossed the wad onto the center of the table. It hit with a thud that quieted the room.

"Bet you what's there you don't make it," I said.

"You got to be joking," the man said. "There's nothin' to that shot."

Maybe there was. Maybe there wasn't. Only one way to find out. One of the regulars counted the cash. It came to $223. All the money I had in the world.

"You're on," the man said.

He chalked his stick three times. When he finally took his shot, his smooth stroke had a hitch to it. The nine ball rattled the edges of the pocket and refused to drop. The room filled with four-letter words as I finished him off and the railbirds cheered me on.

Grandmother never let me leave the house without a clean shirt and pressed pants. New clothes in my neighborhood were as rare as hundred-dollar bills. On my first day of grade school, I walked in with patches on my coveralls and earned another nickname, one I despised.

"Hey, Patches, how you doing?"

"Hey, Patches, nice pants."

"Patches, you know where I can get a set of those?"

Elementary school kids can be a special kind of cruel. In retrospect, the schoolyard and hallway taunts altered my DNA. From the moment I first heard their insults, a fire built and burned inside.

I had no battle plan, other than a determination to prove my worth to anyone who figured me a failure based on my clothes or country accent. My answer to the doubters and bullies was to get up every morning, throw the blinders on, and charge like Billy the bull. Head down, horns up, taking on the world, willing to go as hard and as far as needed to defend my dignity.

I've been a fighter my entire life. Barroom brawls, street fights, beer bottles to the face, pool cues cracked upside my head. I've racked up more stitches than I can count. I've fought bullies and lost, and I've fought would-be robbers and won. My overall brawling record is something like four wins and forty losses.

But I never backed down.

I went through first grade with at least one and, often, two eyes blackened. I did not know it then, but I was fighting for something far beyond the physical. I was fighting for recognition and respect.

My first real test in school came that same year courtesy of Paul "Jeep" Minton. Jeep was four years older, and every time I ran into him he'd bully me. I can't explain my temperament, but the last thing I wanted was guff from a guy named after a four-wheel-drive vehicle.

I got my ass whipped every time we tangled, but he took his share of the beating. Finally, Jeep got tired of picking on me and left me alone. I learned that whatever I couldn't outfight, I could outlast. I could wear down bullies like Jeep, and I could work hard to combat the worst deprivations of poverty. But there was one boyhood challenge that I struggled with even late into my adult years.

We didn't have running water in Grandmother's place. There was a cistern outside, and we drew from it. Grandmother boiled the murky brew before we drank it, cooked with it, or bathed in it. That's because the water quality in parts of rural Kentucky was notoriously bad. Cities in the state may have had plants that cleaned and treated water with fluoride, but most rural areas did not.

Grandmother was a blessing to me in many ways, but she knew next to nothing about dental hygiene. That was one of the reasons she had false teeth. We did not brush our teeth before bedtime or anytime, really. It didn't help that we were always sipping soda and eating sweets.

My teeth have given me problems my entire life. I was so self-conscious growing up that I'd cover my mouth when I talked or smiled. At the age of ten, I went to our dentist, Dr. David Belt, thinking, *Hell can't be any worse than this.* He shot me full of Novocain and gave me fillings, but he was already fighting a losing battle.

A third of my teeth were gone by my early teens. The rest gave me so much trouble that I had them all yanked when I hit eighteen. My dentist put in upper and lower false teeth, but the bottom ones never fit right because the bones in my lower jaw were in such bad shape. I stopped wearing the lower dentures. For a while, I avoided eating anything that required much chewing. Eventually my gums toughened up so that I could eat whatever I wanted if I chewed long enough.

I had no bottom teeth until I was in my thirties, when an acquaintance told me about his dental implants. I had money then, so I flew to Chicago for an oral surgeon to slash open my gums, remove my bad bones, and rebuild them so I could have implants, too. Only one problem—they became infected, causing the worst pain imaginable.

Later on, I found two specialists in Las Vegas who put implants in my jawbone. At age forty I had my first good set of teeth and a full smile.

Tobacco was king in Kentucky when I was growing up. There were no child labor laws governing farmwork. By the second grade I was helping out in the fields of a farmer named Roscoe Lawler.

When tobacco plants get to a certain size, you have to pull ground leaves off the bottom of the stalk. My fellow field hands and I would gather the leaves together, wrap a rubber band around them, and leave them on the ground in the tobacco patch. Then we would pick them up so we could put them on sticks and hang them in the curing barn.

It was hard work even for a boy who stood close to the ground. My pay was five dollars a day plus "dinner"—that's country for "lunch." I remember thinking that if I could just make enough to have $10,000 one day, I would have it made.

Years later, my tobacco field memories came back to me when, oddly enough, I played a friendly golf match with one of my favorite athletes, Michael Jordan, at Rancho Santa Fe Golf Club in Southern California. I recalled that he grew up in tobacco country in North Carolina, so I told him about my first job in the fields of Kentucky.

"Did you ever work a tobacco crop, Michael?" I asked.

A strange look came over his face before he broke into a smile. Michael told me that the most scared he ever got as a kid was working on a tobacco farm. He was up on the fourth tier of a barn when a big black snake started crawling his way. Michael said he was so scared he fell all the way to the ground floor. Luckily, he wasn't hurt, or that might have been the first and final flight of Air Jordan.

To supplement my tobacco wages, I created my own first "full-time" job, at the age of seven. I wanted to mow lawns, which, of course, required a lawn mower. Grandmother wasn't one to simply hand me her hard-earned $40 to buy one. She had to teach me a lesson first.

"I'm going to take you down to the bank and we'll see if I can get you a loan," she said.

Grandmother marched me down to Hart County Deposit Bank, where I met Colonel Luther Caldwell. Little did I know that the "loan application" process was nothing more than a charade; Grandmother already had worked things out with the colonel. He played along and made me sign a note to finance the purchase of a Huffy lawn mower.

Once the papers were signed, I went to work cutting grass for two bucks a lawn. Half of everything I earned was mine; the other half was set aside to pay off the loan. This was Grandmother's way of teaching me responsibility.

At age nine, I switched from lawn boy to paperboy. I took out another bank loan to cover the $90 deposit required to secure a paper route. Make that two routes. I delivered *The Courier-Journal* before school and *The Louisville Times* after school.

Two paper routes a day became quite a slog. This was country living, so the houses were not exactly next to each other. I had to load up my bike's front basket with eighty papers at a time and somehow make my way all over town. I was on that bike four hours a day. On Saturday I did my collections from subscribers, who paid thirty-five cents for the week's daily papers and twenty cents more if they wanted the bigger Sunday edition.

On Sundays, I rode to the town square around four in the morning to pick up the main news sections. Then Grandmother and I would sit on the floor of our home and insert the other sections. I had to pull my bicycle up to the porch when it was time to load all of the bulky Sunday papers. Grandmother would hand them to me, and I'd stuff fifty or so into the huge basket on the front of my heavy-duty bike, careful not to fill the basket too high and tip over. Then I was off and rolling, pumping the pedals and tossing papers onto porches and lawns all over town.

Keeping the routes going in the winter months was a test of my will. I remember one cold and rainy Sunday around the holidays when my mom surprised me by showing up unannounced, which she was inclined to do at times. She played the rescuer role, driving me from house to house in her '51 Ford. It was a tender reunion, a memorable though fleeting moment when she came through for me.

Another memorable day from my paperboy career came when I was ten years old. Snow and ice covered the ground. I was wearing two or three layers of clothes to keep from freezing. Hart County was bone-dry as far as bars and liquor stores, which only created a ripe market for bootleggers and moonshiners.

On that subzero Sunday in January, the county court clerk named Mr. Stewart opened his front door just as I arrived.

"C'mon in, Billy Thurman," he said. "You got to be real cold. I got something here to warm you up."

Mr. Stewart, who had only a tuft or two of hair on each side of his head and nothing on top, escorted me to the back of his house, where he opened the refrigerator and pulled out a jar of clear liquid, along with a single egg.

As I was thawing out, he poured a bit of the liquid into one glass, then another. He took the egg and cracked it open against his ample forehead. Then he swallowed the egg and drank the liquid in one big gulp.

I took a big swig and felt a burn. I thought my innards were on fire. After a few seconds, my body began to glow from the inside out. The bottom of my feet felt snuggly and warm.

(Mr. Stewart, I would later learn, occasionally pilfered the court-house evidence room where the 'shine was stored for criminal trials. I didn't know enough to question what the clear liquid was or where it came from—nor did I care. I also would later learn that the egg was both a shot of protein and a potential hangover cure—a favored nutrition for people who liked their moonshine.)

Between the pool hall and pitching pennies, I displayed early signs of the Walters family gambling gene. My first sports bet came at the age of nine. The wager was $125, every last cent I'd saved from two years of cutting lawns and odd jobs. I bet on Mickey Mantle and my beloved New York Yankees to win the 1955 World Series. On the other side of the wager was George Gatewood "Woody" Branstet-ter, the town grocer, who was equally fond of Duke Snider and the Brooklyn Dodgers.

The Branstetter family lived about a block and a half from us. I was usually at their place, bouncing a ball off the roof or the back of the house with their son, Charles Elwood. I figured the Yankees were a sure thing since the Bronx Bombers had been world champions five of the previous six years. Three of those wins came at the expense of their archrival Dodgers.

I hadn't counted on a crafty left-handed pitcher by the name of Johnny Podres winning two World Series games, including a 2–0 shutout in Game 7. My Yankees lost, and I lost along with them. Handing my hard-earned cash to Woody was the coldest feeling I'd known since that subzero day at Mr. Stewart's house.

But that first betting loss on sports didn't turn me off from gambling. Just the opposite. The thrill of having all my money on the line was nothing less than addictive.

About the time I'd grown accustomed to living with Grandmother and basking in her care, my mother moved back to the area with her second husband in tow. His name was Iman Doyle, a mild-mannered man, perhaps a bit too mild, given my mother's domineering temperament.

Iman and my mom took up residence in a ramshackle rental across the river in an unincorporated community known as Woodsonville. Once they settled in, they notified me that I was expected to join them. This was not welcome news.

By then, my thirteen-year-old sister, Martha, was already married and had a child. Our sister, Barbara, was still under the care of my other grandmother. That left me as the sole focus of my mother's unwanted attention. I didn't like living with my mom and stepfather. Their relationship was tense and so was the household. Iman was targeted by some of my mother's rage, but I bore the brunt. Her temper tantrums and verbal threats would be considered outright abuse by today's standards, but not by the standards of that era.

I lived in fear of my mother's screeching demands. *Mow the grass. Clean your room. Churn the butter.*

I didn't mind the work; I was accustomed to hard work. It was her never-ending threats and the continuous mood swings that took their toll.

"My mom's gonna kill me," I told my best friend, Lester "Boo" Bradway, on more than one occasion, and I wasn't kidding.

I fled the scene at every opportunity. Boo and I rode our bikes around town until the sun went down, picking up pop bottles on the side of U.S. Route 31W, which connects Louisville to Nashville. We exchanged them for cash to splurge on penny candy at the mom-and-pop store a mile down the road. Then we'd play baseball, basketball, and pinball—any activity to avoid returning to a house that was anything but a home.

I wasn't surprised or the least bit upset when my mother's marriage to Iman ended. I went back to live where I was loved, with Grandmother.

As I grew older, I came to realize that my mother's early life was beyond difficult. We eventually reconciled, and I forgave her for everything she said or did. She led an independent life in Louisville before dying of emphysema in 1985 at the age of sixty-three.

3

On My Own

While other kids my age were reading about Tom Sawyer and Huck Finn, I was living a real-life version of their ragtag adventures. Like Mark Twain's fictional characters, I was hustling and hunting for money because I thought it would solve my problems.

I mowed lawns. I delivered newspapers. And then I added a third enterprise—a shoeshine stand—on the Hart County court-house square. My customers were mostly farmers who brought their families into town on Saturdays to shop. Their footwear was caked with cow shit, chicken shit, and shit I didn't care to identify, so my services were in demand.

I charged ten cents a shine and put on quite a show, snapping rags until they popped and finishing in a flourish by buffing boots with a spit polish. Between shines, I'd join a group of courthouse regulars who shot craps in the public bathroom. I usually managed to lose all or most of my day's earnings, which became a pattern for a good part of my life.

Many of my losses were at the hands of a huckster known as Jim Dandy. The nickname came from his gaudy appearance, which included flashy clothing, a billed hat, and gold-capped teeth. Jim Dandy always had a pair of dice in hand, and he would blow on them four or five times "for luck" before rolling.

His blow-and-throw method seemed to work quite well whenever we played. Craps. High Dice. Low Dice. It didn't matter. I thought I was just unlucky until the day Dandy bounced a pair of dice off a wall, and they only showed fives, aces, and treys.

Even at a tender age, I knew that something was up. I eventually figured out that when Dandy blew on his dice, he switched out the legit set for a pair of smaller "loaded dice" known as "Pee Wees," which he conveniently kept tucked in the corner of his mouth so he could consistently roll the same odd numbers.

I never shot craps with him again. But that didn't stop me from pitching pennies with him in the men's room for hours on end. He couldn't cheat in that game.

Gambling was simply a way of life in Kentucky. My friends bet on a daily basis as naturally as they ate supper. We played cards, shot pool, pitched pennies, shot dice, and wagered on racehorses and sports. Basically, we'd bet on anything that moved. We never gave a thought to gambling being immoral or illegal.

Growing up around Munfordville Baptist Church, I learned that some folks considered gambling to be evil. During Sunday and Wednesday evening sermons, the preachers scolded the congregation for engaging in life's pleasures, be it gambling, dancing, or premarital sex.

Frankly, I never bought a word of it.

When I turned thirteen, Grandmother became so ill that she couldn't care for me any longer. I found refuge in the arms of my aunt Nell, who was slowly dying of emphysema. Aunt Nell did the best she could, but I was essentially on my own for a couple of years before she passed on. At fifteen, I had no choice but to leave a place where I knew everybody and everybody knew me, to live with my mother and her latest partner in Louisville.

For me, moving out of Munfordville to the largest city in the Commonwealth of Kentucky was like moving from Mayberry R.F.D. to New York City. And my mom didn't exactly live in a Park Avenue co-op.

Husband No. 3 turned out to be a short, wiry ex-Marine named Van Taylor, who had courted my mother while she was working twelve-hour shifts as a waitress at his truck stop. Van lost the business, but kept my mom. He had twins of his own—a son, Jerry, and a daughter, Terry Fey.

Van managed to support his family with a job at the Brown & Williamson Tobacco factory. I moved into their shabby one-story rental on the backside of the Hazelwood projects, a thrumming cauldron of blue-collar misery on Beech Avenue on the south side of Louisville.

I spent as much time as I could in other places, including a dive pool hall in one of the worst parts of town. With fifteen tables, it was a step up from my uncle's joint back in Munfordville. This new haunt was within walking distance of dilapidated homes and trash-filled yards that lined Bicknell Avenue, the kind of street, even today, where dreams go unfulfilled.

The poolroom regulars sized me up and quickly dubbed me "Country," based on my farm-store fashion, greasy Elvis pompadour, missing teeth, and backwoods drawl. I'd been called "the Kid" at the Q&R and "Patches" in school. What was one more nickname? I brushed off their taunts, found a decent cue, and began picking their pockets. In no time at all, I was taking marks for five, ten, and twenty bucks a game.

My success did not win many friends. One night, a couple of older men took offense after I took a chunk of their wages.

"We want our money back," said one.

"Right now," demanded the other.

Relinquishing my winnings was not an option. I smashed the butt end of a pool stick against one guy's forehead, opening a gash that spewed blood. Then I snatched a fresh cue off the rack and slammed it over the head of the other guy.

To my shock, they recovered and retaliated, which was not part of my plan. I took a beating that day, but hung on to my money and earned some measure of respect among the pool hall regulars. Word spread that I'd fight for every dollar. Of course, a tough-guy reputation only invites tougher guys to come knocking. After that dustup, I went country commando. My homemade weapon of choice was a sturdy, fourteen-inch log chain with one end wrapped in duct tape for a firmer grip. I kept it stashed in my back pocket and didn't have to wait long to whip it out.

While walking home one night with $60 in fresh winnings, two young men jumped out of the shadows. One waved a knife.

"We want your money," he said.

I hit him with my bravado first.

"You don't want to mess with me."

He wasn't impressed.

"Fuck you."

The kid with the knife took a swipe just as I pulled out my steel chain. I whipped it within inches of his head and kept moving closer, swinging and swinging until both would-be muggers disappeared into the darkness.

Score one for the Louisville slugger.

I'd been living with my mother and Van for a short time before they cobbled together a down payment on a two-story home on Rodman Avenue in a slightly better neighborhood a few blocks from Churchill Downs. They claimed the first floor while renting out the second floor to help pay the mortgage. I was banished to the basement and sharing space with another tenant, Barbara Yocum, who would become my sister-in-law.

My mom charged me ten bucks a week to sleep with roaches and bugs, who proved better company than my parental landlords. Both raging alcoholics by that time, they would hole up in their bedroom and go on benders for four, five, six days at a stretch.

As if that wasn't harsh enough, I lost the seminal source of love and support in my life. Grandmother, a woman who loved me when no one else did, died on March 3, 1962, at the age of seventy, due to heart failure. At the time of her death, she had $220 in life savings.

When Aunt Nell delivered the news, I went half out of my mind. I did not eat or sleep for days. At Grandmother's burial, I contemplated joining her in the open grave, inching closer and closer to the edge, until my mother grabbed my collar and yanked me back. The only thing worse than my grief was my guilt.

Grandmother had put me on the right path, but I had abandoned it for back alleys and smoke-filled rooms. I was hanging out with hustlers old enough to be my father, drinking and shooting pool until the lights went out. I only had to look at the sorry asses around me to see my future if I stayed on the same course.

Looking back, I wish I could return the love Grandmother gave to me, to let her know that one seed she planted took root. In the fall of my eighth-grade year, we were sitting together on her porch swing watching leaves tumble from the trees when she reflected on the hard life she'd led.

"The Quesenberrys and the Walters never had it easy," she said. "My girl, Dale, got pregnant at fourteen and never got past sixth grade. Your uncles were all uneducated men who could barely read or write. I want more for you, Billy Thurman.

"Promise me . . ."

I knew what she was about to ask.

"Grandmother, I promise to get a high school education."

There it was. I made a commitment. A promise to Lucy Quesenberry. I did not waver from it. That's the way she led her life and that's how she taught me to lead mine.

Thanks to Grandmother, I never considered quitting school. I'd like to say that after her passing, I resolved to turn my life around. I might have resolved to do that, but my follow-through fell through.

A wiser person might have buried himself in books and obtained an education to elevate his life. I was not that wiser person. DuPont Manual High School was located in the Old Louisville neighborhood with beautiful red-brick Victorian homes. But I hated Manual

High. Hated the teachers, hated the students, hated the *Striving for excellence* vibe.

My worst instincts were my only instincts, and I paid the price.

One morning, I missed the school bus and had to hitchhike. The man who picked me up made his move in the front seat about three blocks from campus. He flashed a smile, reached over, and put his hand on the inside of my thigh.

I had never heard of pedophiles. Grandmother had not warned me. Neither had my mother nor any other adult in my life. Even so, I knew that a strange man grabbing for my crotch was not acceptable. I quickly moved out of his reach, leaned back, and punched the pervert in the face with all the fury and fear he'd churned up.

He was stunned by my swift shot, which gave me time to jump out of the car and race to school. I was a country hick living in the city, but I was beginning to learn about things I had not known before. One lesson: don't hitchhike in Louisville. I stuck to public transportation, mastering bus routes and navigating my way to pool halls around town. A pool hustler can only hustle where he hasn't hustled before, so I roamed the city in search of fresh prey.

My wanderings eventually led me to Churchill Downs, Louisville's storied Thoroughbred horse racing track. Given my instincts, I wasn't drawn to the majestic Twin Spires or the ornate floral gardens or even the grassy infield. I headed for the backside of the track, where there was work to be found mucking stalls, walking "hots" (cooling down horses after hard exercise), and soaping grimy saddles, halters, and bridles that oozed sweat and stench.

I was captivated by the exotic odors, the click and clatter of hooves, and the beguiling beauty and power of the sleek Thoroughbreds. And, oh yes, the sweet smell of money changing hands. I quickly found a job and won the approval of the mostly Black stable hands, who appreciated a kid with country manners, willing to wade into stalls ankle-deep in straw, hay, and horseshit.

Although I was making ends meet working at Churchill, I needed more money to bet. I quit my job at the track to work the early shift at Davis Donut Bakery, a block and a half from our house. On weekdays I worked from 4:30 a.m. to 7:30 a.m. Weekends from 4:30 a.m. to 5:00 p.m. I mopped floors and cleaned trays, in addition to rolling, cutting, frying, and glazing dozens of donuts per shift. Then I went to school.

Working those hours didn't leave much energy for my studies. I didn't do well in class, not because I was dumb, but because I was exhausted. The one subject that perked me up and came naturally to me was math—no doubt the result of all the numbers I crunched as a budding gambler and entrepreneur.

Most kids could focus on learning because their parents supported them. I didn't have that luxury. My teenage years were marked by struggle, and things didn't get any easier when I became a father as a junior in high school.

Now, the odds of a small-town boy with no bottom teeth finding a sweet-faced girlfriend in the big city must have been long, but I was adept at beating the odds. I was athletic and what might be considered "country handsome," so long as I hid my bad teeth by keeping my lower lip sealed.

Sharon Yocum was the girl who caught my eye and didn't look away, in part because we shared a backstory of poverty and neglect. After her parents split up, she lived with her grandmother in The Point, a decaying neighborhood near the Louisville salvage and stockyards. What we lacked in parental supervision, we made up for in raging hormones. First base led to second, and the next thing I knew a baby was in the making.

We had no socially acceptable option other than to get hitched. Besides, I loved Sharon as much as any clueless teenage boy could. She was sixteen—too young to get legally married, even in Kentucky, without parental consent (not an option). So on November 23, 1963, we climbed into my beat-up '51 Chevy and drove 145 miles south to Celina, Tennessee. The sorry vehicle proved a fitting carriage for what would become our wreck of a marriage. The car had a plastic sheet covering the driver's-side window that flapped in the wind. The right front fender was bashed and hung low.

Nobody at the courthouse in Celina, including the justice of the peace who married us, seemed interested enough to ask for proof of our age. (We told them we were eighteen and twenty.) We drove home the same day listening to the radio the entire trip as the nation mourned the assassination of President John F. Kennedy. Another omen of the dark days ahead.

We hadn't told a soul of our plans. We announced the news upon our return to Louisville. Our nuptials, which did not make the society pages, were met with widespread silence and indifference. My mother and Van were thrilled only because it meant that I'd be moving out of their basement and they could charge higher rent.

Sharon and I found a furnished apartment at Fourth and M Streets for $12.50 a week, silverware included. The University of Louisville campus was nearby, not that it mattered—I was still fighting just to stay in high school and keep my promise to Grandmother.

The principal, who knew a hard-luck kid when he saw one, gave me permission to skip study hall at the end of each school day so I could work a second job—the three-to-eleven shift at a Shell station on the corner of Taylor Boulevard and Queen Avenue. When a car rolled in, we were expected to run out, fill 'er up, clean the windows and headlights, and check the oil, wiper blades, and air filter. Every customer presented an opportunity to sell a quart of oil, blades, and filters. Hustling came naturally to me, and the Shell job marked my true beginning as a salesman.

We pushed accessories on our customers like Bible salesmen facing eternal damnation if we failed. The more wiper blades we sold, the bigger our commission. That was my kind of incentive. I also did some grease-monkey work by changing oil, spark plugs, and other engine parts for customers. At the end of every shift, we had to scrub two work bays with kerosene. By the time I stumbled home, I barely had enough energy to take a shower before collapsing into bed.

Manual High's classes were demanding even for students who weren't working two jobs to support a family. If they had given extra credit for sleeping in class, I might have stood a chance. While I had promised Grandmother that I would graduate, I didn't specify the exact high school. In 1964, for my senior year, I transferred to Manual's archrival, the aptly named Male High School. Its academic standards weren't lax, but more practical for working-class kids.

I was the ultimate Male High male—married to a child bride, working two jobs, and the father of Tonia Faye, our newborn baby girl. For most fathers, the birth of a first child is a cherished, life-altering moment. To my shame, I can't recall a minute of Tonia's birth. I didn't go to the hospital, let alone the delivery room. Maybe it was because I had no parental instincts, having never really had a father or a mother. Or maybe I was just too young and emotionally numb to understand the impact a child can have on your life.

Here's what I did know: I would have to work harder to support a wife and child. After graduation—I did it, Grandmother!—I took on a series of low-paying blue-collar jobs, first as a custodian for Brown & Williamson Tobacco, then as a foundry worker for International Harvester. I punched the clock, put in my hours, punched out, and then went drinking and gambling. Sharon and Tonia were basically left on their own. I was far better at being a provider than a husband or father.

The International Harvester job was brutal. The summertime heat index inside the coal-fired plant soared to 120 degrees. As the new guy, I was sentenced to the assembly line. Heavy metal parts plunged down gigantic chutes from three different locations before arriving at my station. I felt like a hockey goalie without protective gear, frantically spinning, grabbing, and lifting fifty-pound chunks of steel before placing them on a conveyor belt for chiseling or grinding.

After my first day on that job, Sharon thought a coal miner covered in soot had entered the wrong house. When I went to sleep at night, my arms felt like lead. It took only two weeks for me to realize I had no future there. I quit and went to work at Jones-Dabney, an industrial varnish and paint company at Twelfth and Hill. I started out on the day shift as a janitor in the research and development department, but quickly slipped into a side hustle booking bets.

Most of my coworkers were Black, which was nothing new to a kid who'd grown up working in tobacco fields and the backside of a track. They were avid gamblers, which rekindled my entrepreneurial spirit. Before long, I became the factory bookie, taking $5 and $10 bets on the races at Churchill Downs and other tracks, along with football games.

As an added service, I offered small payday loans of twenty-five cents interest on the dollar. The terms: $10 to gamble now and pay me back $12.50 on payday. I expanded the operation to include raffles, offering $1 chances on watches I had purchased for $10 at Arlan's department store. I'd sell twenty-five tickets before each drawing, then pocket the profit.

From day one, I joined my coworkers at their two favorite watering holes on West Hill Street. At Nevitt Liquors, a mix of hourly laborers and tobacco executives drank booze out of brown paper bags while playing pool and shooting craps in the back of the red-brick building.

Across the street at the Gremlin Grill, soul and Motown tunes blasted from the juke. The lights were low. Come Friday night and payday, the place shook until dawn. Many a night, I'd play Liar's Poker until I passed out drunk, often with $5,000 in tens, twenties, and hundreds in my pocket.

Every last nickel would still be there when I woke up. My friends Big John and Lefty looked after me. That often meant throwing me over their shoulder, tossing me into the back of their beat-up cars, and depositing me in bed at home.

The routine did not sit well with my red-haired wife. Sharon's sweet disposition sagged with my drunken ways. Not that I gave it much attention. I figured my job was to keep the lights on and the bills paid. The rest was up to her.

I devoted my energy to creating new revenue streams. I persuaded the managers of the Gremlin Grill to let me run Friday and Saturday night games of seven-card stud. It was a "two and four game" (meaning two-dollar and four-dollar limits). Every time the pot reached fifteen dollars, I'd take one dollar for the house. I'd take another buck when the pot reached thirty-five dollars.

The action added up. By closing time on Saturday night, I would have cut five or six hundred dollars out of the pot, with 25 percent going to the Gremlin. The rest was mine.

The lucrative gig didn't last long. One night, a bunch of rednecks who worked at Brown & Williamson Tobacco Co. right down the street stumbled into the Gremlin. *Nothing good will come of this*, I thought. But it was an open game, so I couldn't turn them away.

As the first hand unfolded, a regular player drew a winning card. "Why, you dumb fucking n—r!" one of the rednecks yelled.

All hell broke loose. Guns came out. Shots were fired. The lights went dark. I crawled out the back door with my cigar box full of ones and fives. I bid farewell forever to the Gremlin, which barely had time to miss me. Two weeks later, a mysterious blast leveled the bar to its concrete base.

Just before the place blew up, I received a promotion to the shipping department at the paint factory, which included a raise and a transfer to the 11:00 p.m. to 7:00 a.m. shift. My job was to fill fifty-five-gallon drums with resin, then weigh and stamp them so they could be loaded and shipped to their destination. I dreaded the zombie shift, but it provided a regular paycheck that I desperately needed.

With the raise, Sharon and I purchased our first home, an FHA two-bedroom repo in working-class Highland Park, for $10,000. I barely earned enough to make payments on our mortgage, furniture, and car, let alone food and clothing.

I was nineteen years old and felt like I had already lived two lifetimes.

Little did I know I was about to begin a third.

4

Man on Fire

I bought my first car at age sixteen as a junior in high school. It was a beauty, a red '54 Oldsmobile, two-door, stick shift. I found it at Superior Auto Sales and paid $395, backed by a loan from Dial Finance. The monthly payments came to a grand total of $18.

The car didn't last long. I got into a drag race with friends in the back of Manual High when I lost control and crashed into a parked vehicle, tearing off the front end of that poor ol' Olds.

The monthly payments didn't disappear with the car, so I went back to riding the bus until I paid them off.

At age nineteen, I was looking for a black '65 Chevy. I found that car along with a new career path at McMackin Motors, a mom-and-pop used-car dealership at the corner of Taylor Boulevard and Arcade Avenue.

The owner, John McMackin, offered me a part-time job selling cars. He knew from reviewing my credit application that I was married, had a child, and worked at the paint company. He liked that I could strike up a conversation with a fire hydrant.

I figured selling cars had to be easier than working in a foundry or a factory. It was a hustler's job, and I was adept at hustling. I did think twice, however, about giving up a regular paycheck for a job that paid strictly on commission. I decided to sign on for a trial run at the dealership before giving up my overnight shift at the paint plant.

As Mr. McMackin had observed, I was a natural salesman and within no time I was working his lot twelve hours a day, six days a week. I'd been living by my wits for a decade, thinking on my feet and doing quick calculations to cover my bets. Selling cars wasn't much of a stretch.

From pool halls to tobacco fields to poker tables, I'd already earned a real-world degree in sizing up folks for a sale. In car dealer lingo, it's called "qualifying" a customer. When potential buyers showed up on the lot, I'd kick-start a conversation with a series of innocuous questions designed to match them with a car they could afford.

"What part of town do you live in?"

"Where do you work?"

"How long have you lived here?"

"Who'd you buy your last car from?"

"Who'd you finance with?"

Nine times out of ten, I could gather enough information to fill out a walking, talking credit application without the customer realizing it. Once I determined I had a qualified buyer, I tried every which way to sell a car we had in inventory. If we didn't have a car that fit the bill, I knew at least four other local dealers who might.

The other dealers loved me because they could charge McMackin a bit more than wholesale for a car without having to pay a sales commission. And McMackin could make a tidy profit by charging retail.

If Fay's Auto or Jeff Harvey or the Cook Brothers or any other dealer in town didn't have what I was looking for, I would write down the customer's info and ask Mr. McMackin to get the car at auction.

If I had a customer who really wanted to buy a vehicle, I was going to make it happen. I did not give it up. It was just part of my hypercompetitive personality. My engine did not have an idle. I was high horsepower, revved up and ready to go as soon as I hit the lot each morning. There were times I wish I had shut myself off, but I couldn't. And I still can't today. I get obsessed, maybe even possessed, when I'm in that zone.

"I will find you that car *today*. Not tomorrow or the next day. *Today*."

I learned early on that the auto business was different from factory work because of all the downtime. The secret to success in car sales was to stay busy 100 percent of the time. If there weren't potential buyers milling around, the other salesmen would goof off in the office by chewing the fat, playing cards, or reading magazines.

I also learned something that would become a hallmark of my business career—the more information you accumulate, the more opportunities you create.

When I wasn't on the lot selling, I was in the office searching the criss-cross city directory for people who lived on the same street as my last customer.

"Hi, Mr. Jones, this is Billy Walters from McMackin Motors. I was just wondering if you've seen that car Mr. Vale is driving?"

Regardless of the answer, I kept pitching.

"Yep, it's a 1964 Chevy Nova. I sold him that car and, if you're looking for one like his or a better one, I'd be happy to help you."

I scoured the classified ads every day, jotting down the phone numbers of people looking to sell their vehicles. I knew that some people listed their cars for sale because they couldn't afford the monthly payments. I'd call those folks and tell them we'd take their existing car in a trade and put them in a less expensive one. I called these "trade-downs," and they were just as profitable as a regular sale.

Finally, if I had nothing working, I made cold calls to people who lived in the south end of town.

"Hi, Bill Walters down here at McMackin Motors. We're running a sale today and I thought you might want to come take a look. Our lot is overflowing with cars, and the boss says we're ready to make a deal."

Some folks would engage. Others would tell me to never call back again before hanging up. No matter, I was on to the next call. I just kept dialing until my fingers were numb and my voice was hoarse.

I sold twenty cars in my first month and earned about $600 a week. I wanted to outsell my colleagues every single day, every single week. Once I achieved that, I'd focus on beating my own sales record month after month.

My goals were not limited to just selling a car. I set my sights on building an entire network of customers to ensure future sales. Some salesmen paid a $25 "bird dog" fee for a successful referral. I upped it to $50. I also sent birthday cards and gifts to my best bird dogs and gave away turkeys at Thanksgiving to my best customers.

Within a year, I was selling an average of twenty-five cars a month. By 1966, I raised my average to thirty-two cars a month. At the age of twenty, I sold more cars than anyone in the state.

My commission checks that year totaled $56,000, the equivalent of more than $500,000 in today's dollars. The next best salesman in the state, a twenty-nine-year veteran pushing Pontiacs, took home $22,000. By comparison, the median family income that year was $7,400.

My all-time record: fifty-six cars in a single month. Bad weather, low inventory, economic recession—nothing stopped me. Making money was not a problem. Holding on to it was. By now the gambling demons owned me. The more I earned, the more I put on the line.

Almost every night after work, I'd hit a bar with the guys. We'd pound Maker's Mark—always Maker's, a lot of Maker's—while shooting craps or pitching nickels. Some nights, we'd party and gamble until six in the morning.

Then I'd go home to shave, change clothes, grab a bite, and report to work. I was known as the biggest gambler in Louisville before my twenty-first birthday. I couldn't help myself. The more money at stake, the bigger the rush. The voice of reason played on a reel inside my head every night, repeating thousands of times as I wagered more and more.

If I win this money back, if I get to even, I'm going to quit.

But I didn't know when or how to quit.

Instead, I became the poster child for the old gambler's lament: "The biggest thrill you can have in gambling is making a huge bet and winning. The second-biggest thrill is making a huge bet and losing."

When your home becomes little more than a place to shave, shower, and change, something has to give. Unfortunately, what gave was my marriage to Sharon. Our four years together had produced a precious little girl, but little else. My selfish behavior doomed our marriage from the start. It was all but over within months of our wedding.

That's when Carol Brown came into my life.

Carol had been in the same grade at duPont Manual, but we did not know much at all about each other. She was very popular, outgoing, and friendly. I was married and exhausted from working two jobs.

When our paths crossed after high school at a local drive-in restaurant, we struck up a conversation that led to second and third conversations. That first night, I lied to Carol and told her I had broken up with my girlfriend. She had a date lined up that evening but broke it to go out with me.

Two months later, I gave Carol an engagement ring, along with a confession.

"There's something I need to tell you or someone else will. I'm married and have a baby daughter."

"Oh, no," Carol said.

Oh, yes.

Carol felt like she'd been punched in the stomach. But we talked—I was a good salesman, after all—and she eventually accepted my explanation that my marriage was over except for the paperwork.

The next day, Carol spent the morning crying at work. Her boss at General Electric Supply took her to lunch to find out what was wrong. Carol opened up. She didn't know whether she should give the ring back. Her boss had no such reservations.

"Don't go through with it," he said. "If Billy didn't tell you something as important as that, there's probably plenty of other things he's kept from you as well."

But Carol and I were in love—well, maybe more like lust on my end. On March 25, 1967, the day after my divorce from Sharon was final, Carol Brown and I were married. Shortly thereafter, I found out she carried a secret, too.

She was pregnant.

Seven months later, Carol gave birth to our son, William Scott. I was only twenty-one and had a new wife, a baby boy, an ex-spouse, and a daughter to support. One would think that kind of responsibility might have slowed me down a bit.

Not long after Scott was born, I realized that Carol and I had very little in common. I was committed to trying to make it work because I didn't want our son to be raised in a broken home like I was. I was already divorced and had one child in that situation. I didn't want another.

Still, I continued to run as hard and fast as I could. I scrambled to make as much money as possible during the day before putting every last dollar on the line at night, often in a haze of alcohol and cigarette smoke.

It hurts to say it now, but in my mind back then I was married to Lady Luck and the gambler's lifestyle—the booze, the late nights hanging out with friends, the glory and the guilt.

It never dawned on me that *time*, not money, is the most precious gift a father can give to his family. I still hadn't figured out what it meant to be a dad.

I don't blame Carol. She wanted a traditional husband who worked regular hours five days a week and spent the rest of his time with the family. I just wasn't that guy. I spent seventy hours a week selling cars and the rest of my waking hours gambling. Far too many nights, I came home drunk and busted.

Looking back now, I was a good provider. But I was absolutely never at home. In retrospect, while I loved my family, my true love was gambling. I didn't know it then, but I was addicted.

One of the worst episodes took place at the Domino Lounge. After the owner, Rufus Allen, broke me one night playing cards, I crawled home while devising a sensationally bad plan for telling my new wife what had transpired.

We recently had bought a lovely new home for $50,000 in Heritage Estates, an upscale subdivision. At the breakfast table the next morning, I presented Carol with brochures advertising two new apartment complexes, the Fontainebleau and the Beau Rivage.

"Which do you prefer?" I asked.

She was understandably confused.

"Well, if you had to choose one or the other, which would it be?"

She took a few seconds to scan the brochures.

"I guess the Fontainebleau. Why?"

"Because we're moving there tomorrow. I lost the house last night."

Carol unleashed a righteous fury that I could only accept as my just due. When she finally settled down, she said, "Well, should I call a mover and pack up the furniture?"

"Don't bother," I told her. "I lost that, too."

Rufus called later that day.

"Billy, I don't want your house. Just pay me when you can."

Thanks to Rufus, I got back on my feet. Paid him back every penny. But not before selling the house and buying another one for less money down the street.

By the spring of 1968, my bankroll was back in good shape. To calm the marital waters (at least that was my excuse), I took Carol on a romantic getaway. We were headed to Hawaii's Waikiki Beach for four days of rest and relaxation, starting with a three-day stop in Las Vegas.

You can probably guess the rest.

Caesars Palace had opened two years earlier. It was a modern showplace. The owners had ditched the traditional Old West motif of old-school Vegas venues in favor of an ancient Roman theme. Hollywood had rolled out hit movies set in the era of chariots, gladiators, and lusty bacchanals, including *Spartacus* and *Cleopatra*. Las Vegas joined the toga party.

Caesars ruled with its "anything goes" fantasy park for adults. A few months before Carol and I arrived from Kentucky, Evel Knievel had attempted to jump the spectacular fountain in front of the resort. His bone-crushing crash only drew more legions of thrill seekers. (Years later, a reconstructed Evel would become my golf and gambling buddy.)

When I walked into Caesars for the first time that spring afternoon, I was bedazzled by the brilliant lighting, chattering bells, and clanging coins of the slot machines. The gorgeous cocktail waitresses in bust-boosting tunics made an impression of another sort.

High-end gaming venues are designed to play upon emotions and impulses. As I entered the casino, my addiction kicked in. My legs shook. My heart raced. Gazing out at the casino floor, I felt like a junkie entering a heroin den.

I had no chance. I was the perfect mark. All impulse. No control.

My first stop was a craps table around 2:00 p.m. My plan was to play for three hours, then take Carol to a nice dinner. Within the first two hours, I'd lost one-third of the $3,000 we'd brought. One side of my brain was pleading, *Quit now before you lose it all.* The other side was whispering: *Don't quit now. You can win it back!*

Dinnertime came and went. Carol gave up and turned in for the night. By five thirty the next morning, I'd lost virtually every dollar of our vacation money. Fortunately, the trip was prepaid, but I knew I had messed up. Sure I was remorseful, but that remorse only went so far.

I know my addictions were hard on Carol. She begged me to stop drinking and gambling. And on each occasion, I'd promise to do just that. She told me we didn't need the money. But I could not stop. Still, Carol would be the first to tell you that during our marriage I had an uncanny ability to bounce back after hitting rock bottom. As time went on, she prayed that I would lose badly enough to finally see the corrosive effect my twin curses had on our family.

"Bill, you are in denial about your gambling and your drinking," she would tell me. "You could make something of your life—of our life together—if you stopped."

I could not see it that way. I wasn't drinking all day, every day, like other alcoholics I'd known. And I didn't think my gambling was a problem. I was in denial on both fronts.

When sober, I was a tough guy to beat out of his money. But when I got to drinking and knocking back doubles, my personality changed. I thought I was smarter and tougher than I was. This made me easy prey.

It also made me volatile. If someone said the wrong thing or made fun of me, I reverted to those childhood memories of being bullied. My temper exploded. I went into *I'll show you* mode. And if I couldn't get the best of you, I'd take the worst.

Instead of finding a way to break my self-destructive patterns, I fed my addictions and looked for quick fixes.

Meanwhile, life happened around me.

On July 10, 1970, Carol gave birth to our second son, Derin. I was twenty-three and now responsible for three young children, a wife, and an ex-spouse. Sharon had married a military man and moved with Tonia to Germany, where I sent child support payments.

As if I needed another way to put money at risk, I found a golden opportunity on the golf course.

As a kid, I had been a decent baseball player with good hand-eye coordination. Even though I didn't pick up a driver until my early twenties, smashing a small white ball with a club came naturally. Putting on the greens was like shooting pool on a bigger table. Once I put my mind to it, playing golf came instinctively to me—and quickly developed into another vice.

Big surprise, I made my first golf bet on my first round. It was the late sixties. My buddy (and future brother-in-law) Johnny Humphries invited me to play the nine-hole Bobby Nichols Golf Course in Louisville.

Johnny was the only person I knew who had an interest in golf. As a kid, I never watched it on television for the simple reason that we didn't own a TV set. So when I walked from the parking lot to the pro shop to meet Johnny, he did a double take.

"Where are your clubs?" he said.

"Clubs? What clubs?"

Johnny realized he was dealing with a rank amateur. He had to help me pick out rental clubs and other essentials such as balls and tees, which I didn't know were essential.

You need special shoes? With metal spikes?

We were headed for the first tee when I popped the one question that had been burning in my brain.

"Johnny, how much are we playing for?"

"But, Billy, you've never even played before."

"What difference does that make? We got to play for something or I'm not playing."

We settled on five bucks a hole. The nine-hole course had a tight, tree-lined layout, doglegs right and left, and water everywhere. Nichols Creek came into play on all but one hole. It was not exactly nirvana for someone who didn't know a proper golf grip from Gorilla Glue.

I lost $35 on my first golf match. Johnny won seven holes. To this day, I don't know how I managed to tie the other two. Still, it was love at first swing. Golf became another of my passions. I was so hooked that I made a lighted driving range at the Kentucky State Fairgrounds in Louisville my first stop after work. I'd shake off the weariness from a twelve-hour workday and pound two hundred practice balls before heading out for the night.

Lacking any family instincts, I hit Midland Trail Golf Club in Louisville every Sunday (weather permitting) from sunup to sundown. I usually joined my good buddies Calvin Hash, Danny Matthews, and the Allen boys—Rufus and Hardin. After a round or two or three, we moved to the men's grill to play hearts or spades until the bartenders, Odell and L.C., pushed us out the door at 2:00 a.m.

While drinking late one night with Calvin and Danny at the Domino Lounge, we were talking smack about our golf skills and a bet was born. We had to wait for the sun to come up before driving our drunken butts to the Elk Run Golf Club across the state line in Jeffersonville, Indiana. It was run by Big Jim Barber, who described himself as the "head golf professional, chief bottle washer, and greenskeeper." He ran the pro shop out of an old milk barn.

We showed up that morning smelling like the Maker's Mark distillery.

"What's the cart fee for one hole?" Calvin asked.

"No such animal," replied Barber. "We rent carts for either nine or eighteen holes."

"Well, we have a one-hole bet," Calvin said. "Billy Bullshit here claims he can make at least a bogey on your par five seventh hole using just irons. No woods or putter."

Barber found that proposition one of the most intriguing things to happen at Elk Run in quite a spell. He happily supplied the carts and rode along for the show.

Upon reaching the 516-yard seventh, I pulled a 1-iron out of my bag and blasted a drive down the middle. My next shot with a 2-iron found the fairway. Then I lofted a nice little 9-iron onto the green and used my 1-iron to two-putt for par. Calvin and Danny showered me with twenty one hundred dollar bills.

On another night at the Domino, the alcohol in me bragged about my game so much that the owner of the joint, Rufus Allen, made a bet with me. Now, please note that this is the same bar owner who earlier had won my new house and all the furniture inside of it.

Rufus was in his mid-forties, twice my age, a fun-loving guy with the innate ability to sweet-talk suckers into a trap. When I showed up at his house at 6:00 a.m. to follow through on our bet the previous night, Rufus was dead asleep and still drunk. It apparently wasn't the first time that his wife, Beverly, had to roust her sloshed husband out of bed, get him dressed, and shove him out the door with his golf clubs.

Rufus was a much better golfer than me at the time. Under normal conditions and in a state of sobriety, he would have spotted me five or six shots a side. Fortunately, we had set the game the night before while emptying a bottle of Maker's. The bet was $200 a hole, even up.

We made two loops around the Bobby Nichols nine-hole course. Rufus and his hangover were ten holes down with one hole to play. He couldn't shake the shanks, spraying balls all over the course and beyond. It took me eleven strokes to finish the final hole and I still won.

As I recall, I shot something like 122 for the round. That dreadful score should have made me a surefire loser had Rufus not been sweating booze and shedding dead brain cells with each stroke. I beat Rufus out of $2,200 that day.

Once he sobered up, Rufus wanted a rematch. Riding my $2,200 high, I couldn't wait to get him back on the golf course, thinking I had the stone-cold nuts. When our rematch took place a couple of weeks later, Rufus was sober as a saint and wiped the course with me. He won back his original $2,200 plus an additional $1,000 for good measure. It was just the beginning of a series of intense, entertaining golf matches with Rufus that lasted for years.

Another time, my buddy Calvin Coolidge Hash, a fellow car

salesman and one of my best friends, joined me at Midland Trail for a game. Calvin, a veteran of the Battle of the Bulge in World War II, served under General George S. Patton and was awarded four Bronze Stars for bravery. He was a superb golfer, who shot his age well into his eighties. Calvin gave me two shots a side and promptly won a couple hundred bucks off me.

After the round, Calvin didn't want to play anymore.

"What would it take for you to play me for five hundred bucks?" I asked.

"Give me two shots a side," Calvin replied.

"You got it."

"You're crazy," he said.

I beat him out of $2,000.

That was when Calvin and I realized how much better I played under pressure. From that moment on, Calvin became my partner on the golf course. In the years to follow, we traveled the country playing hundreds of matches together. Calvin remained one of my best friends until his death in 2016.

Most of my life was out of my control, so I found one thing I could control, a necessary quick fix. After playing golf one Sunday, I got to chatting with a family doctor in the men's grill about Derin's arrival and all the responsibilities piling up in my car crash of a life. I told him I couldn't afford any more kids.

"Have you ever considered a vasectomy?" he asked.

Once he explained that I could still have sex without the usual consequences, I was all in.

"Sign me up," I said.

The next day, I broke away from the car lot for lunch and drove to the doctor's office. I swapped a used set of golf clubs for a shot, a slice, and a couple of snips. Then I grabbed an ice pack, limped back to the showroom floor, and sold a couple of cars that afternoon.

5

Falling Apart

In 1967, I walked across the street from McMackin Motors and joined the competition as sales manager at Stevens Brothers Auto Sales. Jim Stevens had recruited me after witnessing my feverish work ethic and prodigious sales records.

"I figured if I can't beat you, I might as well hire you," he told me.

Mr. Stevens had three times the inventory as Mr. McMackin. Even better, he offered me a manager's job, which included a salary plus commission, which paired nicely with my constant need for more income. I earned my keep in no time, breaking *his* sales records.

As my income increased at Stevens, my gambling fever rose with it. I went from betting hundreds to thousands of dollars, and it wasn't going well. After one beating I found myself down $4,000. The bookie holding my debt stopped by the Stevens dealership on a Monday to collect.

I had an envelope ready to go, except it was short $2,000.

Naturally, I had a plan.

"You got to give me one shot to get this money back," I told the bookie.

The shark circled the bait, sensing a chance to double his money.

"What are you proposing?" he said.

"Pitching nickels at that line."

The bookie knew of my lofty reputation in that realm, so he didn't bite. After a momentary pause, I glanced out the window and pointed out two robins sitting on a telephone wire just outside the shop.

"See those birds out there?"

"Yeah."

"They're both facing east."

"So what?"

"I'll bet you the money I owe you that whichever bird flies off that wire first will head west."

The bookie gave me one of those *You gotta be kidding me* looks. "You're on."

We sat there watching for a minute or two until the bird closest to us took flight in a 180-degree turn and went west.

"Marker down," I yelled, breaking into laughter that lasted until the bookmaker left empty-handed.

Ronnie Aldridge, Jim Stevens's brother-in-law, had witnessed the scene. He could not believe my luck, or madness.

"How in the world did you have the balls to make that bet?" he asked.

"Heck, Ronnie," I said, "I've been watching that bird for days. It does the same thing every time."

I worked at Stevens for five years before deciding that I'd learned enough to start my own wholesale used-car business in 1972. As an independent wholesaler, I could buy large numbers of cars from other dealers, rental car agencies, and auctions and then sell them at a profit.

My first car lot was called Taylor Boulevard Auto Sales, a ten-minute walk from the Twin Spires entrance of Churchill Downs. As far as space, my lot was hardly a lot. There was room for only twenty cars. I had to find parking spots—legal or otherwise—up and down nearby streets for an additional forty or fifty cars.

My business quickly outgrew the cramped space, so I moved to a bigger lot along Berry Boulevard. Sales rapidly expanded from twenty cars a week to forty, then eighty. I kept doubling down from there, selling six hundred cars or more a month at my peak. I was netting $60,000 a month, sometimes more.

I would buy as many as a hundred cars over the phone, sight unseen, confident that one way or another I'd sell them all. Once things were rolling, I got cocky at auctions, shouting: "You other fellas might as well put your money away, because no matter what, I'm buying the next thirty!"

Acquiring cars at auctions throughout Kentucky and neighboring states meant that a lot of vehicles would need detailing, tires, trim and paint work, so I built a network of guys who could handle the jobs. I also needed a crew of drivers for pickup and delivery. I found many of them at a local halfway house that was filled with some—I'll be generous here—*colorful* characters.

Frank Odell Gaines was one of them. A good ol' boy from the hills of Frankfort, Kentucky, Frank found his calling as a master safecracker, but needed to polish his getaway skills. He'd done twenty years for various crimes. Although he was much older than me, we bonded as scrappers who'd survived hard times. I eventually trained him to be the manager of my automobile business.

Frank hired other employees from the halfway house. They never complained, appreciated the steady work, were loyal, and watched my back, but they came with some baggage.

Word got around to local law enforcement that I'd hired Frank and other recent parolees, such as Louie Snowden, who'd served twelve years in federal prison for robbing sixty-five banks. Whenever there was a major crime in Louisville, the cops or FBI agents would come by asking about my men. The lawmen did not make any arrests, but I may have sold them a car or two.

The entire time I was wholesaling used cars I never built up any serious working capital. I operated on OPM (other people's money) or what's called the "float." I didn't have to actually pay for a car until the title transferred in my name. I was confident that I would sell it before the title transferred, a constant juggling act for nine years. I felt the pressure every day of having to sell cars to pay off bookmakers. They didn't care that I had a business to run or whether I was drunk, sick, or hungover.

Somehow, some way, I kept the not-so-merry-go-round going. Had I lived a "normal" life, I might have stashed away enough money to own a dozen automobile dealerships. Instead, I slid deeper into debt, despite my sales success.

I'd buy twenty or thirty cars at a time with no money—many through Mike Hockett, who ran the Indianapolis Auto Auction on the east side of town. Mike would become an absolute power broker during his more than fifty-five years in the wholesale automotive auction business.

Back in the late sixties, his Indy auction was a no-nonsense exchange between buyer and seller. It was situated on fourteen acres of blacktop divided into at least four lanes. Up to two hundred cars a day were driven down each lane for a look-see by a few hundred or so dealers. An auctioneer/consignor was stationed in every lane, confirming each sale.

It was organized chaos. My kind of workplace. I moved through two or three lanes at a time like a man possessed. I'd buy one car after another with no money—up to $200,000 in purchases on credit in a single day. Mike trusted me to move the cars before the clock struck midnight on the two- or three-week float on the titles.

Over the years, Mike and I did a massive amount of buying and selling of each other's cars in addition to the auction. We became close, and I still consider him one of my best friends today. But more than once, I put that friendship to a test, such as the time I went to Vegas to gamble while owing him about $150,000.

Not exactly a strategy they teach at Harvard Business School.

My good friend Luther James, who ran junkets for the Riviera Hotel and Casino, went with me. I first met Luther when I was nineteen years old. His backstory was ripped from the same pages as mine, a back-road kid who hustled from an early age. He sold fruits and vegetables from a pushcart along a dirt road for one dollar a day and moved up to selling lumps of coal for fifty cents a bag while running bets on the side from his parents' home in Louisville's Portland neighborhood, a gamblers' den.

At fifteen, Luther spent a summer in Detroit learning the auto upholstery trade before returning home to graduate from Shawnee High in 1952. Drafted into the Korean War, he found himself stationed at nearby Fort Knox, earning off-duty dollars as a bouncer for seven bucks a shift. When he returned to civilian life, Luther opened a seat-cover shop on Seventh Street. Before long, he opened a restaurant out front, which he grew into a string of nightclubs, hotels, and shopping centers.

At the Riviera, I got on a roll playing baccarat and was up $300,000. Luther knew how fast it could all slip away. He had seen this act far too many times. Like a good friend, he shut me down.

"Time to call it a night," he said.

Luther escorted me to our suite, where I paced like a caged tiger. The house money in my pocket was eating me up. I waited for Luther to fall asleep, then hit the casino floor and promptly lost the $300,000, plus an additional $150,000 I didn't have.

Then I went back upstairs and slept as if nothing had happened.

When Mike Hockett found out I'd blown the money, he was as upset as I've ever seen him. It put a huge dent in our friendship for a while.

Looking back, those were some of the worst days of my life. I was out of control when it came to drinking and gambling. Many times, I should have died. And, at one point, I nearly did.

The near-death experience came during one of our rowdy post-auction poker games at a local Holiday Inn. Hockett was there, along with a half-dozen other auto dealers, each carrying several thousand dollars in cash. The TV blared as we battled it out at the card table.

At one point somebody called room service. By then, I had been pounding beers for hours and I needed to take a leak. As I got up to go to the bathroom, there was a knock at the door. It wasn't room service. Three men in masks burst in with guns drawn. They ordered us to shut up and get facedown on the floor with our hands out in order to grab our watches and rings in addition to our stacks of cash.

At that point, my smoker's cough kicked in. I couldn't stop. That's when the beer made me lippy with one of the robbers. Next thing I knew there was a .45 pressed against the back of my ear. I stopped coughing, and breathing, as the trigger cocked back.

"I thought I told you to shut the fuck up."

The room went dead quiet. The lone sound was from the television, and it was ominous—a commercial with guns blazing in a trailer for the new movie *Bonnie and Clyde*.

I never made it to the bathroom. I had consumed so much beer that I couldn't hold it any longer. I lost it right there on the floor with the gun to my head.

As if life wasn't risky enough, I drove back roads to places like Paintsville and Pikeville when I was looking for some action. This was coal country, a couple-hour drive from Harlan County, home of *Justified*, my all-time favorite television series. The high-stakes seven-card stud games started around 6:30 p.m. and ran late into the night, wins and losses reaching $50,000 or more. The table was filled with coal-mine owners and moonshiners, danger being a common denominator among clannish mountain people with an affinity for corn liquor and firearms. I usually traveled with somebody to watch my back, but it wouldn't have made a bit of difference. If the night turned ugly, you had a recipe for homicide, justified or not.

But dead is how I felt when I wasn't playing. I *needed* action. Be it the mountains of eastern Kentucky or the dozen wide-open lounges, bars, and strip clubs singing their siren song on Seventh

Street. Or Louisville Downs, where I couldn't get enough of betting a thousand bucks on every race, badgering bookies in the stands to wager thousands more, and pitching pennies against a wall in a seedy men's room for five grand a throw.

I was about to face some action I never could have imagined.

6

Thirty Days to Live

I had lurched into my late twenties with a load of family responsibilities that did little to slow my irresponsible ways. My second wife and kids played a distant second to dice, cards, and an obsession with proving that I wasn't afraid of anything or anybody.

I can't count the number of times I missed Scott's ball games or called Carol and promised, "We're going to dinner tonight. Get the boys ready."

Only to break that promise again and again.

I loved my family, instilling in my boys the same values that Grandmother instilled in me—respect for people and a strong work ethic. But my way of showing love was providing financially, and not much more.

Gambling sapped whatever energy I had left after working seventy to eighty hours a week. At that point, I wasn't suited for marriage and a family. So life stepped up and slapped me with a notice.

The news arrived via our oldest son, Scott, who was one of the sweetest, most loving children you'd ever meet. He was a people pleaser, willing to do anything to make his mother and father happy.

Scott failed first grade, a setback I blamed on his slight stutter. My solution had been to offer some drive-by parenting: "You're going to have to buckle down and pay attention," I told him.

It wasn't until a rare family outing in late autumn 1974 that I realized Scott was dealing with far more serious challenges than a lack of focus. I'd taken Carol and the boys (Derin was four years old) to see the Kentucky Colonels play in the now-defunct American Basketball Association.

On the way home, we stopped at Frisch's Big Boy restaurant for a piece of pumpkin pie. While waiting for dessert, I asked Scott about his pending report card.

"Hey, Gaga, I'm going to do well," he replied.

"Don't call me Gaga, Scott. Call me Daddy."

Without saying a word, Scott picked up a pen and struggled to write his name on a napkin because he was holding it in his left hand.

"Put that pen in your right hand," I said. "You're right-handed."

Scott tried, but he couldn't grip the pen with his right hand.

Carol and I thought that perhaps Scott had injured his hand jumping on the trampoline in our backyard. The next day, Carol took Scott to the pediatrician for an exam. She called me from his office.

"The doctor wants me to take Scott to a neurologist," she said. "I'm on my way there now."

By the end of the day, we were dealing with news that no parent wants to hear.

Your son has a terminal brain tumor.

The tumor was massive, located behind Scott's left eye within centimeters of the third ventricle that makes up the central part of the brain and facilitates communication between the other ventricles. The neurologist told us that if the tumor grew by even the width of a piece of paper, the ventricle would cut off blood flow and Scott would die.

He gave our seven-year-old son thirty days to live.

The son I worshipped, yet never made a priority. The son I had taken for granted along with the rest of my family.

My god, you talk about guilt. I had failed Scott as a father. All those meals I missed, the countless late nights that I left an empty chair at the table, and an empty place in their lives.

What could I do at this point? The answer was nothing. There was nothing anyone could do.

Doctors told us they could biopsy the tumor to better determine treatment, but even that simple procedure might end Scott's life. After arguing the pros and cons, Carol and I decided in favor of the surgery.

In truth, we were essentially waiting for Scott to die. Sometimes, couples unite in crisis, but not us. Carol went into shock. She cried and cried and cried, while throwing herself into the constant care of our son, never letting him go, and giving him whatever he wanted. Of course, her reaction was totally understandable.

I thought I'd endured pretty much everything, but this was something I'd never imagined. Our boy was facing death and our marriage was crumbling. Instead of being a source of strength and comfort, I was racked with guilt and set about numbing myself with bourbon and beer for six straight months. While I drank heavily, the doctors pulled off a medical miracle. They administered radiation and oral medication in carefully calculated doses that helped our son beat tremendous odds. Although his brain was left damaged, he survived.

My marriage to Carol, however, did not. She wanted a doting husband and a more stable life. At that point in my life, I was not that person.

The end came, predictably, after a night of drinking and gambling. I came home around midnight reeking of cigarette smoke and booze. We started arguing and bickering yet again, loud enough to wake the boys in their separate bedrooms upstairs. I threw a few things I shouldn't have thrown, said a few things I shouldn't have said, punched a hole in a kitchen door, and walked out. I didn't return.

Meanwhile, the rest of my life also was falling apart. My highly leveraged wholesale used-car business was crashing. After three years, Louisville Trust Bank ordered a halt to my nonstop cycle of loans and overdrafts. I owed the bank $200,000. In my higher-octane, energy-to-burn days, I would have focused and sold twenty cars a day. But, after sixteen years in the car business and feeling intense guilt over Scott, I was simply burned out. I was a thirty-something hustler with no hustle left.

If I liquidated every car on my lot, I could put together enough money to pay back either the bank or the body shops, tire dealers, and mechanics who had supported me. I chose to get square first with my friends, which meant I had to sign a note with the bank promising to repay within two years.

After settling up with my suppliers, I took my sorry ass and last $25,000 to the Riviera casino in Vegas, where I let it ride.

Fred Smith, the founder of FedEx, famously pulled off the same stunt in the early seventies. Within two years of the company's founding, FedEx was millions of dollars in debt, primarily due to rising fuel costs. Smith took FedEx's last $5,000 to the blackjack tables at Vegas, where he won $27,000—enough to cover the company's fuel bill for another week.

There are many differences between Mr. Smith and me. One is that he won in Vegas and I went bust.

I was broke, despondent, and just plain whipped and in need of a place to hide out and regroup—somewhere without gaming tables or a stocked bar. Church pews were uncomfortable, so I checked into Our Lady of Peace in Louisville, a treatment center for people with mental and emotional problems, including addictions.

After two long days, I realized that I *would* go crazy if I stayed. So I returned to the real world and began rebuilding my life on the foundation of the one good thing I had: a solid relationship with a strong woman.

Carol and I officially divorced a year later, in September 1976, after nine years of marriage. Carol later married a solid guy, Jerry Cottner, who is a good friend today. Eventually, I came to be a better friend than a husband. I did my best to make up for my failings as a father to Scott and Derin.

I had rushed into two marriages, despite no demonstrated interest in a long-term relationship. Strangely enough, the woman who finally set me straight was not that far away.

She was part of the Humphries family, whom I knew well. I was a longtime friend with her brother, Johnny, who was six years older than me, and her father, Charlie, whom I'd known since 1965. Johnny had introduced me to the game of golf, and Charlie was an avid small-time gambler.

Most of the gamblers I knew were just scraping by in blue-collar jobs, if they had steady work at all. Charlie was an executive at Philip Morris, the powerful tobacco company. Charlie kept his bookie, named Mouse, on speed dial. Every year, he'd take a week's vacation and head to Freedom Hall in Louisville or Rupp Arena in Lexington to watch the state high school basketball tournament. He'd bet $50 on every game.

Charlie and Johnny also were part of the pool-playing after-work crowd at Nevitt's. Before long, they invited me to their Louisville home for Charlie's fifty-cent Friday night poker games.

My first time there, I met his wife, Martha, and their daughter, Susan, a beautiful blonde with sparkly blue eyes. Susan Humphries was sixteen years old. I didn't know it yet, but she was an actress in school plays and an athlete who competed on the girls' flag football team.

As Susan told me years later, she took one look at my haggard face and decided I was closer to her older brother's age, if not her father's. Indeed, my late nights in smoky bars were etched into my bloated, weary face. I looked every bit like "Country," the name most folks still called me back then.

I didn't give Susan a second look. I was married with a child; she was just sixteen. She barely muttered a greeting before fleeing the room.

Years passed, Susan married, and we occasionally bumped into each other around Louisville. As fate would have it, I went to the local trotting track one night and met up with Johnny Humphries and some friends. Susan was part of the group. I learned that she was twenty-six then and divorced.

Our three-year age gap was no longer an issue, even if I still looked a decade older than my actual age. We had much in common. Her parents were like second parents to me. Her brother was like the brother I'd never had. We shared many friends and favorite places around town.

Susan had been around gamblers her entire life and knew that world. She also had a lively way about her. We laughed and talked all night. Being with her made me feel good about myself, which was a rare thing back then.

That first night, I asked her out, and we began dating casually. She was cautious because my second divorce was not finalized. She was also dating another guy, whose intentions were serious, so I had competition for her affections.

Susan had learned a thing or two observing the regular poker games held at her parents' house when she was growing up. She played her cards close to the chest and had a great poker face. She was also a positive and easygoing person. Nothing seemed to faze her, which would prove to be a real blessing for me.

She did draw the line when I drank too much and, on occasion, turned mean. She would just up and leave me in bars, restaurants, or casinos when she saw the first signs of surliness. But she also saw the good in me, even when I couldn't quite see it myself.

After we'd gone out a few times, I decided to get more serious. I worked up the courage to ask her to join me on a junket to Vegas with a group of friends who were also close to her parents.

I am a gambler, after all, but the odds were high that I'd screw this up.

Susan set some ground rules for the trip. She insisted on separate hotel rooms, since we were traveling with friends of her family and she didn't want to disrespect her parents. I accepted the ground rules like a gentleman, but then set the trigger for self-destruction by doing my best to consume the airplane's liquor supply on the flight.

Once we landed, I was so buzzed that I couldn't wait with everyone else for the charter bus. Instead, I hopped in a cab and raced to the Riv, leaving Susan and my fellow travelers behind. It was not the kind of behavior that inspires a long romantic weekend.

By the time Susan arrived at the hotel an hour later, one of her friends found me facedown and blacked out at a blackjack table. Dead broke.

I thought I'd blown it for sure, but Susan, being Susan, made the best of it by hanging out with friends for the rest of the weekend, while I gambled with borrowed funds. If Susan was ticked off, she didn't show it, which both frightened and intrigued me.

Back in Louisville, I showered her with apologies, which she seemed to accept, confusing me all the more. The day after we returned, I sent a huge tulip arrangement to the trucking company where she worked in dispatch. I figured I'd given the other guy who was dating her a huge advantage. I also knew that he'd recently sent her a bouquet of flowers, so I overcompensated and sent her not one, but two dozen tulips, which she loved.

On the card I wrote: "I told you I am twice the man he is."

I'm not sure if it was the tulips or my way with words, but Susan called and laughed and graciously thanked me.

"My desk looks like Derby Day at Churchill Downs," she said.

I figured she was either the most forgiving woman around or she was waiting for the perfect moment to kick me down a flight of stairs. I wagered that she had a soft spot for a rough-edged country boy. So before the tulips had a chance to wilt, I made my move.

A few nights later, I stood outside her apartment door doing my best hillbilly impersonation of a Hollywood rom-com dude. Wearing a Mexican sombrero, leather no less, I knocked with a single suitcase in hand, and put my cards on the table:

"Can I move in with you?"

My bold move paid off. She allowed me to enter instead of kicking me down the stairs.

Almost everyone we know will tell you that Susan was the beginning of a better me. To a man (or woman), they invariably use the same word to describe her—a saint—for staying by my side all these years.

Still, Susan will tell you that she loved my drive and knew in her heart that I would be successful. She has an infinite capacity for forgiveness and positivity. She sees me in the best light, even when I am totally in the dark.

We were married on September 21, 1976. Our wedding day foretold the mad scramble of the years to follow. The only available judge we could find at the courthouse was in the middle of a murder trial. Judge S. Rush Nicholson took a break from the homicide case to marry us.

I didn't have a witness lined up for our ceremony because that would have required forethought and planning. When I spotted Gilbert Hale Nutt in the hallway, I asked him to stand in for my wedding. Gil had been my divorce lawyer and probably figured he'd make some money handling the next divorce a few years later.

After the quick ceremony, Susan went back to her job at the trucking company, and I went back to selling cars. Together, we broke my cycle of fractured relationships. There was no honeymoon, but we've made up for it with our world travels since.

I should have married my third wife first. Not that my first and second wives were to blame, it's just that Susan married the guy who, at thirty years old, was finally, almost, nearly ready to commit to a marriage.

Forty-six-plus years into it, Susan remains the best person I have ever met. She stands side by side with Grandmother as a savior for me. She is a role model in how to live a righteous life. Our love is unconditional.

Susan was not one to lay down the law or demand that I change my ways. She realized I was harder on myself than anyone else. The way she handled me was perfect. She waited for me to finally overcome my demons, but I tested her patience along the way.

The first test occurred shortly after we were married when I went out for a few drinks with friends and came home with my face beaten to a bloody pulp. Oddly enough, the pulping occurred at a Louisville hot spot called the Do Drop Inn, which advertised itself as a place for "Nice People Dancing to Good Country Music."

Initially, everything was as harmonious as advertised, at least for the "nice people." While the band was playing, I pitched nickels for a hundred bucks a rattle with eventual Grammy Award–winning singer and songwriter Guy Clark, known as a "King of the Texas Troubadours." (His many hits included "L.A. Freeway," popularized by Jerry Jeff Walker.)

Naturally I got into a stupid argument with this future Nashville icon. We bickered over a very critical global event—whose nickel was closest to the line. Before we could reach détente, punches flew. I got in a few good licks, but I went down when somebody smashed a beer bottle across my nose. Then some boys in the band jumped in.

We ended up out in the street, where I dove under a car to escape the four of them. At six in the morning, I drove home and knocked at our condo door. I was covered in so much blood that Susan thought I was a degenerate stranger, not that her assessment was far off the mark.

She was about to shut the door on my sorry ass when I managed to mumble, "It's me." Doctors at Suburban Hospital cleaned up my battered face before putting thirty-two stitches in my nose. I spent the next two days with ice packs to bring the swelling down. Later, I had to return to the hospital for surgery to straighten my nose and repair a deviated septum.

Note to self: next time you pick a fight with a band, make it a boy band.

7

Barkeeping & Bookmaking

It was 1975 and Scott's eighth birthday was fast approaching. He badly wanted an expensive parrot and, surprise, I didn't have the money to buy one. So I headed down to the Toy Tiger, a roadhouse haunt famous for wet T-shirt and banana-eating contests, and pool tables with a lot of action.

I hadn't shot pool in a dozen years, but I needed $500 to buy the bird. I was rusty, but after a couple nights, I won the money, bought the parrot, and then packed away my cue stick for good. Desperate to pay the bills, I decided to give the car business one last try. I borrowed $50,000 from my father-in-law, Charlie Humphries, who recently had retired and had, at best, $200,000 in his Philip Morris pension.

Charlie loaned me the money because he knew I loved his daughter. Susan chipped in, too, selling her beloved 1971 VW Bug for $1,800. I tried to make it work. I really did. But my hustle tank was dry and my salesmanship had sailed. Plus, word was out that my line of credit was exhausted.

They say stick to what you know, so Susan and I gathered what little money we had left and invested in a bar called the Patio Lounge. Our partner was Sammy Marrillia Sr., owner of the Prospect Bridge and Backgammon Club, a milquetoast moniker for one of the hottest poker rooms in the country.

We changed the name of the Patio to Butch Cassidy's and featured country music. I did a bit of bookmaking on the side, but had to keep a low profile. The leading candidate for mayor, Bill Stansbury, had vowed to crack down on Louisville's illegal gambling operations as part of his campaign.

Lying low wasn't easy for a guy known as one of the biggest gamblers in town. On Super Bowl Sunday in 1980, our joint was wall-to-wall from noon till midnight. After closing, I locked the front door, emptied the till, and drove home with about two grand in small bills in my pocket.

As I walked to the gate of our condo, two thugs wearing ski masks jumped out from behind a parked car. One of them jammed a double-barrel shotgun in my ribs. The other held a .45 pistol to my head. Both were shaking like it was ten below zero.

Great, I thought. *Amateurs.*

"Calm down. Just take the money," I said.

They took the cash. I braced for them to grab my fake Rolex next, but they had other plans. One of the crooks snatched my car keys, popped the trunk of my Lincoln, and ordered me inside. I knew the odds were not good on coming out of a car trunk alive, but they weren't great on arguing with a shotgun and a .45, either.

The lid slammed shut and everything went dark, including my thoughts. I feared the thugs would drive my car out to some remote spot and either shoot me or abandon me to die.

I'm about two miles and one deserted road from a funeral home.

Instead, they drove off in their own car. I was relieved that they hadn't filled the trunk with lead, but things still weren't looking very hopeful. There was no safety release inside the trunk. It felt as if I was trapped in a coffin, waiting to die.

I screamed and pounded like a man possessed, but the racket did not result in a rescue. I forced myself to calm down, worried that

I'd run out of air. Then I had another panic attack. I frantically dug around in the trunk and found a tire iron. I jammed and jimmied every corner and crevice. Nothing gave.

Finally, with blood dripping from my hands, I grabbed the tire iron and punched a hole through the metal stereo speakers, opening a hole into the back seat.

I shoved my hand against the opening and yelled into the car's interior, exhausting what little energy I had left. An hour slipped by. Then two. I screamed, rested, and screamed again.

Finally, our next-door neighbor heard my cries. He knocked on the door of our condo and alerted Susan to the crazy sounds coming from our car.

I heard footsteps.

"Bill, is that you? Where are you?"

She peered inside and saw a hole in the back seat.

"I'm dying in here," I yelled. "Hurry up, get the keys!"

Thank god she found the extra set.

Susan popped the trunk and set me free. After she helped me to our apartment and into bed, I told her how I ended up in the trunk.

"We're moving! We're moving!" I shrieked, as if the problem was the place we lived and not my reckless ways.

As it turned out, we did *not* move—at least not then.

When I wasn't getting the crap beat out of me or suffocating in the trunk of a car, I was roaming around town throwing good money after bad by shooting dice, betting the ponies, or playing seven-card stud—all while drinking.

More than a few of those high-stakes games took place at the Prospect, Sammy Marrillia's secret garden of poker delight, where the backgammon and bridge games out front were little more than a dodge from local law enforcement. Sammy is a man with as much nerve around a poker table as anyone, and his invitation-only card games drew an eclectic clientele. Among the players was Louisville's favorite son, Paul Hornung, who won the Heisman Trophy at Notre

Dame in 1956. He went on to become a Hall of Fame running back for the immortal Green Bay Packers and Coach Vince Lombardi, who won the first-ever Super Bowl in 1967. While the public knew him as "the Golden Boy," to me he was just Paul. We met in the late 1960s and became good friends. Right around Christmastime 1980, Paul got hooked for about forty grand before promising his wife that he was done if he lost another ten grand the next night. Paul showed up and, naturally, knew everybody at the table. Except for one player, who looked vaguely familiar. Paul wasted no time busting Sammy's balls.

"Who the fuck is this guy?" Paul said. "Are you bringing ringers in on me?"

Sammy played dumb. "He's just a guy from out of town who wanted to play," he said.

Paul knew bullshit when he heard it. No outsiders knew about the game. Then it hit him: the out-of-towner was none other than World Series of Poker champion Bobby "The Owl" Baldwin.

You would have thought Hornung had been stopped one yard short of another Super Bowl ring. He rose up from the table and unloaded his best Lombardi in Sammy's face.

"Sammy, you cocksucker! How could you do this to us? We're buddies. We're customers. I thought we were friends. What's the Owl doing here? How in the fuck did he find out about the game?"

Sammy finally spilled it. He told Paul that I had brought Bobby into the game and that we were partners. Fortunately for us, Paul ended up winning back ten grand. We laughed about that night all the time. Thankfully, Paul never held a grudge.

I first met Bobby at the Horseshoe in Vegas in 1978 right after he won the World Series of Poker Main Event at the age of twenty-eight, then the youngest champion in history. He would win four WSOP bracelets between 1977 and 1979 before transitioning into the executive ranks, among his many titles, the CEO of Mirage Resorts and chief customer development officer of MGM Resorts.

Bobby and I struck a partnership in which I would sponsor

him—but not before I had to hock some guns to come up with enough cash. When I greeted him at the Louisville airport, Bobby carried an Eastern Airlines cardboard box containing all of his belongings, despite having just won more than two hundred grand in the WSOP.

Bobby hung around for about ten months. We were building our bankroll in joints around town before he headed back to Tulsa to spend Thanksgiving with his family. Only *one* little hitch. Bobby left behind our remaining bankroll—sixty thousand in cash. No surprise, I blew it all shooting craps in our finished basement after *our* Thanksgiving dinner.

When Bobby returned from Tulsa the following Monday, I told him I had lost the entire bankroll. Bobby handled it like everything else in his life—no drama. He gave me the time I needed to borrow money and pay him back.

I am proud to say Bobby and I remain good friends to this day.

Even before the thugs followed me home and robbed me, I knew our days in the bar business were numbered. Susan and I were done working long nights surrounded by spilled suds and clouds of cigarette smoke.

The question for us was: *What's next?*

My bookmaking sideline at Butch Cassidy's had gone well enough that I thought it could be highly profitable so long as I did it full-time and avoided getting arrested or robbed at gunpoint.

Like a lot of southern cities in the late sixties and seventies, Louisville's dens of vice and sin ran wide-open day and night. There was no organized crime presence, but there were plenty of local hustlers. It helped that the police department had a hands-off approach toward gambling, as long as nobody got muscled or hurt. That said, I knew I was crossing the legal line from *making* bets to the risky business of *taking* bets.

It didn't help matters that in 1978, the new mayor, Bill Stansbury, was making headlines on his campaign vow to clean up illegal bookmaking. Stansbury had shut down a few operations, but more than a dozen bookies were still taking bets around town. Perfectly content to cruise around in their shiny new Lincolns or Cadillacs, getting down to serious business only on Mondays, when they collected their weekly winnings from losers like me.

Most of them played the same one-sided game, refusing to post odds until game day, which was six days after the official NFL lines were listed in Vegas. Otherwise, it was the day before the game. I ran a few calculations and figured that if I treated bookmaking as an actual business, like selling cars, I could outwork, outsmart, and ultimately outhustle most other guys in town.

And so, amid a crackdown on crime, I launched a full-time business as a bookmaker. Call me counterintuitive or just crazy. I took a very aggressive approach, offering my customers early lines, better odds, and higher limits. I welcomed gamblers of every income and risk level.

My bookmaking operation stayed open twelve hours a day, seven days a week, and ran a variety of promotions. On Friday nights, if you made a minimum of ten plays, I'd let you move the line a half point either way. If you bet the entire card, you could lay $1.05 instead of $1.10.

I hired Frank Gaines, an old bookie himself, and a few other wily veterans to take bets and spread the gospel of Billy Walters in bars, restaurants, pool halls, and poker rooms around town. In exchange, I offered my pitchmen a percentage of the action they brought in.

In no time at all, I was bookmaking full-time, while steering clear of the mayor's posse, which kept busting books from one end of Louisville to the other. In response, I decided to move my base of operations to the town of Crestwood in neighboring Oldham County. After I set up shop in a harmless-looking building, I learned that some bookies were paying off the cops to stay out of jail. I didn't think that was necessary, but I did take a few precautionary measures such as keeping my master betting records on rice paper.

That, at least, proved to be a wise move.

On the first Sunday of the 1982 NFL season, I was in the back office with four of my guys watching the early games on television when it sounded like a car crashed through the front door.

Nope, it was a Kentucky state trooper busting the door off the hinges with a sledgehammer. About two dozen troopers and Louisville vice cops raced in. I grabbed the master sheet and scrambled to the nearest bathroom. I was about to dunk the rice-paper records, which were designed to disappear in water, when one of the cops put a gun to my head and said, "You stick that in, and I'll blow your brains out!"

Screw that, I thought. *No way he's going to* kill *me*.

I stuffed the paper into the toilet. Not exactly the smartest move, because we still had a raft of other gambling records scattered throughout the office. The cops snapped up all the remaining evidence, as well as a stack of cash, two cars, a couple of television sets, and eight phones, including four equipped with our toll-free 800 lines.

All five members of my bookmaking team were arrested, including Frank Gaines and Donald "Jock" Potter, a real-life version of the Jon Voight character Mickey on Showtime's *Ray Donovan*. His resume was more grit than gold. Jock had worked as a racetrack groom, blackjack dealer, and bookmaker. He was funny as hell, too, though the cops didn't seem to appreciate his wit.

During the raid, they found some pot stashed in Jock's '73 Monte Carlo parked out front. When they ordered him to empty his pockets, Jock surrendered every last cent, all seven of them in his pockets.

"Okay," said the cop. "Who's in charge here?"

"Well, normally, the guy with the most money is the boss," Jock deadpanned, meaning Mr. Seven Cents was far from the ringleader.

They hauled us down to the Oldham County Jail on charges of promoting gambling, possession of gambling records, and, the capper, operating a criminal syndication. We each had to come up with $10,000 to make bond. Given that it was a Sunday, Susan could only scrape together $30,000 in cash—enough to bail out three of our employees. That left me and Frank Gaines, who thought nothing of spending a bit more time behind bars.

Our bust made the front page of the next day's Metro section of *The Courier-Journal.* "Gambling Raid Nets Five Arrests" read the headline. The story reported that our operation had been under surveillance for six months. The state police estimated we hauled in $6.5 million in wagers a year, which qualified my operation as one of the largest gambling rings in the state.

As soon as I made bail, I headed to the law office of Frank Haddad Jr. A humble man with a lacerating wit, Frank was a Louisville legend. He commanded respect in and out of court, the go-to guy when you were up to your neck in criminal charges. He wasn't a miracle worker, but he was pretty damn close.

Frank had represented many big-time bookmakers. He took my case, but not before making his.

"Billy," he said, "you've got one of two decisions to make here. You can get out of town. Or, if you stay in Louisville, you can never be involved in any kind of gambling again. From now on, you're going to have a target on your back."

Frank was right. I needed to get out of Louisville. I was thirty-six years old, but looked twice my age. The bags under my eyes carried the weight of hundreds of thousands of dollars in debt, three felony criminal charges, and a young son still fighting for his life.

A few years prior, I made an over-under bet with three friends— Danny Matthews, Hardin Allen, and Knocker Braden—on how long I would live. We wagered $5,000 apiece on that, no joke. The over-under was age thirty-five, given my wild ways. None of my friends took the over. I had beaten those odds, but for how long?

Susan and I agreed that we needed a fresh start. In the end, though, sanity and safety did not guide us. I wasn't born to be an insurance salesman. I just needed to change my location to a place where gambling was legal.

To me, there was only one place for us to go. Las Vegas, baby. When we told some of our friends about our plans to relocate, they regarded it as the equivalent of a dope addict moving into a drug den. They posed a simple question: *What are the odds that an alcoholic and degenerate gambler with no money management skills could survive in a city that ate addicts for lunch and dreams for dinner?*

Even as a child rolling dice, I believed I could make a living as a professional gambler. Call me delusional, but I had a plan. I was at a crossroads in life. In gambling parlance, I wanted to move up from a half-sharp to a sharp. To go from being an average bettor to one who consistently won more often than he lost—and had the chops to move the best betting lines.

The decision was made. In late September 1982, Susan and I headed west to the land of second chances.

8

Heaven

Las Vegas and I had a lot in common back in the early eighties. When we arrived, Sin City was like a weary fighter on the ropes. The Rat Pack glamour of the sixties and seventies had faded, leaving behind a tacky tourist town offering $29 hotel rooms, aging casinos, "all you can eat" buffets, and showrooms featuring stars in the twilight of their careers.

For better or worse, I fit right in. I had met a lot of Vegas people playing in Jack Binion's Professional Gamblers Invitational (PGI) golf tournament. But they knew me, too, as a gambler whose skills diminished in direct proportion to his blood alcohol level. Oh, I was popular at the casinos because, in their opinion, I couldn't hang on to my winnings more than a day or two. I was a sucker with a capital *S*. But I could be a dangerous sucker because I would bet it all—without a worry about going broke again.

In those days, Vegas was a volatile place with a violent undercurrent. The Jewish mob that ran the city in the forties, fifties, and sixties—led by the likes of Meyer Lansky, Bugsy Siegel, and Moe Dalitz—were largely replaced in the seventies by organized-crime families such as the Chicago Outfit and its psychopath-in-chief, Anthony "Tony the Ant" Spilotro.

Spilotro was a human powder keg with a short fuse who inspired the Joe Pesci character Nicky Santoro in Martin Scorsese's 1995 mob classic *Casino.* Spilotro overcompensated for his pint-size stature (five feet, two inches) with a reputation for murder and mayhem.

The Ant took sadistic pleasure in torturing his victims with ice picks, hammers, blowtorches, and other industrial-strength tools. He'd been linked to nearly two dozen murders in a rampage that set the city on edge.

Spilotro became known as the leader of the notorious Nevada-based crime ring dubbed "the Hole in the Wall Gang." The group was comprised of safecrackers and thieves known for smashing through walls and the roofs of high-end homes, luxury hotel rooms, and expensive stores. The gangsters later expanded their reign of terror to include loan-sharking, arson for hire, and strong-arming the city's top gamblers and bookmakers for a "street tax."

One of their targets was my friend and betting partner David "Chip" Reese, an A-list poker professional. I met Chip in the late seventies at a PGI tournament, and we became friends right from the start. Chip was originally from Centerville, Ohio, a suburb of Dayton. He went to college at Dartmouth, where his exploits in poker and bridge led his fraternity brothers to christen the "David E. Reese Memorial Card Room." Chip was on his way to Stanford Law School when he won $60,000 in a professional poker tournament during a stopover in Vegas. He never left town.

The Ant and his minions harassed Chip and other pros during the World Series of Poker by demanding a piece of their action, punctuating each request with an ominous "Unless..." And nobody in his right mind wanted to find out what "Unless" meant.

In the late seventies, Chip secured the rights to lease the poker room at the Dunes from the previous owner, Johnny Moss, a real rounder and multiple WSOP winner who had lost $200,000 to Chip in a poker game. Moss couldn't pay the debt, so he forked over the keys. Virtually every table in the Dunes had at least one or two cheaters playing Texas Hold'em, seven-card stud, or Deuce-to-seven lowball.

For a time, the Dunes was the only place in Las Vegas to play serious high-limit games. Chip knew the big pots would disappear if he didn't clean up the cheating, so he brought in an enforcer. Not a muscleman, but a professional manager by the name of Doug Dalton.

Doug had arrived in Vegas in the sixties from San Diego, where he made ends meet by dealing blackjack and playing in low-limit games. After taking command of the Dunes private room in 1978, he carved out a stellar career that took him to higher-ranking positions at the Golden Nugget, The Mirage, and the Bellagio, where he ran the celebrated poker room named in honor of my friend Bobby Baldwin.

During his first night as shift manager at the Dunes, Doug let it be known that the games would be run honestly and problem players would be dealt with appropriately. Troublemakers were hauled into his office for a one-time warning that went something like this:

"Might as well tell your wife and kids to get ready to move back to California."

"What do you mean?"

"You throw any more cards or mouth off to a dealer one more time and I'm kicking you out of here for good. Then I will blacklist you in every poker room in town. Your call."

"You mean it?"

"You know I mean it. And I can do it."

"I'm sorry, Doug. It won't happen again."

And nine times out of ten, it never did.

One day, a short, stocky guy got pissed and threw his cards at a dealer. Doug made a beeline to his table.

"Look," he said, "you need to calm yourself down or you will have to leave."

The very next hand, the guy did it again.

"You're out," Doug said.

At that point, as Doug later told it, everyone in the room froze, because this wasn't just any half-sharp Doug had just eighty-sixed. It was Tony Spilotro's driver, Sammy Spiegel, another guy with dead eyes.

On his way out, Spiegel stopped for a few final words with Doug, and the room fell silent again.

"Doug, I like you," Spiegel said, "and for that reason I'm leaving. But don't ever do this to me again."

Afterward, Doug called Chip to give him a heads-up.

"One or both of us might get killed because I just threw out Sammy Spiegel."

To ensure my survival as a newcomer to this Wild West, I sought the guidance of the Cowboy, longtime Las Vegas casino owner Lester Ben Binion, the ultimate Vegas insider, a font of insight and common sense, and, in his own day, nobody to mess with.

Benny was like a crusty character out of a Larry McMurtry novel. His nickname sprung from his Texas roots—he once shot and killed a man "cowboy style"—and from his role in bringing the National Finals Rodeo event to his adopted hometown. Today, Benny's life-size bronzed statue—on horseback, no less—dominates a lobby in the South Point Hotel, Casino & Spa.

Benny built a gambling and racketeering empire in Depression-era Dallas. He cultivated a reputation as a cold-blooded mob boss whose rap sheet included moonshining, concealed weapons charges, and a couple of murder convictions. Thomas "Amarillo Slim" Preston, poker ace and human nature expert, proposed this epitaph for Benny: "He was either the gentlest bad guy or baddest good guy you'd ever seen."

Born and raised in tiny Pilot Grove, Texas (population 193), Benny relocated to Nevada in the early fifties when living in Dallas became a bit too dicey for him and his millions. He brought poker and glamour to Las Vegas in the form of Binion's Horseshoe, a sprawling downtown

"Glitter Gulch" casino known for its late-night two-dollar steak special, single-deck blackjack tables, sky-high limits, free drinks to players and, shall we say, frontier justice when dealing with cheaters.

Benny's motto was "People want good whiskey, cheap, good food, cheap, and a square gamble. . . . Make the little man feel like a big man." Night after night, the Horseshoe delivered all that and more before Benny lost his casino license in 1953 due to some federal income tax issues. His oldest son, Jack, eventually took charge and Benny assumed the title of director of public relations. He had walked the dark side, but later in life, he was widely regarded as a benevolent presence and source of great wisdom. In 1970, he also happened to create the World Series of Poker.

Benny was pushing eighty when I sought his guidance about living and gambling in Vegas. Before we left Louisville, I had visited with Benny many times and came to know him and his family. When I asked to meet after settling in, he invited me to dinner in his corner booth at the Horseshoe coffee shop.

The sage of downtown Las Vegas quickly dispensed some wise advice.

First, he told me to avoid one particular guy, whom we both knew well.

"He's a snitch," Benny said.

His second tip was to give me the name of Harry Claiborne, his longtime lawyer, in the event I needed a good one in a pinch.

Benny saved the most important bit of advice for last. As someone who'd once put fear in the hearts of his own adversaries, he cautioned me to avoid another particularly dangerous man.

"Billy, if you're going to live here, you really need to stay below the radar. The one guy you don't want to cross is Tony Spilotro. If he finds out you're here, you'll have to make some tough decisions. He will insist you pay tribute to him, and I can't help you there. If you don't ante up, he'll hurt you or have you killed. Your choice will be to either pay up or leave town. Those are your only options."

Benny had already played his ace in the hole with Spilotro. A few years earlier, Billy Baxter, a professional poker player and good friend of mine, answered the phone at his place in the Regency Towers to find the Ant on the line. Here's Billy's version on how that went:

"I got to talk to you," Spilotro said.

"Tony, it's ten o'clock at night."

Spilotro could not have cared less.

"I'm at Winchell's Donut House. I need to see you right now. I'll be waiting for you."

From the tone of Spilotro's voice, it was not an invite that Billy could turn down. He hightailed it over to Winchell's.

"Let's cut right to the fucking chase," Spilotro began. The Ant proceeded to explain in no uncertain terms that he wanted 25 percent of their book from Billy and "the other Fatty," meaning Doyle Brunson. And, if he caught either one of them taking one bet without getting his cut, he was going to stick an ice pick twelve different times into the "big fat bustle gut" of Doyle.

The mobster left no room for further debate.

The next morning, Billy met Doyle to relay Spilotro's warning, including the specific number of stabs he'd threatened. Doyle pointed to Billy's then ample waistline and cracked, "What's wrong with *your* stomach?"

Jokes aside, both men had a big fat problem on their hands. They decided to reach out to their friend Jack Binion, who spoke to his father, who agreed to meet with them to discuss the threat.

According to Billy, Benny was blunt. "I hate to tell you boys, but you've got yourself in a bad spot. If you can get Tony to come down here, I'll talk to him."

This was the Vegas equivalent of the Godfather requesting a sit-down with a rival mob boss. Billy called Spilotro to inform him that he and Doyle were friendly with the Binion family, and that Benny wanted to meet him at the Horseshoe for a little chat.

"Oh, you got that old motherfucker involved?" Spilotro replied.

Indeed, they had. Spilotro showed up with a couple of his killers in tow only to see that Benny was fully staffed in that department as well. Benny knew better than to get caught in the cross fire. Instead, he played his usual role of peacemaker.

"Tony, these two fellows are friends of my son. They're good ol' boys. Is there any kind of way you could give them a pass?"

A long pause ensued before the Ant replied:

"You know, Benny, I'm gonna do that for you."

Soon after arriving in town, I met with another Vegas player, although he was no Benny Binion.

Dr. Ivan "Doc" Mindlin was an orthopedic surgeon who was a degenerate gambler, but one who had lucked into a highly sophisticated operation of another kind. He would serve as my connection to the legendary betting syndicate in Las Vegas known as the Computer Group. Beginning in the late seventies, the Group had made a killing by placing bets against the posted Vegas line based on a computer model created by a math whiz named Michael Kent.

Doc and I had never met, even though I had been placing bets— what's known as "moving money"—for the Computer Group indirectly through a bookmaker in Pittsburgh, who was moving money for the Group in New York. At one time, the New York operation— headed by Jimmy Evart and Stanley Tomchin—had the largest sports-betting market in the country. Eventually, I would establish an even bigger sports-betting operation with more places to bet than Jimmy and Stanley.

Upon moving to Vegas, I thought it wise to meet face-to-face with Doc because of his connection to Michael Kent and the Group. I found him outgoing and charismatic. There was no hint of the guile and deceit that I'd come to know later. In our first meeting, Doc confirmed our arrangement—I could continue to move large blocks of the Group's money as an independent contractor.

I needed my own partner to take advantage of the Group's edge. The first person I approached was the aforementioned poker pro Billy Baxter, better known as "BB."

When Susan and I first arrived in Vegas, we were upside down about $300,000. We stayed with Billy and his wife, Julie, for a couple of days before renting a house. BB and I had first met in the seventies in Las Vegas at the PGI. Right from the start, I felt he was my alter ego, a slightly different version of me.

He, too, was a southern boy who'd grown up hard, fast, and ready to wager on just about anything. He was the city marbles champion of Augusta, Georgia, at age nine and a pool hustler by sixteen.

In no time, BB was taking his crack-shot pool winnings to the back room of the high-end Alpine Lounge, where serious money could be made playing gin and poker against local lawyers, bankers, and businessmen. Billy's parents wanted him to be a dentist, but he dropped out of college after quickly deciding that he preferred pulling aces to pulling teeth.

Billy once beat the owner of an illegal joint called the Paisley Room out of $40,000 in a gin rummy game. Instead of paying the forty grand, the owner offered Billy an interest in the Paisley. Billy accepted, which proved to be a bad move. The law eventually shut down the place. Billy was later busted on felony bookmaking charges and did a stretch in state prison, where he was assigned to a chain gang overseen by shotgun-toting prison guards and their snarling dogs. He was thirty-six when his ten-month sentence ended.

BB and Julie then beat it out of Georgia for the friendlier confines of Vegas, where he quickly earned a reputation as a boss gambler. He went on to win seven World Series of Poker bracelets and bankroll a string of successful business ventures. He also managed and promoted three world-boxing champions.

I pitched Billy to partner up on my venture with the Computer Group. He turned me down flat (telling me later that he couldn't trust a guy who went broke that many times). He suggested I try Doyle and his bankroll.

Doyle "Texas Dolly" Brunson was a different breed of gambler. Competitive by nature, he had won the mile run in the 1950 Texas interscholastic track meet. An All-State high school basketball player, he starred on the Hardin-Simmons University hoops team before he broke a leg at twenty that never fully healed, ending his dream of one day playing in the NBA.

Doyle turned to a more competitive game that he could play while seated. While still in college, he honed his card-playing skills and eventually jumped full-time into games across Texas, Oklahoma, and Louisiana before moving to Vegas in 1970.

He settled in as a professional gambler and became the first player to win $1 million in poker tournaments. Doyle would go on to win ten of the coveted bracelets awarded to winners in the World Series of Poker. He also wrote three books on poker strategy, including *Super System*, the bestselling poker book in history.

Along with a bum leg, Doyle had an Achilles' heel. Though he was successful in most other forms of gambling, he had never scored big on sports wagering. Following BB's advice, I offered Doyle a partnership with the Computer Group.

We swung into action late in the strike-shortened 1982 NFL season. The first weekend as partners, we lost so much of Doyle's money that he nearly went into shock. On Monday morning, he called BB and screamed, "You've never done anything worth a shit! This man bets every game on the fucking board! We lost a million dollars this weekend!"

BB replied gently in his soft Georgia peach of a drawl: "Well, Doyle, what can I tell you? I ain't that smart."

As luck and the Computer Group would have it, our fortunes turned the next two weeks. We won back the million dollars and were up $220,000. But the sweat of high-risk, high-volume wagering proved too much for Doyle, and our partnership ended shortly after it began.

Looking back forty years later, no one believed that we could win making such a large number of bets.

I was running out of options when it suddenly hit me: Why not pitch my friend Chip Reese, the best poker player on the planet? Chip loved to bet on sports. But, like Doyle and other great players, his world-class skills at poker did not carry over to sports betting.

Chip was drawn to other gamblers with killer instincts. He knew that I played to win it all, so he was interested when I suggested we partner up to cash in on the edge provided by the Computer Group's high-tech system.

I asked Chip to stake us to $5,000 a game to start. He agreed to back me so long as we established a ceiling on the amount of money that he was willing to risk on any single wager. He also demanded that we split our winnings fifty-fifty.

That arrangement didn't sit well with some of Chip's friends, who viewed me with suspicion. One of them suggested that Chip keep track of my bets with this newfangled device called a fax machine, which transmitted information via hardwired telephone lines.

Back then, faxes were the size of washing machines and cost five grand apiece. We bought two of them. One was hooked up in Chip's house, the other in the home Susan and I rented at the Sahara golf course. The information we faxed Chip gave him the data on every bet we made, providing him peace of mind.

Throwing my chips in with Chip was like enrolling in Professional Gamblers Business School. Until then, I had been a poor money manager. Chip was simply the most disciplined money manager I've ever known. He was skilled at minimizing risk wherever and whenever possible.

To leverage our money carefully we agreed to never risk more than 3 percent of our bankroll on any single wager. The size of each bet was based on our analysis of the opportunity. The more we spread our bets out, the more we reduced our risk profile.

Chip had learned these lessons the hard way. As a younger player, he'd been cheated and busted numerous times in shady card rooms. He became adept at protecting his downside—as well as his backside—by leaving a table when things didn't feel right. He also vowed never to throw good money after bad.

Eventually, we had hundreds of thousands of dollars riding on big games during college football season. As careful as we were, we still sweated through our shirts and shorts watching those games in our condominium. When things got intense on the field, Chip, Susan, and I would put bowls on our heads as helmets and take three-point stances on the carpet to form an imaginary goal line stand to stop the opposing team from scoring.

We had fun with it, enjoying the kind of action that gamblers live for. My partnership with Chip put me on a roll. Under his guidance, I worked on honing my skills at poker. Under my guidance, Chip honed his golf skills, a combination that proved to be very profitable for both of us.

Susan and I were on our way to enjoying a seven-figure income. By this point, I had my life in order. (Or so I thought.) Yet I was still driven, frantic even, about proving to casino dealers and pit bosses that Billy Walters played hard and fast and without fear.

Alcohol was still a problem for me, drowning out common sense and caution. When I drank heavily, I risked going all in until the lights went out. One night, I committed a typical act of self-sabotage after taking Susan to a lovely dinner at the Horseshoe to celebrate having $1 million in our bankroll for the first time.

After dessert, I suggested that she head on home because I wanted to play a bit of blackjack.

A *bit* of blackjack turned into another reckless binge of gambling and drinking that ended at 4:00 a.m. When I dragged my sorry, drunken ass home and into bed, Susan asked, "How'd you do?"

"Well, it was really, really bad."

"How bad?"

"I lost the entire million. Plus two hundred thousand in credit."

"Don't worry about it," my rock of a wife said. "We'll get it back."

Susan's faith in me was rewarded. Before long we were flush enough to move out of our rental into a condo we bought next to Chip's place at the Las Vegas Country Club. In the early eighties, LVCC was *the* place to live in Vegas, home to the city's biggest movers and shakers. Members included crooners Robert Goulet, Wayne Newton, and Jerry Vale; Senator Paul Laxalt; Merv Adelson, the real estate developer and television producer who was married to Barbara Walters; Irwin Molasky, a powerful Las Vegas developer and cofounder of Lorimar Productions; and Moe Dalitz, the dignified former mob boss turned leading Las Vegas philanthropist, developer, and a founding father of the LVCC.

The country club's eclectic membership was a testament to Vegas as the second-chance capital of the world—and the only city in America where gamblers and mobsters were seen as respected members of the community. I never felt more at home.

Chip would pop over for breakfast in the morning. Bobby Baldwin lived a few doors away. Doyle was down the street. Stuey "the Kid" Ungar, a future Poker Hall of Famer, had a place right around the corner. We had our own little neighborhood of real-life rounders—including Sarge Ferris, Billy Baxter, and Puggy Pearson—"action" men who talked trash with the best of them.

As the new kid on the block, I spent countless hours closely observing one Hold'em hand after another as Doyle, Bobby, Sarge, Chip, and Stuey—the best gin rummy player in the world—squared off in their game rooms, man caves, and poolside patios.

Watching the strategies of the best of the best play out, I was reminded of a quote from a Prussian general who said, "In the whole range of human activities, war most closely resembles a game of cards." My mentors took me into their war rooms, where I learned when to advance, when to retreat, and how to protect my flank, as well as the importance of patience.

They taught me how to chop, chop, chop in a Hold'em tournament by picking up small pots, accumulating chips, playing with discipline for position and big cards, while thinking three, four, five moves ahead. For me, the key was balancing patience against greed, gaining control over my ego and emotions, and knowing when to walk away and live for another day.

Looking back, I was in heaven, the happiest time of my life.

Around that time, Doyle Brunson steered me to a different kind of light. After surviving a cancer scare in the 1960s, Doyle considered his recovery a miracle that he attributed to the prayers of his wife, Louise, and friends, as well as the guidance of Bob Tremaine, his former college basketball teammate who had become a Baptist minister.

Later, Louise developed a tumor that also disappeared, and their daughter had a remarkable recovery from scoliosis. When his daughter died unexpectedly of anorexia at the age of eighteen, Doyle found solace in Pastor Bob's teachings and regular Bible study classes held at Doyle's home, just a few doors from our place. Many who attended had addictions and challenges of all kinds. When Doyle and Pastor Bob invited me to attend, it awakened my long dormant spiritual side first kindled by Grandmother and her Southern Baptist beliefs.

I welcomed that reawakening, which helped me cope with my drinking, my son's intellectual challenges, and feelings of emptiness that overcame me at times. Susan joined as well and supported me.

It was much easier to stop fixating on money when I finally had some in the bank. Between Chip's strict money management system and the Computer Group crushing the bookmakers at their own game, I had accumulated about $3.5 million in the early 1980s. This windfall allowed me to pay off my debts to Susan's dad, the bank in Louisville, and my hero of a lawyer, Frank Haddad Jr.

Frank had performed yet another legal miracle by plea-bargaining my three felony bookmaking charges in Kentucky down to a single misdemeanor for possession of gambling records. I walked away with little more than a parking ticket, paying a $2,000 fine and receiving six months probation. The conviction was later fully expunged and removed from my record.

Once again, there was no shortage of money to gamble with. I bet a lot of it on head coach Bo Schembechler and his underdog Michigan Wolverines in the 1984 Sugar Bowl game against the Auburn Tigers and future Heisman Trophy winner Bo Jackson. The game opened with the underdog Wolverines at plus 4½ points, a line that never moved.

I started making bets on the game and didn't stop. When I added them all up, I had bet more money on Michigan ($1.5 million—more than $5 million in today's dollars) than I had intended. I overshot the runway by $500,000! That made the game painful to watch.

Almost too painful.

Leading, 7–6, midway in the final quarter, Michigan saw Auburn go on a seven-minute, sixty-one-yard drive that seemed to last an eternity. It didn't help that the Auburn quarterback handed the ball to Jackson, one of the greatest athletes in the century and the game MVP, on what seemed to be every play. It was excruciating. With sweat pouring down my back with his every step, Bo marched the Tigers all the way to the Michigan two-yard line with twenty-three seconds to go.

I was dying a thousand deaths. If the Tigers scored a touchdown, I was screwed.

Michigan called a time-out. When Auburn placekicker Al Del

Greco trotted onto the field, my heart fluttered. His nineteen-yard field goal was good!

The final score was Auburn 9, Michigan 7, which meant I won the bet by 2½ points and survived a $3 million swing. Nearly four decades ago, it was like winning $10 million.

And it only fueled my desire to play higher.

9

The Eighteen Hole Hustle

After we moved to Vegas, I found no shortage of local hustlers and fast-talking tourists to test my growing golf skills against. Take Jimmy Chu, for example.

He rolled in from Tulsa, a friend of PGA Tour pro Raymond Floyd and Bobby Baldwin. Jimmy boasted that he could beat anyone in Vegas at gin, backgammon, and golf. Well, that might have been true, but we assembled an all-star lineup to take him on—Stuey Ungar (gin), Chip (backgammon), and me (golf).

Jimmy lost at every last game and left town six figures lighter.

When matching up, my game plan was simple: one way or another I needed to get my opponent to agree to higher stakes than he was comfortable playing for. I wanted their ass puckered so tight you couldn't pound a flax seed up it. The tighter they were wound, I figured, the worse they would play.

Another example was tennis pro Bobby Riggs, famous for his "Battle of the Sexes" tennis match against Billie Jean King. In addition to his racket skills, Bobby fancied himself as something of a shark with a club in his hands. He played out of La Costa in San Diego.

I was practicing on the driving range at La Costa when Bobby introduced himself and asked me if I would like to play. When he walked away, my longtime professional caddie Mike Nuich told me to avoid him. He said Bobby had reduced himself to hustling hotel guests. But when Bobby approached me again the next day, I couldn't help myself. The prospect of beating a would-be thief proved too enticing.

We set up a two-day match. I won $1,500 the first day. I could tell after the round that Bobby was in shock. This outcome was totally foreign to him. On day two, I won $1,700 off Bobby. A good loser, he was not!

Afterward, I was having lunch at the club, waiting to collect from Bobby, when a waiter stopped by and dropped a check on the table.

It was not the check I had expected.

"Mr. Riggs says this is on you," said the waiter, leaving me the bill for Bobby's lunch.

I gladly paid up.

And not so gladly, eventually, so did Bobby.

Trust me, I didn't always win. Sometimes even a hustler gets hustled. Dewey Tomko was the first guy to win any serious money from me. "Dew Drop" was a former kindergarten teacher and one of the best poker players in the world. He also happened to be a near-scratch golfer who took no prisoners.

The first time we played, I lost $25,000 to Dewey. That was the beginning of many a battle. Eventually, we grew weary of beating our heads against each other and decided to join forces and play as a team.

Freddie Barnes, a bookmaker, was another gambler who taught me that, just like at the racetrack, there are certain horses for certain courses. Freddie lived in a simple apartment in Mobile, Alabama, and drove an old yellow Cadillac Eldorado. We had first met at the PGI in Vegas. He never worried one whit about losing hundreds of thousands of dollars a year playing golf, but he played hard for his money.

Being able to play Freddie in his hometown of Mobile was like trying to get a corner table at Cracker Barrel on Mother's Day. Every golf hustler in the land was trying to get a piece of Freddie's action. After I had made a game with him, I thought no one else in Vegas knew about it.

I thought I was being sneaky, but guess who walked onto our flight to Mobile at the very last minute?

None other than my friend, the professional poker-playing, golf-hustling Walter Clyde "Puggy" Pearson. Somehow, Pug had caught wind of my travel plans and my golf rendezvous with Freddie and his bankroll.

If you looked up the word *rounder* in the dictionary, odds are you would find a picture of Pug. Talk about a character; he owned an RV that he called "the Roving Gambler" with a slogan painted on the side: "I'll play any man from any land any game he can name for any amount I can count, provided I like it."

Pug's educational background, if I remember correctly, topped out in the fifth grade. Self-educated and self-made, Puggy was consistently the best golfer in our Vegas group. He was blessed with a big heart and a fabulous short game. His putting only got better when the heat was on.

Pug plopped down in the seat next to me on the plane and pulled out a backgammon board with the full intention of breaking me on the way to Mobile. We played the entire flight and broke about even.

Once we landed, I let Freddie know that I had a new game in mind: Puggy and I would play against Freddie and his regular partner, Tommy Marr, at the Grand Hotel's two courses. Pug and I gave Freddie two shots a side, knowing Freddie was at least four shots a side worse than the rest of us.

The fairways at the Grand were lined with pines, magnolias, and ancient oaks. Freddie couldn't hit it more than 220 yards off the tee, but his lollipop drives were finding the fairway, setting him up perfectly on every hole. I teed off with a 3-iron on most holes instead of a driver, which negated my length advantage, but kept my ball in play. Puggy, on the other hand, couldn't hit it straight to save his life. We lost every team bet for three straight days. In this case, the lambs got the butchers.

I had to call Doyle to borrow $25,000 for a bankroll because we were broke.

"What do you need money for that game for?" Doyle asked, figuring Puggy and I had the nuts, until I explained that Puggy had been living in the trees for days.

"Fine, I'll loan you the money," Doyle said. "But you'll need to get it from a guy in Kentucky who owes me."

Of course! I called an old friend, whom I had met playing pool in my younger days in Kentucky. His name was Josh Crabtree, and he agreed to pick up the cash from John Y. Brown, who just happened to be none other than the governor of Kentucky. Who knew? Josh collected and drove through the night to Mobile to deliver the twenty-five grand the next day.

I told Pug our team game was over. He could still join the bets, but I would be playing solo against Freddie and T-Marr. After some intense lobbying on my part, Pug finally agreed to go to the rail.

Fortunately, my strategy worked. After the smoke cleared, I won our money back and $50,000 more from Freddie.

Then Susan, Pug, and I headed back to Las Vegas.

Some of my best battles in the late eighties on the golf course took place at Canyon Gate Country Club in Vegas with former PGA Tour pro Jim Colbert on the other side. These battles were more about competition than money. We must have played at least thirty times one year and the bet rarely varied: $20 Nassau five ways (front nine, back nine, and total, with automatic presses on both nines). It was usually Gene McCarlie and me against Colbert and a rotating cast of gunslingers. It was blood money down to the last dime.

I loved partnering up with Gene, a Mississippi-born Las Vegas transplant. We hit the links at Canyon Gate CC, the Sahara, Las Vegas CC, Spanish Trail, or wherever we could find a tee time. We took on all comers. And if we couldn't find a game, we'd head to the first tee and try to beat the pants off each other for twenty bucks and bragging rights. It was pure old-school, mano a mano—no gimmies, no relief, play it where it lies.

Which brings me to perhaps our most memorable duel at Spanish Trail. I'll let Gene tell the tale:

Going into the eighteenth hole, Billy had me down a hundred dollars. The eighteenth on the Lakes course is a dogleg par-five bending to the right. There are creeks and ponds all over that damn hole. I hit my drive right down the middle, but it's right close to a lake, where there's a lot of ducks and geese and fowl floating around. And a black swan, which evidently was startled by my ball landing a bit too close for comfort.

Well, Billy doesn't so much as slow the cart down as we get closer to my ball. I can remember it like it was yesterday. The swan's got his wings spread out looking like a 747 doubly pissed at this vehicular intrusion.

Immediately, Billy flies over me from the driver's seat like he's been ejected from a fighter jet and starts scurrying to the middle of the fairway. Meanwhile, this fucking swan attacks me like I just killed one of its babies.

I'm out of the cart as fast as I can escape, the swan still after me like a gourmet dinner. Billy is hysterical with laughter, which instantly makes me think he knew damn well that the black swan would react exactly as it did if we invaded its territory.

Well, as God is my witness, I get to my ball and it's smothered in swan shit. And remember, it's summer in Vegas, about a hundred and fifteen degrees, so there's steam coming off my ball.

"Billy," I said, "I got plenty of balls. I'm just going to drop another one."

"You're not going to drop another one."

"What are you talking about?"

Billy said you're going to have to take a penalty stroke if you don't hit that ball right there. Gamblers' rules.

I pull out a three iron and hit that son of a bitch, and I swear you couldn't script what happened next. The shit flies off and hits me smack in the face. I've got sunglasses on, but I've still got shit in my eyes, hair, all over my shirt. And I swear that you've never smelled anything worse than freshly baked black swan shit. I ran over to the lake and washed off my face and hair.

I ended up making par and tying the hole. I should have been awarded a medal for playing the damn thing where it lay. What that guy wouldn't do to win a bet. Incredible.

From the 1970s into the mid-'80s I traveled the country playing golf for big money—El Paso, Dallas, Knoxville, Nashville, Southern California, and all over Florida. I only teed it up if I believed I could win at least $5,000. Otherwise, I kept on looking until I found the right match.

One of my favorite places to play was South Florida. Back then, cash was king, thanks to boatloads of bookmakers, drug dealers, Ponzi schemers, and scammers straight out of *Ocean's 11*.

Tyson Leonard, a former Clemson running back from Myrtle Beach, was one such character. Tyson liked to say he made his money in nightclubs, aluminum, and camper covers. Maybe he did, but I knew him as one of the biggest bookmakers in the South. He was also a loudmouth jerk who loved to show off. He may have been a shark in Myrtle Beach, but in West Palm Beach he was more like a pigeon just waiting to be plucked.

Cruising around in a personalized golf cart with his shirt off, Tyson loved to bring wads of cash and his Myrtle Beach entourage to Breakers West Country Club. Tyson couldn't break one hundred to save his life, but he was smart enough to recruit a couple of good players to team up with. All of this made him an inviting target.

Susan and I were staying at Turnberry Isle when I got word that Team Tyson had blown into town. I called my friend Angelo Kokas, a union power broker from Chicago, and we drove up to Breakers West in Palm Beach County to play Tyson and Charlie Webster. I had made a game with Charlie, Tyson's right-hand man, to play a $10,000 Nassau per man.

Angelo and I won $120,000 the first day from Tyson and Charlie. A couple of days later, we beat them again. The third time we played, I had a different partner—my gambling buddy Dewey Tomko. We negotiated a million-dollar freeze-out, meaning no one could quit until one team had lost $1 million.

Chip and I were in for a quarter million each. Dewey put up the other half million. We were playing a $40,000 Nassau per man. At those stakes, a team could lose $240,000 a round with no presses.

I called Chip Reese back in Vegas, who was my betting partner, to inform him of our bet.

I added that we were giving Tyson Leonard a shot a hole on his ball.

"A shot a hole?" Chip screamed. "Are you crazy?"

"Don't worry about it," I told him. "This is the nuts."

"You can't give *anybody* a shot a hole in a team game."

Word spread about the million-dollar freeze-out, so naturally a pack of buzzards showed up in golf carts hoping to squeeze even more money out of Tyson.

It was a show of shows, and Tyson could not help himself. Pretending he was back playing college football, he broke from a huddle on every tee box with one guy putting grease on his club, another placing his ball on a tee, another making sure he was aimed correctly. Between holes, Tyson stripped down to basically his underwear, dumping water on his head, and having Charlie rub lotion on his back.

It was a three-ring circus. After four or five hours of this slow-play nonsense, we had only played seven holes. I lost patience with Tyson's antics and gamesmanship. It didn't help my mood that Dewey and I were one down at that point.

Dewey, the coolest of heads, reminded me that we still had plenty of time to take Tyson's money. I calmed down, and sure enough, Tyson dumped multiple balls in the water on the next two holes.

We won the match. Not once. Not twice. But three days in a row.

Going into the fourth day, Dewey and I were up $450,000. But when we showed up for the next round, Team Tyson was nowhere to be found.

"Tyson had a heart attack," Charlie told us. "He went back to South Carolina."

My ass. He faked a heart attack to get out of the freeze-out. We never did finish the match, but Tyson, to his credit, paid us what he owed. In gold coins.

"Keep your head down" is a golf maxim heard on every course in the country. Vegas had its own unique slogan for golfers: "Watch your back." The major courses at the time, among them the Las Vegas Country Club, the Dunes, and the Desert Inn were home to predators in polo shirts with golf bags full of tricks.

Dropping balls to improve their lies? Check.

Magnetic putters to move their marks closer to the hole? Check.

Paying off bag room attendants to bend the lofts of your opponent's clubs? Check.

Injecting mercury into the liquid center of an opposing player's balls to send them sideways? Check.

Slip a mickey in someone's drink to throw off their game? Double check.

My good buddy Doyle Brunson once accused me of doing just that. Which hurt my feelings. We were at the Sahara Country Club (now the Las Vegas National Golf Club), renowned as the boozy playground of Frank Sinatra, Sammy Davis Jr., and Dean Martin. To this day their favorite seats at the clubhouse bar are marked with brass nameplates.

When Doyle and I arrived to play that day, the temperature was hovering right around 110 degrees. After the front nine, Doyle ate a tuna sandwich and had something to drink. Suddenly, he began to feel dizzy, which made him play like a twenty-handicapper.

"Billy, did you put something in my drink to screw me up?"

"No, Doyle," I said, "you did that all by yourself."

I couldn't blame him for being suspicious, I guess. Most golfers in Vegas figured that, if you weren't trying to get an edge on your opponent, you just weren't trying. There were two standard approaches. You could either cheat on the course or out-negotiate the other guy on the first tee.

The majority of guys I played were not cheaters. But we knew them when we saw them, and we adjusted our bets accordingly. In poker, a "nut peddler" is a player whose intentions are to only bet on sure things. In golf, it's the same principle.

Take Michael O'Connor, a nut peddler if there ever was one. We played in a game without betting each other a couple of times, and neither of us broke 90. We were both doing the same thing—throwing off and setting a trap for another day and another match.

When that day came, I had $30,000 to my name. We agreed to play a $10,000 Nassau (separate bets for ten grand on the front nine, back nine, and the eighteen-hole total). The first hole at the Dunes was a dogleg left par-four. O'Connor made a six. I made a four and he pressed (another $10,000). Now I was looking at a potential loss of $40,000—more money than I had.

On the second hole, a par five, O'Connor dumped his approach shot in the water. I was thinking this guy couldn't play a lick. On the third tee, O'Connor pressed again. Now we were up to a $50,000.

It was dead summer in Vegas, a hundred degrees in the shade, and O'Connor's cart mate had a cooler full of vodka and orange juice. I thought: *How sweet it is!* I was playing a guy in desert heat and he was downing screwdrivers like water.

Pretty sweet indeed. I shot 75 and beat O'Connor out of eighty thousand.

Little did I know that Chip, Doyle, and Jack Binion were laughing their collective asses off. They knew O'Connor was the lockup artist of all lockup artists—he only bet on a sure thing.

Turned out, O'Connor thought he was setting me up. That slowly dawned on me the next day before our second round when ten guys from around town showed up. All of them wanted to bet on O'Connor.

They figured I'm just some hillbilly from Kentucky.

I was all too willing to give them some action. I bet them anywhere from $1,000 to $5,000 each. As a precaution before we teed off, I made O'Connor throw me his ball and I tossed him mine.

"You mark my ball any way you want," I told him, "because I'm going to mark yours."

That way if anyone in his peanut gallery switched balls on me, I'd know it.

No matter. When it came time to play, O'Connor reached for the light switch, but it didn't turn on. He couldn't break 90 that day. I won another sixty thousand, plus fifteen more from the boys on the rail.

I hadn't downed my first Corona before O'Connor demanded another match. I beat him again. When the smoke finally cleared three days later, I had won a total of $490,000.

To his credit, O'Connor paid me at the golf course after each match ended.

Jack Binion was so afraid I'd get robbed after winning so much cash that he sent a limo and a couple of security guards to the Dunes every day. Their job was to escort me and the cash back to the cage at the Horseshoe.

Jack wasn't acting entirely in my best interest. He knew that, sooner or later, likely sooner, I'd lose all that money and more at his casino. Which I did.

On any given day, Vegas offered almost unlimited action from book-makers, drug dealers, and wealthy businessmen. No one had more gamble than Jamiel "Jimmy" Chagra.

In Vegas, you couldn't get a background bio or rap sheet on everyone you were gambling with, though that would have been nice. I only learned later that Jimmy was by way of El Paso and his money came from a massive marijuana, heroin, and cocaine oper-ation linked to major crime families that stretched from Colom-bia to Mexico and across the Western world. The smuggled goods were shipped into the U.S. by Jimmy's private fleet of freighters and planes.

In the late seventies, Jimmy made Vegas his second home. He en-deared himself to local bartenders, dealers, waiters, and waitresses by tossing around hundred-dollar bills like party favors. One story had it that he paid off a $50,000 mortgage for a cocktail waitress who was raising three kids on her own.

Jimmy fancied himself a boss gambler, a gross exaggeration that routinely lured a school of sharks chumming for his cash at poker, pool tables, and golf courses around town. His net worth was said to be in the neighborhood of $100 million or more in the early eighties.

It wasn't long before I learned of Jimmy and his frequent visits to Las Vegas. I knew a gambler and pool shark in El Paso named Timmy, so I called him to get a line on Jimmy. He reported that Jimmy's best game by far was pool, but that I could beat him. And that Jimmy didn't stand a chance against me in golf because he couldn't break 100 on a decent course.

The next time I hit Vegas, I packed my sleek friend Mr. Bala-bushka, the Stradivarius of pool cues named after its famed Russian-born maker George Balabushka. Even though I hadn't played pool competitively in years, it still felt like home and Uncle Harry's to me.

As I expected, Chagra was in town, but he was closed off by a group of "fence-builders," sharps who had kindly constructed a protective wall around Jimmy and his money. When he played poker, the table was already full and stayed that way until he quit.

That didn't stop other sharps from trying to gamble with him, including Dewey Tomko, Gus Poulos (brother of a major Wichita crime figure), and Jack "Treetop" Straus. A bookmaker and World Series of Poker legend, Jack was famous for once being down to his last chip—"a chip and a chair"—only to come back and win the tournament's main event. They had a standing golf game with Chagra every day.

Jack and Gus had already played so poorly on the golf course against Chagra that they ran out of money. Jack called me with a proposition: he'd get me in the game, but I had to give him half of whatever I won.

I said sure, though I'd never met Jimmy. I joined them on the first tee at the Tropicana golf course. Playing it cool, I didn't ask for a bet. The first nine, I must have shot 50. I was topping balls, spraying shots, doing my best to impersonate a hacker.

Dewey, in the meantime, had developed a serious case of the shanks. Normally he could have beaten Jimmy with one hand in his pocket, but he had the shanks so bad that he paid off after the front nine, forfeited the eighteen-hole bet, and did not play the back nine.

We were preparing to tee it up for the back when I turned to Jimmy and said the magic words.

"You want to make a little bet?"

"Sure, what do ya want to play for?"

"Let's make it ten thousand."

I won the first hole of the back nine. Jimmy pressed. I won the second. He pressed. By the time we finished, I was up forty thousand.

Then Jimmy uttered some magic words of his own:

"You want to play an emergency nine?"

Did I ever.

"I'll play you for the forty thousand," said Jimmy.

"Sounds good," I said.

Suddenly, I heard a low-lying buzz. It wasn't mosquitoes. A sleek police helicopter was monitoring our round. I noticed then that Jimmy had a gallery—what seemed like a hundred maintenance men cutting grass and raking bunkers. They were much better groomed than most in that field.

Ah, the FBI.

I can play in front of any crowd, feds or no feds.

When the back nine was over, I had won three bets and $120,000. Jimmy owed me $160,000. He told me to meet him at the Horseshoe that night.

When I walked in to settle up, he was playing cards. Thirty minutes later, he handed me $160,000 that he had won playing blackjack. Easy come, easy go.

The next time I saw Jimmy was at the Silver Bird casino. By then, big surprise, I'd blown my end of the $160,000 that I'd won from him playing golf. Jimmy was there to play poker, but the game never materialized. I asked him if he wanted to play some pool. (I was broke, but Doyle and Sarge had agreed to stake me.)

"If you can't run five or six racks, you got no business playing me in pool," Jimmy said.

"I can't run five or six racks, but I'd like to play you some pool," said the spider to the fly.

"C'mon, I've got a table at the house," Jimmy replied.

We agreed to a $200,000 freeze-out at $10,000 a game. In order to win, you had to be twenty games ahead. And you couldn't quit until one of us got there. Doyle had never seen me play and expressed concern we were getting set up, especially because we would be playing on Jimmy's home table.

But I knew something that Doyle didn't know. I already had a line on Jimmy from someone I trusted.

Susan, Doyle, and Sarge went along for the show. We rode over to Jimmy's home, which was decorated in fortress chic. The multimillion-dollar mansion was surrounded by palace walls, iron gates, bodyguards carrying shotguns, and a pack of dogs snarling and snapping at the end of a leash.

We entered the front door and stepped into the foyer. It was more like a holding room featuring a gleaming tile floor and massive doors on each side. An electronic lock clicked, and a door slid open to reveal a four-foot-by-eight-foot table.

Jimmy's house. Jimmy's table. Jimmy's rules. No problem.

Our host had no idea that I'd cut my teeth playing pool at Uncle Harry's. Before he knew it, I'm up eighteen games, on the edge of winning the freeze-out. By that point, I knew more than a bit about the legend of Jimmy Chagra.

A Las Vegas newspaper once called him "the undisputed marijuana kingpin of the Western world." I'd long since learned that the streets of El Paso, Texas, were littered with the bodies of people who had crossed him. Word was that he may have tried to kill an assistant U.S. attorney investigating his drug dealings; and that he'd killed his own brother in a dispute with a crime boss.

This information didn't shake me, but I did not do any trash-talking, which wasn't my style anyway. I won the last two games and started to unscrew my friend Mr. Balabushka when I heard Jimmy say: "I want a chance to win my money back."

"That's fine," I said. "As soon as you pay me the $200,000, we'll play some more."

Jimmy's big black Lebanese eyes stared a hole in my head.

It was two thirty in the morning. Sarge had long since taken a cab home. Susan and Doyle were sound asleep on couches.

Jimmy kept staring.

I woke up Doyle and asked if I should take Jimmy up on his request.

"No problem," he said.

Doyle went back to snoring, and Jimmy and I went back to his pool table. I was two games shy of taking home another $200,000 when Jimmy started mumbling. I had no trouble deciphering: "Motherfuckin' pool hustlin' sons of bitches get fingers broke. Bad things happen to motherfuckin' pool hustlers."

My grade school nemesis Jeep Minton was nowhere near as threatening as Jimmy Chagra. But a bully's a bully whether you're in a first-grade hallway or a drug dealer's den. My policy—not the smartest—was to stand my ground and fight back if I had to.

I stared into his coal-black eyes and called him out.

"You told me if I couldn't run five or six racks, I had no business playing you in pool. I never ran five or six racks. If you think you're going to keep me from winning your money, you got that wrong. I'm gonna win this money."

Which is exactly what I did.

By the time the last ball dropped, it was 6:45 in the morning. I shook Susan and Doyle awake. Jimmy was still mumbling and grumbling as we walked into the foyer, but Doyle calmed him down.

The next day, Susan and I were at Doyle's house when he got a call from George Poulos, Gus's brother, a tough guy from Wichita.

"Jimmy will only pay half the four hundred grand," he said.

After some back-and-forth, Doyle hung up the phone. Poulos had only been out of prison a short time and had a reputation as a killer. I became concerned and called two friends of mine from Louisville, who came out to watch my back.

A couple of days later, Benny Binion joined the negotiations, and Poulos decided he no longer had an interest in our money. Doyle went to Jimmy's house and collected $200,000. He still owed us another $200,000.

In the spring of 1979, news broke that Jimmy has been indicted on federal drug-smuggling charges. At that point, I was broke again. I needed my half share of the $200,000 he owed us. The night before Jimmy headed back to El Paso for his drug trial, we met in the Sombrero Room, the Mexican restaurant at the Horseshoe. It was just the two of us, seated at a table in the back.

"Look, Jimmy," I said. "I need the money you owe me."

I'll never forget what happened next. Jimmy looked at me with those big black eyes. Only, this time they were filled with tears.

"Billy," he said. "The world is closing in on me."

And he started to cry.

"Jimmy, it's all right. You're an action man. I'm an action man. You go down there and take care of yourself. I know you're going to win that trial. When you come back, we'll straighten things out."

I never saw Jimmy Chagra again.

As the story goes, Chagra was facing life in prison when the U.S. district court judge overseeing his drug-smuggling case was shot to death outside his San Antonio home on May 29, 1979. Nicknamed "Maximum John" for the severity of the sentences he handed down, John Wood Jr. was the first federal judge to be assassinated in more than a century. It took years and thousands of man-hours, but FBI investigators claimed to have unraveled the mystery: they claimed that Chagra had paid a hit man $250,000 to kill Judge Wood. The alleged hit man, who was later convicted and sentenced to two life terms, was Charles Harrelson, the father of actor Woody Harrelson. Jimmy got off on the murder rap, but was convicted for drug smuggling. He spent twenty-four years in Marion, a maximum-security prison in Illinois, before being paroled. He died in Arizona in 2008 at the age of sixty-three.

10

The Computer Group

It was Saturday, January 19, 1985. The day before Super Bowl XIX between the San Francisco 49ers and Miami Dolphins.

Susan and I were on vacation with her parents in a rental house on the Intracoastal Waterway in Fort Lauderdale. Suddenly, there was a loud pounding on the front door.

Ten FBI agents came barging in, guns drawn, terrifying Susan and her mother, who was asleep. Thankfully, Susan's father had gone fishing early that morning.

The storming of our rental unit was one of a series of nationwide raids on the biggest betting day of the year. We had no idea that we had been targeted as part of a nationwide federal investigation into alleged bookmaking by the Computer Group and people reputed to be linked to organized crime.

FBI agents armed with search warrants had raided forty-five offices and homes in twenty-three cities. They seized gambling records, betting charts, and two Texas Instruments data terminals, along with checks payable to twenty-one individuals totaling more than $200,000 from Doc Mindlin's Vail, Colorado, vacation retreat.

When the raiders struck, I was downstairs in a basement office dialing football and basketball bets on a bank of phones flown in the day before on Eastern Airlines. The FBI agents jumped in and answered the ringing phones in search of proof that I was operating as a bookmaker.

Instead, all they got was confirmation that I was making bets, not taking them. When all was said and done that day, no arrests were made. The FBI gathered everything they could find and left. We cut the vacation short and forfeited the security deposit on the rental house.

Later, we learned that the FBI raids were set in motion on December 3, 1984, when Nevada district court judge Lloyd D. George signed an order "authorizing the interception of the wire communications of William Thurman Walters, Glen Andrews Walker, Dominic Anthony Spinale, and others yet unknown" over phone lines tracked to C&B Collections, a phone bank operation I had set up off the Strip under a name guaranteed not to get any unwanted phone calls or solicitations.

A few weeks after signing that motion, Judge George signed another order adding Dr. Ivan Mindlin, Susan Walters, Arnie Haaheim—one of my close associates—and another set of phone numbers to the list of authorized interceptions. On January 2, 1985, Judge George extended his order yet again. Court records reveal that during much of 1984, the FBI had been investigating the Computer Group for operating "an illegal gambling business." It alleged that William Thurman Walters ran a "large bookmaking operation" to make legal and illegal bets for the Computer Group, and that C&B Collections was little more than a front for organized crime.

We were organized all right, but not criminals. We were the nation's biggest sports-betting syndicate. Our origins traced to a geeky softball player tinkering on his computer in 1972, the kind of nerd one finds at the circulation desk of your local library.

Michael Kent was a twenty-seven-year-old math and computer wizard when he wrote the code that birthed the Computer Group. His regular job was developing nuclear submarine technology at the Westinghouse Electric Corporation in Pittsburgh.

As the center fielder on the company softball team, Mike let his analytical mind wander one day and found himself contemplating softball statistics in place of nuclear physics. His team had won a couple of league titles, but Mike wondered if there was a way to quantify success in softball beyond wins and losses.

For answers, Mike turned to his trusted friend, a high-powered, high-speed computer he had used on the job to program a sleeker, more efficient nuclear sub. Working after hours, Mike applied his expertise to handicapping his softball team's relative strengths and weaknesses. The results were impressive. His teammates were amused. Mike's calculations added mathematical heft to their bragging rights. The computer had provided power ratings and measurable values.

But so what? There was no real application to Mike's findings—they simply had no practical use. Or did they? Mike soon realized he had created a model that could be applied to college and professional sports. Why not use it to analyze college football, which had a huge national following with sports fans and (drumroll) avid sports gamblers?

Mike was not a big sports gambler himself, but he knew a ripe market when he saw one. He dug for information at his local library and bookstores. He searched NCAA football guides, which listed scores and statistics, as well as local and national newspapers and handicapping resources like the GoldSheet.

Once he compiled the stats, Mike wrote a computer program that accounted for every variable he could imagine. He studied the relative importance of first downs and turnovers, scheduling, home versus away scores, travel distance and various modes of transportation used by teams, the impact of weather conditions and field altitudes, and each team's comparative performances against shared opponents.

Mike worked on this side project an average of two hours a night for several years. He then wrote the computer program that pioneered the use of algorithms and probability theories to predict power-rated numbers in sporting events against the official Las Vegas line produced by mere mortals who were working with pen and paper. His creation proved to be a groundbreaking formula for wagering on college and professional sports.

He tested his program in Pittsburgh, home to legions of illegal bookies. When Mike found point spreads with the numerical difference he was searching for—three points or more—he pounced. During football season, he bet $2,400 each week on NFL games. He made so much money that within three years he was betting $50,000 a week through a network of friends that helped mask his identity from wary bookmakers.

One local bookmaking operation, Steel City, led by characters with comic book names like Bobo and Primo, stopped taking any bets after they got wise to Mike's network. He took that decision as motivation to quit his day job. He relocated to the far friendlier gambling environment of Las Vegas, arriving just in time for the 1979 college football season.

At first, the shy computer wizard was intimidated by the Vegas vibe. Who could blame him? He was understandably nervous about carrying wads of cash in and out of loud casinos packed with drunks, thugs, mobsters, and their henchmen.

Even so, Mike realized Vegas was the perfect environment to unleash his brilliant concept. He created a small "pool" of betting partners—generally around $100,000 total per pool—and decided who could participate and how much interest each person could acquire.

In 1979, a neighbor in Mike's apartment complex introduced him to Doc Mindlin, who was a slender, unimposing, and charming fellow on the surface. Doc had been raised in upper-class Montreal, the son of a prosperous real estate developer. Doc became an orthopedic surgeon, practicing and teaching at Monmouth Medical Center in New Jersey.

As Doc told it, he taught himself computer programming and, in addition to his surgical duties, began trading in commodities. He landed in Sin City in 1971, looking to put those computer skills to the test betting college basketball and major-league baseball games.

If you were writing the sunny side of Doc's life, it would read something like this: accomplished surgeon with an excellent reputation around town; deeply respected expert witness in complex medical cases; well-regarded in-house physician for several hotels on the Strip.

The darker side revealed Doc to be a heavy gambler known to carry six-figure debts. His surgical career was sidelined after a 1981 auto accident in Florida damaged Doc's right (operating) wrist and caused serious back and neck injuries.

As *Sports Illustrated* reported in a March 1986 article, "There is definitely a Jekyll-and-Hyde quality to the life of Dr. Ivan Mindlin of Las Vegas."

Based on years of personal experience with him, I can say without pause that Doc is simply one of the most conniving people I've met in my life. He saw Mike Kent's odd brilliance—and revolutionary computer program—as gambling gold. Doc ingratiated himself with Mike by playing the father figure and spinning stories of his own fascination with computers to determine the spread. Mike agreed to work with Doc in the late 1970s. Within a few years, Doc had convinced Mike to let him oversee the Computer Group operation so Mike could concentrate exclusively on handicapping. As the Group's success grew, so did Doc's ego and greed. In 1986, he went so far as to promote himself to *Sports Illustrated* as the brains behind the Group.

As previously mentioned, I connected with the Computer Group in the late 1970s when I was one of the biggest bookmakers in Louisville, moving money for a guy in Pittsburgh, who was, in turn, moving money for Jimmy Evart and Stanley Tomchin in New York. That arrangement lasted until I got arrested. By the time we moved to Vegas in September 1982, the Computer Group was crushing it. Mike had upgraded his software program, which was performing more and more like a crystal ball, winning north of 60 percent of their bets, earning millions in the process. Their success rate was nothing short of phenomenal given that, at times, they were betting one hundred games a week. They were raking in so much money that Doc persuaded Mike to send hundreds of thousands of dollars offshore to avoid paying taxes on his earnings.

Susan and I had been living in Vegas for about a year before I finally met Mike in person. Our meeting was brief; I can't even remember where it occurred, only that Mike wasn't much for small talk. My first impressions of him held up. Despite playing softball, Mike seemed more like an academic. He was casually dressed and a complete square; shy, bearded, and slightly overweight. He appeared to be naive to the cutthroat ways of the gambling world, yet he was shaking up that very world by the early 1980s.

My job with the Group was to do what I did best: to move millions of dollars every weekend and protect the Group's identity. To that end, I recruited a small army of runners and beards to place bets on our behalf. Thankfully, in Vegas, there was no shortage of needy gamblers willing to put in long hours in exchange for a few hundred bucks a week and the inside scoop on the games we told them to bet.

"Chicago Gary" was my man on the street in charge of a crew of at least thirty runners. Gary looked like he'd just blown in from the Windy City. He was rumpled, balding, and a no-BS guy, the spitting image of Sergeant Bilko, the scam artist played by comedian Phil Silvers in his 1950s television show.

Seven days a week, Gary's team of runners fanned out to their respective casinos and sportsbooks around town, sitting tight, waiting for their Nextel walkie-talkies or beepers to chirp or buzz with our instructions. The Computer Group operated like this: Mike would determine our betting numbers on selected games. He would pass on those numbers to his brother John, who would update the information with the latest injuries and send the final numbers to a contact in New York and to me.

I worked with Susan out of our home office at the Las Vegas Country Club. Susan and I had phones in each hand and were betting everywhere we could, including through Glen Walker, who ran the C&B betting room for me. Glen took the orders and passed them out to everyone in our office. Then I beeped the games and numbers out to Chicago Gary and his runners.

It was a call chain for printing money. When the time came to make our move, our team made hundreds of bets around the country in the time it takes to brush your teeth. On an average weekend with pro football and college football and basketball in full swing, we placed bets totaling more than $10 million.

"Alabama minus 2½, a hundred thousand, go!"

"Florida plus four up to forty thousand, go!"

"Georgia-Tennessee under forty-five, up to fifteen thousand, go!"

As the games played out, Susan and I charted every bet by hand—the number we bet, how much, with whom—and posted that information to a master account. At the end of the betting day, we'd work until eleven or twelve every night, adding up multiple bets on hundreds of tickets, using an adding machine. Together, we'd then compare each individual ticket to look for any mistakes and reconcile them down to the penny. After that, we would enter each ticket into its specific account and update our master sheet. It was every day and it was exhausting. Some nights, we didn't get to bed until one or one thirty in the morning.

I never knew exactly how much money the Computer Group won. One report put a single year's profits at $25 million. As word got out and our reputation grew in gambling circles, law enforcement became interested in our numbers and success.

As partners in our own betting operation, Chip and I were rolling right along with the Group. Then, in December 1984, Chip reported that the heat was on. A large-scale federal investigation into illegal bookmakers was underway, according to word on the street.

I didn't think twice about it. I hadn't done any bookmaking since my bust in Kentucky, and I knew the Computer Group wasn't breaking any laws. Bookmaking? Organized crime? Not us.

Still, Chip didn't like what he was hearing. He ended our partnership.

Turned out, Chip was right.

The heat *was* on.

On us.

While researching this book, I filed a Freedom of Information Act (FOIA) request with the U.S. Department of Justice for all documents related to the Computer Group. The FBI had compiled 22,836 pages on our little operation, but I was only able to obtain sixteen heavily redacted pages. One of those pages stood out to us. It was dated December 10, 1984:

FOR INFORMATION OF THOSE IN RECEIPT OF THIS COMMUNICATION, CAPTIONED CASE INVOLVES AN ILLEGAL GAMBLING GROUP KNOWN AS THE "COMPUTER." THIS GROUP MANIPULATES AND CONTROLS THE BETTING LINE IN LAS VEGAS WHICH ALSO GIVES IT CONTROL OF THE BETTING LINE THROUGHOUT THE UNITED STATES. . . .

AN ATTEMPT WAS MADE BY CHICAGO LCN OVERSEER OF OPERATIONS IN LAS VEGAS [NAME REDACTED] TO TAKE OVER THE "COMPUTER GROUP." . . . THE "COMPUTER GROUP" ARRANGED FOR REPRESENTATIVE OF NOW DECEASED GENOVESE LCN MEMBER ANTHONY RUSSO, AKA "LITTLE PUSSY," TO INTERCEDE ON HIS BEHALF AND FOR HIS EFFORTS RUSSO RECEIVED APPROXIMATELY $50,000.

Translation: the FBI believed the Computer Group engaged in "illegal gambling," could somehow "manipulate" and "control" betting lines across the country, and was in the process of being taken over by organized crime in Las Vegas ("LCN" is shorthand for La Cosa Nostra).

Wrong on every count.

I only wish I'd known what we were up against before the FBI came banging on our front door.

11

The Investigation

The FBI special agent leading the Computer Group investigation was Thomas B. Noble. I should have immediately sensed trouble in the surname. Agent Noble was trying to make a name for himself by trashing ours. He was reckless, clueless, and out of his league in targeting our operation.

As we would discover, Noble had been an agent for only about a year and a half and investigated a grand total of one bookmaking case when he came to believe (mistakenly) that he had stumbled across a massive illegal bookmaking operation controlled by organized crime. Fresh out of the FBI Academy, he was dispatched to the Las Vegas office and assigned to an investigation of Dominic Spinale, Tony Spilotro's right-hand man.

Our problems began when Noble observed Spinale associating with Glen Walker, the supervisor of my betting office who, unbeknownst to me, was catting around town with Spinale for some extra cash. The FBI tailed Walker to our C&B office on West Spring Mountain Road. It didn't take Noble long to figure out it was home to a sports-betting operation.

Noble thus linked Spinale, an organized-crime figure, to Walker, who was connected to the most successful sports-betting group in the country. Being a righteous crime fighter, the agent decided to make a case against these allegedly corrupt men. And, along the way, he hoped to accelerate his rise within the FBI.

Like a lot of lawmen, Noble believed there was no such thing as a group of successful bettors. He assumed—wrongly—that we had to be booking well. He persuaded his boss, the special agent in charge of southern Nevada, to obtain wiretaps for our betting office at C&B.

The feds listened in as we placed bets morning, noon, and night. They also obtained search warrants for locations in nearly two-dozen cities, including Vail, Pittsburgh, Salt Lake City, Houston, New Orleans, Mobile, El Paso, and Chicago.

Noble's investigation would never have happened if not for Doc Mindlin. His greed and stupidity helped the FBI connect a series of make-believe dots. First, in an attempt to make some money outside of the Computer Group, Doc opened a betting account in Spinale's name at the Stardust, one of the city's largest casinos and home to the world's first major sportsbook. The Stardust bookmaking operation was opened in 1976 by none other than Frank "Lefty" Rosenthal, a front man for the Chicago mob who worked without the benefit of a gaming license. (See Robert De Niro as Sam "Ace" Rothstein in *Casino*.)

Doc might as well have sent a telegram to Special Agent Noble to confirm his suspicions about the Computer Group's ties to orga-nized crime. The agent was evidently unable to grasp the vast legal difference between a bettor (a person who bets) and a bookmaker (a person who accepts bets).

Doc's arrangement with Spinale proved that Doc had violated our simple agreement   in exchange for a percentage of profits, the Computer Group numbers would not be shared with anyone else, and no one could bet outside the Group. But Doc couldn't play by the rules. Desperate to ingratiate himself with the city's Gucci-wearing elite, he passed around our numbers to Vegas power brokers such as Irwin Molasky and Merv Adelson, and, of course, Spinale, which linked us to Spilotro and the Chicago mob, at least in the minds of the FBI.

Adding to his stupidity, Doc also bet with Bob Martin, the premier oddsmaker in the country who was fresh off a thirteen-month stay in federal prison for felony bookmaking. Still, the death blow for the original Computer Group was Doc's association with Spinale, Spilotro, and the Chicago Outfit.

After the FBI raids, Jimmy Evart and Stanley Tomchin simply disappeared. Jimmy moved to Spain. Stanley, a world-class chess, backgammon, and bridge player, went undercover to points unknown on the West Coast. That's when Mike Kent began asking questions that he should have raised from the beginning: *How was the Group run? What happened to his research after he passed it on to Doc? How much money was the Group making? How is it that Doc has homes in three states and I'm living in a condo in Vegas?*

After the FBI came knocking, I called my miracle-working lawyer and friend Frank Haddad Jr., who was a former president of the National Association of Criminal Defense Lawyers (NACDL). He recommended that I hire Oscar Goodman.

Everyone in Vegas knew Oscar. He was a brilliant, flamboyant criminal defense attorney and a former NACDL president himself.

My mistake was in forgetting that Oscar's clientele included organized crime figures such as Meyer Lansky, Nicky Scarfo, Lefty Rosenthal, and Spilotro. He was a known mob attorney, which put me in bad company. I was trying to keep a low profile and distance myself from organized crime. By the time I realized that mistake, I'd already paid Oscar a $50,000 retainer.

Smart, Bill, real smart.

In need of some practical advice about how to get out of this mess, I checked in with my friend Ned Day, the best investigative reporter and newspaper columnist in town. Everybody in Vegas who was anybody read Ned's column in the *Review-Journal*. Week after week he took no prisoners, particularly when it came to the mob. This may explain why Ned's car was torched in July 1986. Luckily, only his golf clubs were in it. The hard-nosed columnist, whose mission in life was to get under the skin of local politicians, mobsters, and prima donnas, described the torching as "the happiest day in my life."

Ned grew up in Milwaukee, the son of a Hall of Fame bowler. He spent his youth hanging around bowling alleys and pool halls. He was a New York Yankees fan and liked to place a bet now and then on sports. Obviously, we had a lot in common.

It helped that Ned had more connections in Vegas than the phone company. In those days, he was dating a woman whose roommate was dating Larry Leavitt, chief of the Justice Department's Organized Crime Strike Force in Vegas.

I told Ned the FBI had the whole thing wrong. "We're not booking, but they must not know the difference."

Ned had done some digging into the case, which was being presented to a grand jury. He told me that the prosecutors knew the Group wasn't booking and suggested I meet with Agent Noble to explain the difference between betting and bookmaking and persuade him we weren't committing any crimes, organized or otherwise. You do that, he said, and the case should go away.

Based on Ned's advice, I consulted Oscar. He did not agree with Ned, not one tiny bit. His animosity toward the strike force and FBI agents working on the force went back decades.

"There's no way you're talking to this FBI agent," he said. "It ain't gonna do you any good."

"All I'm going to do is explain the difference between betting and bookmaking," I said. "What harm can it do?"

"You're being naive," replied Oscar. "There's nothing good that comes out of you talking to a fucking FBI agent."

In retrospect, I wish I had listened to Oscar.

Noble had made a couple of attempts to engage me in a conversation and each time I had taken a pass. The third and final time came right after I had talked with Oscar.

I had just returned home from having major gum surgery and new implants inserted to replace the teeth ruined by Grandmother's sugarcoated cooking. The doorbell rang and Susan answered. There stood FBI special agent Noble, once again in my (badly swollen) face. My patience had long since worn thin with Agent Thomas Noble.

"We're closing in on your friends in La Cosa Nostra," he said, hoping his Sicilian reference to the Mafia would loosen my tongue.

I shut the door in his face and called Oscar, who shared my sense of outrage. He filed an official complaint with the head of the strike force, which ordered Noble to stay away from me.

Even after that, I kept thinking, *What do I have to lose by meeting with Noble?*

In January 1986, I called Noble to set up a meeting at White Cross Drugs on the north end of Las Vegas Boulevard. I requested that Oscar not be notified of our meeting or any subsequent meetings. I also told Noble that I needed something in writing to make clear that my sole purpose was to explain the difference between betting and bookmaking. I was not trying to cut a deal to implicate anyone; I wanted an agreement that stated I was simply trying to educate Noble that we were not doing anything illegal and I was receiving nothing in return for me or Susan.

Noble went and talked to Eric Johnson, a prosecutor in the Las Vegas Organized Crime Strike Force. Then he called back: "We have a deal."

A few days later, we returned to White Cross Drugs. Noble had the two-page document that said exactly what I asked for, signed by Johnson. I read it and signed. At that point I felt like we had an agreement.

On January 22, I met Noble at the Mount Charleston Lodge, a hidden gem nestled among juniper and ponderosa pine trees in Kyle Canyon, forty-five minutes outside Las Vegas and far from prying eyes. Looking back years later, I find it odd that Noble showed up without another agent or a tape recorder. He took not a single note during our hour-long conversation. How often does that happen?

He had rented a modest room. We sat at a table as I explained everything the Group was doing, including how our strategy worked, and how this made for a successful betting—not bookmaking—operation.

"These are not organized-crime people," I said. "Take Dale Conway in Utah. Dale Conway is a poker player. He wouldn't know a mob guy from anybody—he's one of my beards I met at a poker tournament in Vegas."

Later that same week I went to a boxing match with Ned Day, hoping he'd heard something from his sources in the FBI. He had.

"Billy, this case is dead," Ned said. "Don't worry about it."

A few months later, the Justice Department got a stark reminder of the legal hurdles to come when the strike force sent Johnson to Salt Lake City to claim in court that the government had the right to keep $75,179 in cash as evidence, along with other items seized in the raid of our beard, bettor Dale Conway.

At the hearing, Johnson informed district court judge Bruce Jenkins that the Computer Group "is not your typical bookmaking operation."

"You're talking about over a thousand hours of tapes that have to be listened to," he added. "You're talking about 216,000 pages of computer printouts that have to be reviewed. We believe that bookmakers from coast to coast, from a number of states, have been involved in this. It's set up like a corporation. If your honor would like, I can even show a chart demonstrating the vast complexity of the case."

Judge Jenkins didn't need a flowchart to understand that the federal government believed it had uncovered a massive national network of illegal bookmakers tied to organized crime. Billy Walters was a bookmaker. Glen Walker was a bookmaker. Dale Conway was a bookmaker. On and on and on.

But the savvy judge had some rather pointed questions for the strike force attorney Johnson. When the lead prosecutor finished answering, Judge Jenkins ordered every dollar of the money seized in Conway's home returned, along with everything else taken during the raid that had remained in the government's possession.

The strike force had struck out.

Nearly eight months after the cross-country raids and the failed attempt at indictments, Special Agent Thomas B. Noble was transferred to the Chicago office of the FBI.

No sooner had Noble exited stage left than "the Ant" entered stage right.

When news spread that I'd hired mob attorney Oscar Goodman, my public profile went through the roof, and I had showed up on Tony Spilotro's radar. Word came down that he wanted to see me. An offer I could not refuse.

We met at Oscar's law office. After we were introduced, Spilotro and I walked out of the office and onto an adjacent back patio. He looked exactly like somebody nicknamed "the Ant" should look: short, but with a distinct set of eyes.

Ice pick eyes. Empty. Dead.

We talked for about twenty minutes. Spilotro never threatened me. He didn't have to. Virtually every soul in town knew his reputation. He quietly told me that before the FBI raid, Doc had routinely shared the Computer Group's numbers with him. But now that Doc was no longer part of the Group or privy to our numbers, he wanted me to provide them to him.

"I'll get back to you on that," I said.

I did not get back to him. In fact, I did everything I could to avoid Spilotro. But I couldn't avoid going to the bathroom when I was playing in a poker tournament at the Golden Nugget.

Waiting for me was one of Tony's men, mob enforcer Fast Eddie DeLeo.

"The little guy wants to see you," Fast Eddie said.

Playing dumb, I said, "What are you talking about? What little guy?"

"You know who I'm talking about."

"Eddie, I gotta get back to the game," I said. "I'll see you later."

When I returned to the poker table, I kept one eye on my cards and the other on Fast Eddie, who was hovering nearby. When he headed for the restroom himself, I headed for the hills, leaving all my chips on the table.

That night our home phone rang. It was John Spilotro, one of Tony's four brothers. Our number was unlisted. Or so I thought. I had no idea that Spilotro had several Metro police officers on his payroll who had access to unlisted numbers.

I was told to come to the Food Factory restaurant in the morning.

I had been preparing for that call for years.

"We've got to get outta here right now," I told Susan. We packed in record time. Then Susan and I flew back to Louisville and rented a house under a friend's name.

Eight months later, Tony Spilotro and his brother Michael were found beaten to death in a shallow grave in a cornfield in Indiana. We did not mourn their loss.

With Spilotro dead and gone, it seemed safe for us to fly back to Las Vegas. Upon our return, we threw a party in celebration. Chip Reese, who lived next door, was among the first to arrive. He had been living with iron bars on his condo windows for years as protection from the Ant and his henchmen.

I figured my future in Las Vegas was bright again with Spilotro and crew out of the way. Little did I know that another storm was brewing.

12

Spinning Wynn's Wheel

I first met Steve Wynn shortly after we moved to Las Vegas in 1982. I was playing poker at the Golden Nugget when the famed owner approached me.

"Why don't you play more over here?" he asked.

I had an excuse at the ready. His assistant card room manager was my good friend Bobby Baldwin.

"If I win here, Bobby could take some heat," I said.

Truthfully, I had no desire to gamble at the Nugget—other than playing poker—because the blackjack limits ($10,000 per hand) were much lower than at the Horseshoe ($25,000). The Shoe also offered single-deck blackjack, while the Nugget dealt from six decks. And normal commission on baccarat at the Horseshoe was 1 percent less than the Nugget.

Thus, my polite pass to Wynn.

This was not something I did lightly. I was playing in a poker game with Wynn a few nights a week and he was a live one—someone who usually lost. I also wanted to stay friendly with Wynn as long as Bobby worked there. Not to mention the fact that Wynn was well on his way to becoming Mr. Las Vegas, a powerful figure known to hold a grudge.

Wynn had first stepped into the spotlight in 1967 at the age of twenty-five by buying a 5 percent interest in the Frontier Hotel and

Casino. Four years later, he leveraged his way to a controlling interest in the Golden Nugget, thanks to his high-profile position in the liquor distribution business and an improbable Mormon bank connection. Two years later, at thirty-one, he became the majority shareholder. Wynn would go on to build an impressive collection of resort hotels and casinos—The Mirage, Treasure Island, the Bellagio, Wynn Las Vegas, and Wynn Macau, to name but a few.

Even the casino mogul's most severe critics—and there is no shortage of them—have a grudging respect for his ability to stay in business despite numerous probes by local and federal law enforcement. Throughout the years, Wynn has been accused of everything from sexual assault and indecent exposure to money laundering and condoning narcotics trafficking in his hotels. His luck finally ran out in 2018, when he was forced to resign from his casino company following allegations of rampant sexual misconduct spanning decades.

But at the height of his power, Steve Wynn was a good guy to know and a bad guy to cross. He had a well-earned reputation for a hair-trigger temper and a take-no-prisoners approach to business.

I managed to make him a sworn enemy with the spin of a wheel.

Vegas is crawling with sketchy characters pitching the next foolproof plan for beating the house. Roulette, blackjack, craps, slots, sports betting—you name the game and there are a dozen hucksters ready to pitch their revolutionary systems for beating the odds, some legal, most not.

"Just front me the money. If you win, we split the profits. If we lose, well . . ."

On one occasion, a couple of con men pitched me on their ability to identify certain biases in roulette wheels that enabled them to accurately predict where the bouncing ball would land.

"We just need you to bankroll us," they said.

"I'll pass," I replied.

I told Chip and Doyle about that pitch and they about laughed me out of the room. Serious gamblers will tell you that roulette is pretty much a sucker's game—a 47.37 percent chance of winning—in part due to the addition of the green zero and double zero to the eighteen red and eighteen black numbers on every American-made wheel. (If you have a math allergy, please skip ahead.)

Let me run the numbers for you. That adjustment to American roulette wheels means you are pushing your odds against winning on a single dollar bet by 2.56 percent, or 38 to 1, with a payout of only 35 to 1. This gives the house a 5.26 percent mathematical edge on every bet. In Europe, where the wheels have just one zero, those odds are 2.7 percent.

While I told the con men to take a hike, I was intrigued by the idea that there might be a way to tilt roulette odds in a player's favor. Being an all-in kind of guy, I paid $4,000 to buy my very own American-made wooden roulette wheel.

I took that baby apart, piece by piece, in our living room. Once I broke it down and stripped it of the *Casablanca* glamour, I realized the wheel was just the sum of its collective parts, like any other mechanical device, subject to the same wear and tear as a washing machine, blender, or lawn mower.

For example, the "frets"—dividers between pockets—should function in the same way on every spin to dispense a completely random sequence of numbers. But what if a wooden wheel was twenty-five years old and not properly maintained? The frets could, in theory, become loose and alter the distance the ball traveled. The wheel shaft and bearings were other potential sources of bias if they became worn or loose over time, which could cause the track to tilt slightly in one direction and favor certain quadrants on the wheel.

After a lot of deliberation and tinkering, I began recording results on a couple of wheels at the Golden Nugget. I didn't choose them by scientific means, they just happened to be located on my route to the Nugget poker tables, where I hung out most nights. To get the figures I wanted and build a database of three thousand spins, I paid a small crew twelve bucks an hour to play the dollar minimum every time the two Golden Nugget wheels were open. Later, we did the same with roulette wheels in other locations.

Once we gathered the data, we fed the results into a special software program. We discovered that the Nugget wheels and several others around town showed a hint of a bias, but not nearly enough to overcome the house odds.

I kept digging. It was routine throughout Las Vegas for casinos to designate one of the zeros as no bet for a big player, knowing the odds still leaned heavily in their favor. I figured I would take my shot if I detected a roulette wheel biased enough to spin off a 10 percent net advantage.

Eventually, I felt we had accumulated enough data on the bias of a wheel at the Golden Nugget. I took my shot, and it was a big one. I brought $450,000 and began playing the five numbers our computer analysis liked: 7, 10, 20, 27, and 36.

Six hours later, I was down to my last $50,000 and thinking to myself, *Boy, you're an idiot.* Before I could tear myself away or go bust, the numbers started hitting. Twelve hours later, I was up $50,000, while wondering if the stress and sweat were worth it.

For a change, I took the money and ran. But I knew I'd be back at a roulette wheel.

One quick note: I placed my bets before the wheel started spinning. As far back as the 1970s, there were players in Las Vegas who used timing or computing devices that calculated which quadrant the ball was likely to land based on where it dropped when the wheel started spinning. Players would have earpieces or electronic devices in their shoes or boots to get the feedback on how to bet. However, if players started winning large amounts of money, the casino would simply make them bet before the wheel spun. Their advantage evaporated. This strategy only was effective if the player could find a casino that was asleep at the wheel, no pun intended.

As it happened, I was at Caesars in Lake Tahoe in February of '86 when I found a wheel I thought I could beat. Only one little problem: I had my hands full playing Hold'em in Amarillo Slim's Super Bowl of Poker tournament, where I got on a heater and won the main event against the likes of Doyle Brunson, Chip Reese, and Al Jay Ethier, the pride of Bristol, Rhode Island, which put a little extra money ($175,000) in my pocket. A few weeks after Slim's tournament, I flew back to Tahoe with some numbers I liked.

Damn if I didn't win $2 million of the emperor's money on that roulette wheel. I had Caesars wire the money to its sister hotel in Vegas, where I took Susan and another couple out to dinner and afterward played some more roulette without any advantage. I won an additional $600,000!

It was not good for a couple of reasons. One, I was trying to *lose* on that roulette wheel to take some heat off the Tahoe score. I didn't want the casino figuring out what I had discovered about the wheel's bias. My second reason was that the Computer Group investigation was in full swing and IRS agents were crawling all over town checking into my finances. Not that I had anything to hide, but I had seen their act before—seize your money and argue about it later.

My IRS friends were swarming because, during the bookmaking bust back in Kentucky, the feds had confiscated a half day's worth of gambling receipts from the morning games of a single NFL Sunday in 1982. After a few mathematical somersaults, they concluded (erroneously) that I owed $7 million in unpaid taxes, interest, and penalties. It was bull, but they were intent on collecting the money and forcing me to fight to get anything back.

One morning, the lead agent in the Kentucky case came knocking on our front door at the Las Vegas Country Club. Also present was a massive moving truck parked out front. It wasn't a subtle hint. I instantly recognized him. Before answering the door, I ran out back and stashed my bankroll—$35,000 in hundreds—in a watering can by the pool.

When I returned and opened the door, the IRS man was steaming.

"If you don't pay thirty thousand dollars right now, we're coming in and confiscating every stick of furniture in the house."

The last thing I wanted was IRS agents hauling furniture out of our house or knowing I had a stack of cash lying around for them to ask questions about. So I told him that I might know someone who'd lend me the money.

"Who?"

"Jack Binion down at the Horseshoe."

"Let's go."

With the revenue agent at my side, we drove downtown for an impromptu meeting with Jack.

I introduced the agent to Jack. "He says if I don't give him thirty thousand right now, he's going to take all our furniture. Is there any way you can loan me the money?"

Enjoying the moment, Jack hemmed and hawed before giving me one of those looks that said, *Billy, never a dull day at the office around you.*

"Yeah, Billy, I guess we can do that."

I went into the cashier's cage, signed a marker, and handed the agent $30,000 in cash. We rode back to the house. I didn't invite him in for a beer, so he left with an empty moving truck.

Problem solved. I went to the pool and fished out my own $35,000 in cash in the can. Susan had to stick the soaked bills in the dryer. This, by the way, was my first and only experience in literally laundering money. For my next spin at the roulette wheel, I changed venues to the Golden Nugget in Atlantic City, owned by my then-friend Steve Wynn.

At that time, Wynn and I were golfing buddies at the Las Vegas Country Club. During one round, we started talking about roulette and we negotiated a game. These were the ground rules: I could bet up to $1,000 per number at his Atlantic City casino. In exchange, the house would eliminate a zero from the wheel. I was required to put up a minimum $1 million deposit as a show of good faith.

That sounded like a bet I could take, so I did—but only after my guys scouted out a wheel with a perceived bias that I believed worked for me. Feeling confident, Susan and I chartered a Learjet for the trip to AC. We were met on the tarmac by the Golden Nugget limo. When we arrived at the hotel, we were greeted by two smiling hotel executives and a casino host. After depositing $1 million in cash in the cage, I wandered over to the wheel I liked.

I asked the dealer which one of the zeros he was going to bar.

"Can't do it," said the dealer.

When I complained, he called over the shift boss, who called over the casino manager, who called over casino president Daniel Boone Wayson.

"Sorry, Billy, it's against the law in Atlantic City to bar any zeros," Boone said.

"That's impossible," I replied. "Steve Wynn and I made this game in Vegas. Steve owns this goddamn place. I never would have flown to Atlantic City in a million years if I was going to bet two zeros."

Boone informed me that Steve likely didn't know the law. But he'd call the gaming board to see if they'd make an exception.

He called. There would be no special permission.

If I had won betting a wheel with two zeros, it would have raised suspicions because of my background and reputation as a professional gambler. So I headed for the bar and proceeded to put a big dent in their Corona supply. I managed to get drunk and lose the entire million dollars at a blackjack table.

Susan and I flew back to Vegas the next day. I was so mad at myself I could barely speak. The phone rang as we walked in the door. Guess who?

Wynn wasn't calling to apologize about the roulette debacle. Instead, he invited me to play golf. I accepted his invitation and we teed it up a couple days later. We briefly discussed Atlantic City, and I told Steve I couldn't play there again because I wouldn't play a wheel with two zeros.

A few weeks later, while playing poker together at the Golden Nugget, Steve invited us to join him and his wife, Elaine, at the U.S. Open golf tournament on Long Island.

"We'll take the helicopter," he said.

I knew what he was thinking.

"Steve, I won't play a roulette wheel with two zeros."

"Don't worry," he said. "I figured out what we can do. You're betting the same amount on every spin. It will be easy to track what you've bet on an hourly basis and then figure out what the house percentage would be. We will take half of that, figuring one zero, and I'll pay you in cash comps out of the Golden Nugget in Vegas."

Gamblers with math minds think alike.

"That will be fine," I said.

We negotiated a new game. This time I'd put up $2 million and bet $2,000 per spin on five numbers.

At the Golden Nugget in Atlantic City, I found the same wheel I liked and bet the same five red and black numbers over and over— 7, 10, 20, 27, and 36—until the casino shut down at 4:00 a.m. When the wheel finally stopped spinning, I was up $3.2 million.

After a few hours of sleep I went back to the casino floor and what do you know? They had the same roulette wheel, right where I had left it a few hours earlier. I played the same set of numbers and jumped off a winner again, which attracted some unwanted attention.

I looked around and every pit boss and floor manager was sweating my plays. Four or five hours later, I was still winning, when a fresh face sat down next to me and started talking.

What do you know? It was a member of the New Jersey Division of Gaming Enforcement with a brand new hard-on for Bill Walters. He was looking for anything illegal or improper. Good luck with that.

The guy could have stuck a .45 to my head and I would not have been able to tell him one way or the other what was wrong with that wheel. Whatever the issue was—the bearings, the frets, the *whatever*—all I knew was it showed a bias and, yes, I had some numbers I liked to play. Everything I did was perfectly legal.

I was up another $600,000 by 6:00 p.m. Mr. Enforcement had more company, a posse of beefy men in expensive suits sporting permanent frowns on their faces.

Yeah, it's time to get the hell out of here.

I went to the cashier and collected a check for $5.8 million, which included my $2 million deposit. Trust me, Steve Wynn did not take kindly to losing $3.8 million to his golfing buddy in less than forty hours.

Word got back to me that Wynn sent the roulette wheel to the manufacturer to check for a bias. They found nothing wrong. Steve then supposedly sent the wheel to be examined by some NASA scientists who'd helped put a man on the moon. They tore it into itty-bitty parts and still came up with nothing.

Thus marked the beginning of a bitter feud with Steve Wynn that lasts to this day. It also marked a true awakening. When you lose in casinos—as 98 percent of people do after being plied with alcohol and battling sucker's odds—everything favors the owners. But when hundreds of hours of time and thousands of dollars of investment uncover a *legitimate* mathematical edge, the powers that be get very angry.

Case in point: Steve didn't mind at all when I lost the million dollars playing blackjack on the previous trip to Atlantic City. Or the more than $500,000 I lost in the Golden Nugget playing baccarat and blackjack.

But when Wynn lost that roulette money to me, you would have thought I'd waltzed into his mansion and put my elbow through one of his Picassos.

After winning $3.8 million at the Nugget, I played several Atlantic City and Las Vegas casinos before word spread and the operators wouldn't let me play anymore. I went to plan B and recruited some partners to play the wheels I liked.

One of my beards was Maurice "Mo" Moorman, whom I had known from our days in Louisville. Mo was a first-round draft pick of the Kansas City Chiefs and a starting offensive lineman on their 1969 Super Bowl championship team. After football, Mo was a successful businessman with his own beer distributorship in Louisville.

I asked Mo if he would do me a little favor and play some roulette for me in Atlantic City. He rightly asked what was in it for him. I said I would give him 25 percent of whatever we won. That did the trick. So I gave him the following instructions: Go to a particular bank in Louisville and ask for a girl named Mary, who would give him a cashier's check for $400,000. Catch a flight to Philadelphia, where a limo would be waiting to take him to a casino in AC. Then deposit the money in the cage and play some high-level craps.

"Show them some speed," I instructed. "Let them know you are a serious gambler, not just some jack-off."

As luck would have it, Mo won about twenty thousand. When he called me that night, I outlined step two of my plan.

"Go over to Harrah's in the morning. You're looking for a guy named Uncle Jack. He'll be waiting by a bank of phones in the hotel lobby. He's going to introduce you to a man named Stan, who's going to tell you how to stack your chips and play a specific system on the wheel."

Off Mo went and played the Harrah's wheel. He later told me that after two or three hours he was down sixty grand before suddenly hitting three numbers in a row. The dealer was not pleased.

"We're shutting this wheel down," he told Mo.

"Shutting it down?" Mo replied. "I'm sitting here a big loser and you honestly believe something's wrong with this wheel?"

"We're shutting this wheel down."

That's when Mo said the dealer pointed behind him and said, "If you want to talk about it, they'll talk about it."

Mo said he turned around and saw two guys who looked like Dobermans. Big. Strong. Salty looking.

"Hey," Mo said, "why you shutting this wheel down? I want my money back."

"If you know what's best for you, you'll leave it alone."

Mo said he took one more look at their size and their faces and decided to leave well enough alone.

After Mo's cover was blown, I turned to Ivy Ong, an unassuming sort who had made his money as a builder in California before blowing most of his life savings gambling. I staked Ivy to the tune of $500,000 and set him up at a fancy Atlantic City hotel. He brought his wife and two kids.

After his first day at the designated roulette wheel, Ivy walked away happy. He was up six hundred thousand, earning him an upgrade to the penthouse suite, a comp, of course. Since Ivy had established himself as a high roller, the resort invited his wife and kids for a boat ride. While they cruised around AC on a yacht, Ivy picked up where he'd left off. He added another couple hundred grand to our growing pot of money.

Then the pit boss yanked the wheel. He tossed Ivy out of the penthouse suite and kicked his wife and kids off the yacht.

Ivy was in tears when he called and told me what had happened. The guy who had lost everything in life finally wins, and they throw him and his wife and kids out on the street.

I've had a few defining moments in my gambling life, but that was one. It opened my eyes to the unwritten code of casino misconduct: beat us, and we'll ban you.

From that moment on, I promised to never lose another dime inside their smoky rooms. I was done with any casino games, other than poker and sports betting.

I was forty years old and on the verge of a rich new chapter in my life.

13

Making the Turn

Dewey Tomko and I were sitting at a table at the World Series of Poker when I noticed a tall dude eyeballing our game.

"You know that guy?" I asked.

"Yeah, that's David Leadbetter," Dewey said.

Dewey explained that David was a renowned golf instructor for many top professionals. He had just moved to the United States from England and worked at the Grenelefe Golf and Tennis Resort in Haines City, Florida.

David's clients have included Nick Faldo, Greg Norman, Ernie Els, Nick Price, Charles Howell III, and Michelle Wie. He's also written several best-selling instructional books on my favorite game.

I asked Dewey to set up a lunch with David so I could ask him to help take my game to a higher level. Given the caliber of his clientele, I was a little nervous when we met. I opened with a confession that may have made David wonder what he was getting into.

"I've never played a serious round of golf without grease," I said.

David certainly understood how applying grease on the face of drivers and long irons reduced the amount of spin, which was what caused a ball to slice or hook. Back then, pros on both sides of the Atlantic were suspected of adding "a little dab will do ya" to their hair before they played a round. I think what surprised David most was how using grease was part of the everyday rules we played by.

Before David, I'd taken a few lessons from Bob Hamilton, a legendary pro from Indiana and five-time PGA Tour winner. Bob was a short-game wizard, but I wanted to improve my overall game.

During my first session on the range with David, I teed up my wooden Ping driver and promptly demonstrated what happened to my shots without greasing the clubface—I sliced the ball fifty yards to the right.

I half expected my new instructor to hand me a jar of Vaseline and flee back to England. To my lasting relief, David stuck it out with me, and our friendship endures to this day. Thanks to him and his teaching protégé, Simon Holmes, my de-greased game improved tremendously.

As an all-in sort of guy, I became—stop me if you've heard this before—obsessed with golf once we moved to Las Vegas. I was determined to become as proficient as possible for someone who wasn't exactly born on the back nine of a country club.

During the past four decades, I've had the privilege of being tutored by—and befriending—some of the world's best teaching pros, including Leadbetter, Jimmy Ballard, Jim Hardy, Dave Pelz, Peter Kostis, Pete Cowen, Randy Peterson, Dennis Sheehy, John Redman, Billy Harmon, and his brother, Butch Harmon.

If none of those professionals were available, I was more than willing to take tips from caddies, cabdrivers, and bartenders. It's also true that I've learned a lot just by associating with more than a few golf legends. After working with Leadbetter in Florida, for example, I'd occasionally head to the Bay Hill Club & Lodge, owned by Arnold Palmer and home to other top pros. Dewey and I would join a half-dozen pros, throw money in a pot, and choose up sides. When Mr. Palmer was in town, he would join us on occasion. Afterward, he'd sit at the card table for a wicked game of hearts. He was the King, but just one of the boys around us.

In between lessons, I practiced compulsively, pounding balls on the range for hours at a time, chipping and putting until my hands were red. When I wasn't honing my game, I was playing money matches from Las Vegas to South Florida to Southern California.

My favorite tournament of all time combined my twin loves of gambling and golf. It was the Professional Gamblers Invitational, the brainchild of Doyle Brunson.

In his younger days, Doyle barnstormed Bloodthirsty Highway, a covert poker circuit strung across Texas, Oklahoma, and the Southwest with stops in back-room parlors and underground gaming dens. His skilled poker and travel buddies were Bryan "Sailor" Roberts and Thomas "Amarillo Slim" Preston. They were robbed and beaten many times on the road, before settling into Vegas residency.

Doyle came up with the idea of the PGI in 1974 to keep his high-rolling buddies in town after the World Series of Poker ended in June. He and Jack Binion, owner of the Horseshoe, figured they'd simply shift the venue from felt tables to grass fairways and greens.

What started as a $200-a-round wager at the Dunes golf course quickly morphed into a weeklong annual event played on multiple courses around town. The sixty-four invitees were selected, paired, and handicapped by Jack.

When I was first invited to play in the PGI in the late seventies, the entry fee was $5,000, a minimum $1,500 a round ($500 Nassau over three days), and another $500 for expenses.

Jack said he wasn't interested in hosting small fish who saved their money to play in his tournament. He wanted professional gamblers, hustlers who lived to sweat six figures on a single match. Every participant was a true-blue stickup artist who thought nothing about doctoring his handicap. This forced Jack to do a lot of reconnaissance, checking hometown sources to see how the local stud golf gamblers would fare under the gun in his tournament.

Once Jack set the handicaps—at least to the extent possible, given that the invitees were renowned hustlers—he threw the USGA Rule Book out the window.

Maximum of fourteen clubs in your bag? Carry as many as you want.

Putt like you're playing pool? No problem.

There was only one steadfast rule that Jack enforced—you played your ball *exactly* where you found it. No free drops. No relief. Cart paths, sprinkler heads, ground under repair, play it where it lies. No arguments.

I held my own in my first PGI, but eventually I wised up and, like a few other gamblers, rented a place in Vegas for the summer to play practice rounds before the tournament to be more competitive.

In those years, my cash flow was often in flux, to put it mildly. For the real big matches of several hundred thousand dollars, I relied on a stake horse a few times when I was broke. One of those willing to bet on me was Fred Ferris, whose nickname about town was Sarge. The son of a Lebanese-born railroad worker, Sarge was born in 1928 in Waterville, Maine. He rose from abject poverty to become a World Series of Poker event winner in 1980 in Deuce-to-seven draw over Doyle and Bobby Baldwin, winning $150,000.

Small and skinny with a hooknose, Sarge was never destined to win any beauty contests. Naturally, we called him "Handsome." Sarge's card-playing skills were a thing of beauty, however. He was tenacious, committing 100 percent to everything he did, especially poker.

I'll never forget the night at the Golden Nugget when Sarge and Sam Angel stayed long after everyone else had quit playing. Sam's nickname was "Stubby" because his physical dimensions were five-two by five-two. It could just as easily been "Stinky." Sam was a well-known Vegas character, peddling mostly fake versions of expensive jewelry when he wasn't drinking too much and playing poker.

Stubby could be funny in a prickly Don Rickles kind of way, but mostly he was obnoxious, a crusty drunk who cussed out dealers while he inhaled beer and salted peanuts for breakfast, lunch, and dinner. And that brings me to the stinky part.

Stubby wore a colostomy bag, which he used as a weapon at the poker table. One night he was off the rails and headed for broke. Most of the pros had evacuated the area because every time Stubby lost a hand he'd open his colostomy bag, releasing a stench that made the cards curl up. You can only imagine the rancid smell of crap, beer, and peanuts wafting out of that bag.

Sarge was the only one who stuck around to finish off Stubby. Sarge had played with him before and came prepared for Stubby's crappy bag of tricks. Whenever Stubby unleashed a blast from the bag, Sarge lit a match and held it under his nose. He went through an entire book of matches, until he'd won every last nickel Stubby had.

Sarge and I shared a determined approach to gambling. He didn't know a golf ball from a grapefruit, but he knew I could play as well as any of the other gamblers, especially under pressure. He bankrolled me in matches where the swing in wagers could run two or three hundred thousand dollars a day. Sarge didn't ask whom— or how—I was playing. But he knew that I played without fear and was a consistent winner. That's all that mattered to Sarge, and we became great friends.

Sadly, in early 1989, Sarge asked me to help get his affairs in order after he'd been diagnosed with a terminal brain tumor and lung cancer. He was just sixty years old. "The doctors tell me I have weeks, not months, to live," he said.

We all lose people along the way, but this one hit me especially hard.

Sarge asked me to accompany him when he met with his attorney. When I walked into the law office, I almost fell over when this ponytailed guy with hair down to his waist greeted Sarge. He did not look like your typical buttoned-down lawyer. But when I noticed the tears for his client running down Richard Wright's cheeks, I wanted him to be my attorney, too. And he has been ever since.

Sarge died on March 12, 1989—only hours after playing his final high-stakes poker game. I honored our friendship by helping his daughter, Kelli, straighten out Sarge's financial affairs and making sure she received everything she deserved.

The other good thing that came from my grief over Sarge's death was the decision to give up drinking and smoking. His death forced me to confront my own mortality. But first I got myself in a heap of trouble.

Shaken by Sarge's death, I went out with a friend, drank too much, and broke my own promise to stay the hell out of casinos. I ended up drunk and gambling at the Horseshoe at 2:00 a.m., pushing the casino's sky-high limits.

Five years earlier, after attending Benny Binion's eightieth birthday bash, I had lost a million dollars in a single drunken session at his casino. Then I won $2 million betting sports and went back to the Horseshoe—tell me if you've heard this story before—and got drunk and lost that, too.

This time I was up $550,000 in baccarat, betting $50,000 a hand, when the casino manager, Ted Binion (Benny's youngest son), cut the limits. In response, I lived up to my nickname of my younger days—"Wild Bill from Louisville"—and made a complete ass of myself. There's no other way to put it.

Chips went flying all over the room. Ranting and raising hell, I cussed out the croupier, the pit boss, Teddy, and the entire Binion family—which nobody in their right mind would have done unless they were begging for a one-way ticket to the desert.

Their only option was to kick me out of the casino.

My good friend Gene McCarlie was Jack Binion's right-hand man and the shift manager that night. He escorted me onto Fremont Street, where I proceeded to curse him with every awful word I knew. I then stumbled across the street to the Nugget and plopped my drunken butt down at a blackjack table.

My phone rang. It was one ticked-off Teddy Binion. He said something and I exploded.

"I'm not taking that crap from anybody!" I yelled.

Teddy said he was on his way over.

"Well, c'mon then," I told him.

While tracking me down inside the Nugget, Teddy bumped into Doug Dalton, who was running the swing shift in the poker room that night.

"Where's Billy Walters?" Teddy said.

Doug saw the serious intent in Teddy's eyes and decided to protect me from myself.

"I don't know," he said. "Haven't seen him all night."

That's when Teddy headed deeper into the casino and Doug noticed the pistol in the back of his waistband.

My phone rang again. This time it was Doug.

"Teddy's looking for you," he said, "and he's got a gun."

I was not drunk enough to have a death wish. I got out of Dodge.

The next morning, I woke up sick to my stomach—and not only from the booze or my near-death experience.

Filled with remorse, I called Jack Binion.

"Jack, I'm sorry. I don't know what I was thinking disrespecting Teddy and the family like that."

"Well, Billy, I don't think you were thinking," he replied. "But, trust me, I've seen worse. We're good."

Sarge's death and my humiliating night at the Horseshoe proved a turning point—no, *the* turning point—in my life. After years of stops and starts and stumbles, of promises made and broken, I finally said, "That's it. I'm done smoking and drinking for the rest of my life."

I quit right then and there. Cold turkey.

I was tired of making a fool of myself. I'd long been in denial about having a drinking problem, mostly because to me an alcoholic was someone who drank every day or was drunk most of the time. In my mind you couldn't work like I worked—seventy or eighty hours a week—and be an alcoholic. Plus, I would go three weeks or more without taking a sip. But when I did drink, I didn't stop. Drinking changed my personality and affected my decision-making—and not in a good way.

I was ready to quit smoking, too. I was coughing a lot and smoking had killed people I cared about, including my mother and my aunt Nell. Unfortunately, I replaced one vice with another after throwing out the cigarettes by stuffing my face with food. I gained thirty pounds and my waist size ballooned from thirty-four to forty, seemingly overnight. I couldn't get my pants on. One evening, Susan and I went to dinner with Jack Binion and his wife, Phyllis. Jack looked at my big belly and started laughing, which was all the incentive I needed to stay out of the refrigerator.

I took up racquetball at Jack's suggestion. The first time I played him, Jack spotted me ten points even though he wasn't that good, either. I literally had to lie down during the match because my back hurt from carrying around that big belly.

I'm a competitor, so the belly had to go. I hired a dietitian and kept playing racquetball until I lost the thirty pounds and began beating Jack often enough to spot *him* ten points. I also got even more serious about my golf game.

One of my favorite golfing buddies in those days was the rounder and roving rambler Puggy Pearson. I told my all-time Pug story in April 2006 during his memorial service at the Bellagio. We were playing at Canyon Gate CC against Tommy Fisher and Mike Sexton, two guys not wholly unfamiliar with six-figure wagers. Here's what I said to Pug's family and friends at the service:

We were on the eighteenth hole at Canyon Gate CC and Puggy hit his drive down the right side. Puggy was playing a Titleist ball imprinted with a La Costa logo. Now, we're all pretty sure that Puggy's ball went in the water. The other three tee shots landed on the left side of the fairway. All of a sudden, we heard

Puggy scream to us, "My ball's in the bunker," and he quickly hit a shot onto the green.

This didn't smell quite right to our opponents. So they drove up to the green as fast as they could before Puggy could get to his ball. Mike took one look and said, "Pug, this ball is a Titleist all right, but it doesn't have a La Costa logo on it."

Pug instantly hung his head. You could tell he was embarrassed. He'd been caught cheating red-handed. After a long pause, he looked up and said, "Boys, I've learned a valuable lesson today."

"Yeah, the lesson is that you shouldn't try to fuck your friends," Mike said.

"Oh, I've learned a lesson all right," Puggy said. "I'll never play another ball with a fucking logo!"

Without a doubt one of my finest hours in golf came two years later in February 2008 at the magical Pebble Beach Golf Links on the Monterey Peninsula. The opportunity to play in the AT&T Pebble Beach Pro-Am is perhaps the most coveted invitation for an amateur golfer. I didn't care at all about hobnobbing with celebrities or professional golfers. I craved the competition on one of the most spectacular stages in the game.

Leading up to the AT&T, my handicap had spiked to 11. I hadn't picked up a club since the beginning of football season the previous fall. I'd been distracted by far too many business obligations, and my trusty putter had failed me. Out of desperation, I brought five different flatsticks to Pebble, none of which found the hole during early practice rounds.

Before the tournament began, I went to the practice green and met a sales rep showing off some extra-thick putting grips—the same kind K. J. Choi made famous a year earlier with his win at the AT&T. I tried putting with one and suddenly I couldn't miss. The fat grip felt firmer in my hands and forced me to putt with my shoulders.

When I expressed interest in the grips, the rep delivered the bad news: these were new models that wouldn't be available to the general public for months. I applied the old Kentucky charm and slipped him a Franklin to put one of the unavailable grips on my most reliable putter.

The oversize grip was just what I needed. With veteran tour caddie Zak Williamson reading the greens I rediscovered my golden touch. In another lucky stroke, my assigned partner was Fredrik Jacobson, a Swedish pro whom I really liked. Freddie and I didn't have a strong first round, but we managed to post a 7-under 65 on the Spyglass course.

The next day at Pebble, Freddie put on a show with five birdies and an eagle. Combined with my one gross birdie, we shot 62 for a total of 17-under par after two rounds.

On Saturday at Poppy Hills, Freddie again went on a tear with a 31 on the back nine. With my improved putting, I was steadily making pars, with net birdies on several holes. We shot another 62 and had a five-stroke lead going into the final round on Sunday.

I was both thrilled and nervous to see our names at the top of the Pro-Am leaderboard. We played Pebble again and put on a clinic of ham-and-egg golf, with a touch of good fortune blended in.

The 145-yard par-3 fifth hole proved a harbinger. I pulled an 8-iron long and left of the green. My ball landed near a grandstand in matted-down grass behind a narrow bunker with next to no room to the pin. Freddie's ball was safely on the front edge of the green.

I told Zak that I was going to pick up because I didn't get a stroke on the hole.

"Take a swipe at it anyway," the veteran caddy said. "You may surprise yourself."

Well, I more than surprised myself when I took a hard swing with a sand wedge, which slid perfectly under the ball. It popped up from a thick lie and rolled straight into the hole. The fans in the grandstand erupted in cheers.

Pebble Beach magic!

Our lead ballooned to eight strokes. If I was ever going to throw off (inflate my score), it would have been on the back nine. Instead, I went on to shoot 40 on the back, my best nine-hole score of the tournament, and we went on to a record runaway win. I was still on a high when the killjoys piped up. Our victory provoked some grumbling from the sore losers and skeptics who were suspicious of a "Las Vegas gambler" with an 11 handicap. The word *sandbagger* was tossed out more than a few times.

The bad-mouthing dissipated a bit when a hole-by-hole analysis of our scorecards determined that my lowest eighteen-hole score was 83, well within my handicap range. Still, the critics wondered how I managed to perform so well under pressure.

Answer: I had probably played in more high-pressure matches than any other amateur in the field. Freddie making sixteen birdies and two eagles that week didn't hurt. Oh, by the way, I was invited back to the Pro-Am in 2012. My pro and I finished dead last. This time, no one moaned about the "sandbagger."

The majority of matches I now play with my friends are for bragging rights and maybe a few bucks. No matter where or how I play, I will always cherish that magical week on the Monterey Peninsula.

14

Two Steps Forward & Back to Court

After I said goodbye to drinking, smoking, and casino gambling, my life improved significantly—at least for a while. I stopped burning through money and began accumulating it for the first time, elevating our net worth into solid seven figures.

In 1987, I launched an investment company, Berkley Enterprises, which borrowed Susan's middle name. I was ready to try a more traditional line of business, and the late 1980s was a good time to invest in real estate.

The savings and loan crisis had hit like a hurricane during that period, resulting in bankruptcy for more than 1,300 financial institutions with total assets of nearly $600 billion. Taxpayers lost as much as a half trillion dollars in what, at the time, was the worst financial collapse since the Great Depression.

A friend of mine, Eric Nelson, was an auctioneer who sold distressed properties at fire-sale prices. Eric knew I had some cash to invest, and he taught me how to quickly buy and turn around non-performing assets for substantial profits.

I bought and sold virtually everything Eric brought to my attention. My strategy was simple: buy properties at a substantial discount, make the most money as fast as possible, and then move on to the next deal.

In Phoenix, for example, I acquired a shopping center on Bell Road for $25 a square foot and an apartment building for $10,000 a unit. I also scooped up first mortgages on thirty-eight condos in Chandler, Arizona, for pennies on the dollar and 1,200 finished lots in a gated community in Tucson for $10,000 apiece.

The business suited me. My financial affairs stabilized along with my once-chaotic personal life. I spent more time with Susan, and together we became more active in the community, including getting involved in local charities. The timing was right for stepping out. Las Vegas was transforming into a true metropolis, an oasis of glittering lights with five-star resorts and convention hotels.

Two years earlier, in 1985, my youngest son, Derin, moved in with us. He'd been struggling back in Louisville, and Carol had her hands full taking care of Scott. A big (six-foot-one) outgoing kid, Derin had started playing football and basketball in the seventh grade, motivated to do well in school because playing on a team required at least a C average. Then, in October of his sophomore year during tryouts for the junior varsity basketball team, he tore his ACL. The knee injury marked the beginning of a downward spiral. Without sports as motivation, Derin started hanging with the wrong crowd—cutting classes, smoking pot, sneaking out at night. When he lashed out and slapped Carol, it was time for a change.

He was fifteen when he moved in with us. I quickly laid down the law, utilizing the carrot-and-stick approach. We gave him $75 a week in allowance and I found him a job that paid $100 every Saturday. Money-wise, he was fine. Then I hit him with the stick:

"Here are my rules," I began. "You don't get a girl pregnant. You don't get arrested. You don't go to jail. You make As and Bs. If you do that, you and I are going to get along."

We enrolled him in Bishop Gorman, an elite private high school, with the help of a friend, Michael Gaughan, who was a big donor to the school. Derin was admitted on probationary status and quickly found his footing with the honor society crowd. He made straight As his first year. As a reward, we bought him a new Toyota Supra. From there, he kept on getting all As and Bs—minus one C+ in AP Physics—right up until graduation day.

In the meantime, Michael Kent and I had reconnected. Mike had figured out that Doc's double-dealings had led to the demise of the original Computer Group. He was determined to reorganize and move forward just as the 1986 college football season approached.

Mike needed a place to bet legally, so I hooked him up with a buddy of mine. Gene Maday was the owner of Little Caesar's sportsbook, a classic Vegas haunt tucked into a run-down strip mall on the north end of the Strip. A transplant from Detroit, Gene had operated Checker Cab in Vegas before opening Little Caesar's casino and sportsbook in 1970. Under Gene's benign neglect, the floor of his joint was more tape than carpet. Cigarette smoke hung in the air like drapery. Racing forms and parlay cards were scattered everywhere. Calling the place a "dive" would have been a compliment.

Dedicated degenerates swarmed to the stand-alone book, wandering around with twenty-four-ounce cans of Old Milwaukee in hand. When the book's highly regarded lines were posted—etched in black markers on white tote boards—the clientele scrambled to the pay phones out front. An old-school joint: pure *Vegas, baby.*

Little Caesar's quickly made its mark as the place for monster action. Gene and his expert handicapper, Bob "Toledo Blackie" Black, accepted wagers as high as anyone in the country.

By welcoming big bettors, Little Caesar's lured the likes of Kirk Kerkorian, founder of the MGM Grand and a certified Las Vegas business legend. Kirk's heart didn't start pumping until he had six figures on a game. I witnessed this firsthand when he pulled into the parking lot at the Dunes, rolled down his window, and tossed a sack full of cash into a car Gene and I were waiting in.

I proposed to Gene that I'd move the money that Mike was betting, while also placing bets for the both of us. Gene loved the idea. He relished the chance to get an inside track to Mike's numbers—not just for himself, but also to shade his line however he wanted. This was seventh heaven to a big-time bookmaker like Gene.

Life could not have been sweeter, until August of 1989 when an investigative book called *Interference* stirred the pot in our gambling game.

Author Dan Moldea reprised the story of the Computer Group investigation and inferred that no one was indicted because Merv Adelson, the head of Lorimar-Telepictures, was involved with the Group. Adelson's then-wife was television star Barbara Walters, who happened to be best friends with Nancy Reagan, the wife of President Ronald Reagan, a connection that was questioned but never reported by Moldea due to a lack of documented evidence.

That said, a Justice Department source cited in the book told Moldea: "The problem is that the Justice Department knows it's an organized-crime operation, with some embarrassing links to major celebrities in the worlds of sports, politics, and entertainment. This whole investigation has been stalled for political reasons."

That inference did not sit well with certain folks in the Justice Department and strike force.

Six months later, the FBI came calling yet again on the morning of January 5, 1990—just two weeks before the five-year statute of limitations on the Computer Group case was set to expire.

I was sleeping off an all-night poker game when a swarm of agents came barreling in at eight in the morning. Susan was in her pajamas and robe, already up with the dogs. She was forced to endure the indignity of a body search before being allowed to dress.

Two of the strike force agents showed up in my bedroom. I had to blink a couple of times before recognizing the big block letters FBI on their jackets.

"You're going to have to get dressed," one said.

Perhaps concerned that I was packing a weapon in my boxer shorts, they demanded I dress in front of them. No shave, no shower, nothing to make myself presentable. Adding insult to indignation, they slapped handcuffs and leg-irons on poor Susan before we were paraded out the front door of our upscale Rancho Bel Air home.

The perp walk had one objective—to publicly shame us in full view of our neighbors and friends.

We had known for weeks that indictments were in the offing. Oscar had pleaded with members of the strike force to let us voluntarily surrender downtown. Instead, the feds chose to play the PR game and humiliate us.

As I was escorted to a waiting van, I glanced down at the morning's *Review-Journal* in our driveway. We were front-page news: "Indictments Target Betting Group in LV" screamed a headline.

I can't begin to tell you how angry I was to see Susan subjected to that kind of treatment. My animosity toward the FBI and Department of Justice multiplied tenfold that morning.

Shackled and silent, Susan and I rode down to the federal courthouse, where seventeen others connected to the Computer Group were formally charged. Interestingly, Michael Kent, Dominic Spinale, Merv Adelson, and Irwin Molasky were not among them. Those of us who were charged faced a total of 120 counts of alleged conspiracy, violations of the Interstate Transmission of Wagering Information, and Use of Interstate Facilities in Aid of Racketeering.

There was not a single charge involving bookmaking or ties to organized crime. Repeat, not one. This time around, the government changed its tactics by concocting a new genre of crime in the indictment. They called it *organized betting*.

The charges were based on federal statutes that prohibited illegal bookmaking. They claimed those statutes could be expanded to criminalize the activities of what it called a *business enterprise*. In doing so, they alleged that members of the Computer Group had violated federal law by using wire communications facilities—that is, a telephone—inside and outside the state of Nevada to wager with legal and illegal bookmakers.

The stakes were sky-high. If the government successfully prosecuted the Computer Group for placing bets with bookmakers, the entire landscape of sports gambling would change and recreational gamblers who placed wagers across state lines would be committing a federal crime.

After being fingerprinted and stashed in separate cells, Susan and I were left to stare at the same sad-sack lunch: a soggy bologna sandwich. Our lawyer saved the day and our digestive systems. Oscar arrived and secured our release.

Before we gathered in Oscar's office, prosecutors made their opening move. They wanted to make a deal. If I agreed to plead guilty, they would drop all charges against Susan.

Nice. The feds were playing the get-your-wife-out-of-jail-free card.

Susan was stunned.

"Is there any chance I could go to jail?" she asked.

Oscar is a lot of things—bombastic, a lover of Bombay Sapphire gin—but he does not coddle his clients.

"Susan, you're not guilty of anything. But anytime you go before a judge and a jury, anything can happen. So yes, there's a chance you can go to jail."

Susan began to cry.

I knew what I had to do.

"This is real simple," I told Oscar. "I'm going to plead guilty to the charges and they'll release Susan."

Susan stopped crying.

"Bill, we need to go somewhere and talk," she said.

We retreated to a fast-food restaurant down the street from Oscar's office. Susan waited until we were seated in a booth before speaking up.

"We haven't done anything wrong," she said. "How can this happen in America for betting on a ball game? You are *not* pleading guilty."

Susan and I were among fourteen defendants who eventually went before a Las Vegas jury in January 1992. The media covered every moment of the landmark trial. I understood the significance as well, and brought in Rick Wright to replace Oscar, who was, frankly, still upset at me for ignoring his advice and meeting with Agent Noble. In retrospect, it was the right move. Rick proved to be the game changer.

The prosecution made some lineup changes as well. Eric Johnson, the lead prosecutor on our original case and still part of the Organized Crime Strike Force, decided to sit on the sidelines this time around. He passed the prosecutorial reins to Jane Hawkins Shoemaker, a second-year assistant U.S. attorney.

We found it interesting that Shoemaker had clerked for—how's this for a coincidence?—the Honorable Lloyd D. George, the same U.S. district court judge who had authorized the FBI wiretaps and multistate raids on our operation six years earlier.

So Judge George had an attack dog in the fight. We feared that, if he stayed on the case with Shoemaker leading the prosecution, our defense was dead on arrival. With that in mind, in June 1991 Oscar filed a motion to have Judge George recused, citing judicial misconduct in the judge's order that I appear at an unprecedented secret hearing before the court—without Oscar present—to discuss the legal ramifications of my private meetings with Noble. Generally, such motions are tossed like yesterday's trash, even more so given that Judge George wielded enough clout that the Las Vegas federal courthouse where our trial was held was later renamed in his honor.

Believe it or not, in late July, our long shot came home when Judge George stepped aside despite writing in his decision, "There is absolutely no evidence of bias, prejudice, or impropriety by the court." He was replaced by senior U.S. district court judge Clarence

Newcomer, a wise old soul from the streets of Philadelphia who had presided over many bookmaking and mob-related cases.

Suddenly, we had a glimmer of hope.

Still, we were scared. Believe me, the line between guilt and innocence is extremely thin when you and your loved ones are forced to fight for your freedom in federal court.

On the surface, it appeared that our case became even more daunting when Mike Kent agreed to testify on behalf of the government in exchange for a grant of immunity from prosecution for any criminal charges, including tax fraud and tax evasion related to his offshore accounts. This potentially did not bode well for the rest of us—if he did not tell the truth.

In her opening statement, prosecutor Shoemaker took great pains to describe the Computer Group as an interconnected betting and bookmaking behemoth, a massive operation in thirteen states churning out millions of dollars a year in profits. In short, ladies and gentlemen of the jury, ours was a sprawling *criminal enterprise*.

Our co-counsel, Kenny Hense, a former prosecutor and expert on gambling law, conceded that, yes, the Computer Group made staggering amounts of money at times, but it was hardly an evil bookmaking empire. He questioned why it had triggered an investigation that cost millions in taxpayer dollars and tens of thousands of hours of FBI manpower.

Not surprisingly, Mike Kent was first up as the government's star witness. He testified for hours on end about his computer genius, his gambling past, and the inner workings of our operation, but, in reality, his account only helped our case. All Mike did was tell the truth. We were bettors—nothing more, nothing less.

The tide truly began to turn the next day when FBI special agent Thomas Noble was subjected to a withering cross-examination. Hense relied on Noble's original January 1985 affidavit for search warrants as a road map to attack his credibility and his insatiable drive to indict the Computer Group.

Our defense attorney didn't stop there. He got the FBI agent to admit that, when he prepared the original affidavit for search warrants, he didn't know what the Computer Group was doing. Instead, Noble testified, he "wanted to believe" bookmaking was involved.

When Hense questioned Noble's gambling knowledge, the special agent folded like a deuce-seven offsuit Hold'em hand.

"I first need to say I am not a gambling expert," he admitted.

Noble then conceded that he had "limited experience" with gambling, adding: "I will tell everyone in this courtroom I'm not a gambling expert."

But our Doberman defense lawyer wasn't finished:

HENSE: Let me ask you this: Before you got involved in this investigation, did you ever hear anybody on a tape or anything else make a lay-off bet? Do you know what it is?

NOBLE: No, I had never heard it.

HENSE: But you put in an affidavit that these were lay-off bets according to the tapes that you listened to, and you wanted search warrants; isn't that right?

NOBLE: Yes.

HENSE: Okay. And that's not true. You didn't even know what a lay-off bet was on the tape, did you?

NOBLE: I knew what a lay-off bet was, but I wasn't sure if what I was hearing was a lay-off bet.

HENSE: Then how can you put it under oath in an affidavit?

NOBLE: Because it asked for a state of mind or belief and that was my belief.

HENSE: No, it was what you wanted to believe, isn't it . . . ?

NOBLE: Obviously, yes.

When Noble finally left the stand that day, you almost felt sorry for him.

He admitted that he knowingly misrepresented his knowledge of an undercover IRS bookmaking operation when he sought permission for the original nationwide raids and withheld that information from the defendants during discovery.

The case turned even more bizarre when the judge threw out charges against an actual bookmaker, James Proctor Hawkins. He ruled that Hawkins had been wrongfully charged as part of a conspiracy to place unlawful bets. The *Review-Journal* reported that the trial had turned nonsensical, like an *Alice in Wonderland* skit. The government was prosecuting legal bettors while letting an actual bookmaker go free.

The final blow to the government's case came courtesy of Roy Woofter, the last witness for the defense. Woofter was considered a community pillar in Las Vegas, a sage and reputable attorney who had previously served as the Clark County district attorney and was the current Las Vegas city attorney.

Woofter testified that I had sought his legal advice in late 1984 during a meeting at the Horseshoe brokered by Benny Binion. After I shared my concerns about the legality of our bets placed with a group across state lines, Woofter told the jury he researched the applicable case law and concluded that what we were doing was not illegal in his expert opinion.

Woofter also testified that, after the federal raids in January 1985, I called him to inquire, "Roy, do you still stand by your advice that it's perfectly legal to bet across state lines?"

And he said, "Yes, I do. Why?"

"Because," I said, "I just got raided by the feds."

And here's where the case turned extra juicy: by the time prosecutors decided to seek an indictment from a different grand jury in 1990, the government evidently knew that it had a losing hand on the bookmaking charge. They had long since realized the Computer

Group was merely a group of organized bettors. So they played fast and loose by deciding *not* to instruct the 1990 indicting grand jury of the pertinent law, even though they had previously made clear to the 1985 grand jury that mere bettors were not in violation of federal law.

In his folksy yet devastating closing argument, Rick Wright put the government on trial, starting with Noble's imaginary bookmaking belief.

This started with the FBI listening in to people's telephone calls. And Mr. Noble listened in and thought, to his untrained ear, he was hearing a massive interstate bookmaking operation. . . . And he ran and ran and ran with it. And he gave it to the Strike Force, and they've been running with it ever since. Seven years since the raids. In fact, this Sunday is the seventh anniversary of the raids before the Super Bowl. That's how long this has been hanging over these people waiting for our day in court. . . .

Next, Rick turned the jury's attention to the FBI wiretaps on Susan's and my phones, which recorded more than ten thousand conversations during a period of some fifty days. He noted that there was not a word about bookmaking in the wiretap transcripts.

And these defendants happened to be in the crosshairs of the Strike Force. And they were in those crosshairs because of the mischaracterization of the evidence by Mr. Noble. You get in those crosshairs, and you don't get out. . . . Now, they latch on, and they're like a dog. . . . And the only way you shake them is through a jury verdict. . . . These are pit bulls.

After ten long days, our case finally went to the jury. If we needed any reassurance prior to the official verdict, it came from two alternate jurors, who had been dismissed from deliberations and were free to talk to the press.

"I feel if there was a conspiracy in this situation, it was the government against these people," alternate juror Linda McConnico told the *Review-Journal*. "It opened my eyes to a lot of things my government does that I guess I was really blind to. I was rather angry at the waste of taxpayers' money I've seen in this case."

Alternate juror Richard Morgan agreed: "My own personal opinion is these people have been under the gun for seven years. If that had happened to me, I would have felt I was being harassed or persecuted."

After three days of deliberations, the jury returned its verdicts—outright acquittals on sixty-four counts. I wanted to cry and scream with joy.

The jurors were unable to resolve the remaining fifty-four counts, but they were said to have voted 11–1 in favor of acquittal. (The lone holdout was a former police officer who had failed to disclose his occupation on his juror questionnaire, a rather pertinent piece of information.)

It was a victory for us. And an unmitigated disaster for the FBI and the U.S. Attorney's Office.

"This was just a terrible waste of money," jury forewoman Deborah Palladino told the *Review-Journal*. "The agony these people went through nobody should have to go through."

Afterward, in an interview with the *R-J* reporter who covered the case, I took the high road.

"I wouldn't want to wish this experience on my worst enemy, but I'm a better person for having gone through this," I said. "The bottom line is I'm glad I live in the United States. If this were another country, you wouldn't even get a trial and a chance for things to get straightened out."

A few days later, the federal government announced its intention to drop all remaining charges.

About a month after the verdict, I was walking into the Bank of America building downtown when I ran into Kurt Schulke, the newly appointed head of the U.S. Attorney's Organized Crime and Racketeering Strike Force in Vegas.

I stopped him and introduced myself. Schulke had attended our trial, and I was concerned the strike force would stay on my case forever. I had heard stories about how vindictive the feds could be.

I asked Schulke point-blank if there were any hard feelings. I'll never forget what he said.

"Billy, we don't meet many people like you. Don't worry about it."

Unfortunately, in other dark corners of the Department of Justice, there were people with very good memories carrying very big grudges.

All I knew at that point was that Susan and I were free.

15

Cat & Mouse

To guard against any more feds banging down my door, I made a few strategic moves in late winter 1992.

First, I consulted with a gaming specialist at Greenberg Traurig, one of the larger law firms in the world. On his advice, I created Sierra Sports Consulting. I took out a business license in my name, leased office space in an industrial park under my name, and put a Sierra Sports sign on a front door that remained unlocked during business hours.

I hired former Las Vegas Metro police officers James "Arky" Handley and Bobby Hitt and put them in charge of security and compliance. Both were licensed to carry firearms, which was important because the only way you could bet on sports was in cash. And I was moving millions of dollars around Las Vegas on a weekly basis.

I knew from my years with the Computer Group that size and scope mattered when it came to squeezing that critical mathematical edge in playing the odds. To accomplish that, I set up a war room similar to those used by investment firms Goldman Sachs and JPMorgan. But at Sierra, we were betting sports, not trading equities.

I hired Daniel Pray, an aptly named devout Mormon and brilliant software programmer from San Diego, to build a computer network that enabled thirty employees to input information within seconds of checking with major bookmakers around the country. This was, in essence, an early in-house version of DonBest Sports, now considered the gold standard for online odds and betting.

Daniel's computer program gave us access to as close to real-time odds as you could get. To achieve that goal every morning, my employees called a prioritized list of bookmakers to learn their numbers and limits on every game. Those calls continued throughout the day, updating the posted lines and limits. This allowed me to instantly calculate the overall percentages and total market on games I liked.

For the beards who bet for me, the questions were the same: *What percentage do you have at 6 points? 6½?* Ten employees called ten different beards at a time, at which point I did a quick count and knew exactly how much we could bet indirectly on any single game. When it came time to finally make our moves, we sprinted out of the blocks. My team of workers speed-dialed their contacts, filling orders like rush hour at Chick-fil-A. The beards we could trust not to scalp were given both numbers. Those we couldn't trust were given just one. On a real big play, we gave beards both numbers and took our chances.

To say I was obsessed with information would be like saying Tom Brady could play a little quarterback. Remember, this was back in the eighties, before the internet and easily accessible 24-7 sports coverage. So how had we conducted in-depth research on each player and team without those resources? I cleaned up! Literally.

I made a deal with the head of the crews who cleaned the passenger planes that landed at McCarran International Airport day and night—at least sixteen hours a day. Why passenger planes? Because each plane was littered with newspapers—and the local sports sections—left behind by travelers. My crew went to the airport multiple times each day to pick up all the newspapers from across the country. They got papers such as *The New York Times, The Boston*

Globe, *The Miami Herald*, and *The Chicago Tribune*. Then we had another team of guys who did nothing but read the sports sections of those newspapers to glean any and all information on teams, players, and coaches.

They scanned local game coverage, sports columns, interviews with owners, coaches, players, and anyone else associated with the teams. We searched for scraps of information about game plans, injuries, players' personal and professional lives, their friends and acquaintances.

To supplement Sierra Sports, I set up a separate Vegas operation that featured partners and runners equipped with two-way Nextels and beepers. Their job was to lie low and sip drinks at the legal books in town until it was time to bet.

As head of compliance, Arky made it clear that, on every bet of $10,000 or more, our team members had to file a Currency Transaction Report, a bank form used in the United States when a customer makes a currency transaction of more than ten grand.

We also made sure no one offered an opinion on a game, to remove any suspicion of aiding and abetting a bookmaker. At full tilt, Sierra Sports ran like a nonstop fire drill from six in the morning until eight at night. We placed thousands of bets from the college football season beginning in late August straight through to the Final Four in early April.

Sandwiched around and in between was a full slate of NFL, NBA, MLB, PGA Tour, and NHL games to wager on. Each year, our operation dealt with hundreds of millions in dollars of "gross handle"—the amount of money we bet on an annual basis.

Operating at that level and with that amount of money 24-7, 365 days a year was nothing less than a test of survival. We went to insane lengths to make sure that most bookmakers never knew the primary source of our wagers.

I never wavered from the mission: getting the best possible number and price on every game. And no matter the obstacles, via trial and error, I became the best in the world at finding that number and concealing the source.

The business of sports betting might seem like quantum physics to the general public. At the highest level, it is closer to psychological warfare between bettor and bookmaker—cat and mouse, hunter and prey. The posted line is just a way to trigger the game.

Some cynics assume that my goal was to put every bookie out of business—but nothing could be further from the truth. Bookmakers strive for balance. They never want to tilt too far on one side of the action. Bookies breathe easiest in the middle, taking equal money and profiting off the 10 percent juice.

If a bookie was destroyed, it meant he either closed his shop or reduced his limits. Neither scenario did me any good. My goal was to keep the bookmakers *in* business and expand their limits. This served to increase the size of the market, which meant more potential profit for me.

The smartest bookies had solved this riddle and wanted to do business with me directly. They wanted to know straight from the horse's mouth what games I liked. If they were smart, they took my information and profited by shading their line and forcing customers to the other side, extending limits.

A smart bookmaker knows there will be winners and losers. They also understand that there is no business if there are no winners. Translated: the smartest bookmakers are open to all comers—just like baccarat, blackjack, and craps. The brightest bookmakers know they can use smart money for their own benefit.

Early in my career, the major-league bookmakers were Bob Martin, Johnny Quinn, Gene Maday, and Scotty Schettler. Following in their footsteps are Nick Bogdanovich, Jimmy Vaccaro, Richie Baccellieri, Matt Metcalf, and Chris Andrews. They are grand masters of the art. They know how to book.

How smart are they? Well, Nick ran the William Hill U.S. sportsbook operation and then oversaw Caesars Sports trading for nearly a decade before being hired as sportsbook manager at Circa. Jimmy is the senior linemaker at the sports-betting network VSiN and vice president of sports marketing at the South Point Hotel, Casino & Spa. Richie B., who ran the counter at the MGM, Caesars, and the Palms, now works as the director of product development at Circa alongside Nick. Chris Andrews, legendary oddsmaker Jack "Pittsburgh Jack" Franzi's nephew, is the sportsbook director and Jimmy's sidekick at the South Point, owned and operated by Michael Gaughan, another Las Vegas legend.

In 1992, Jack Binion was Nick Bogdanovich's boss at the Horseshoe. I could bet $25,000 on a game of college football at eight o'clock Monday morning, and $50,000 on a pro football game. The last thing I wanted to do was put a dent in Jack's book, but he insisted I should be the first guy to bet with Nick, befitting the fact that my account number was 101.

"I want you to bet early with me, and I want you to bet direct," Jack said. "Because I'm going to take the business one way or the other, either from you or a follower."

Jack knew that if Nick got the bet directly from me—for example laying nine on a game, betting the favorite—it would give the Horseshoe an edge. Based on my bet, Nick might immediately take his number to ten while continually monitoring the market to make sure he stayed a half point ahead of the crowd. A poorly run book could easily end up with too much money on one side. When the game kicks off, they are no longer booking. Instead, they are gambling with the house's money on an uneven game.

By taking my money early, Jack was giving his sportsbook manager the entire week to adjust his line and limits based on bets for or against me.

I had a similar arrangement with Tommy Elardi and Bob Gregoria at the Frontier. I worked with both of them for years and never had one disagreement.

Jimmy Vaccaro, then the main man at The Mirage, was another

go-to guy. From his side of the counter—and in those days The Mirage book was booming like the fake volcano out front—Jimmy was happy to take my action because he wanted to know what the sharps were doing.

"Here's what I can give you," Jimmy said the first time we sat down. "Thirty thousand a side on the NFL. Twenty thousand a side on college. No totals."

We shook hands. Never once did I break my word with Jimmy or vice versa. Never once did he change a line on me, or refuse a bet, because, frankly, he wanted to know what I knew. And I never doubled back on a game on him. I never sent a runner into The Mirage without introducing him first.

That's respect.

Once my reputation as a wizard of odds was established, I had to deploy beards to do my betting with some bookies because they didn't really understand the art of bookmaking. Another reason I used beards was to get access to bigger limits and to get more volume across the globe. As a result, I was able to expand my market.

As an example, in England when we were doing business with William Hill, if an account won as much as two weeks in a row, his limit might be reduced from $10,000 to $50 a game regardless of how he won. Instead of removing a finger, the books cut off the entire arm. That was their mentality. That's how drastically winners were punished.

Paddy Power of Dublin, Ireland, was even worse. They only offered a $500 limit. If an account won three bets in a row, they would close the account. Over the years, I had two hundred accounts at Paddy Power that lasted an average of four days. Sadly, that's the way many legalized bookmakers operate today.

These bookmakers end up costing themselves a lot of money. Gamblers do win, and some can win for a period of time. Almost every one of them, however, eventually will lose.

Imagine if casinos ran their entire operations the same way—

you start winning at the slot machines and you get kicked out. If that were the case, every casino would be a graveyard—completely empty. That's why the pros who run casinos understand there are going to be winners.

Obviously, the longer I could protect and disguise the sources behind my bets, the longer I could continue to take advantage of our wealth of information. I realized over the years that if one guy gets thrown out, I've got to find another guy.

If you were casting a movie about sports gambling, the supporting actors would be the beards and partners employed to make bets on my behalf. They play the roles of high rollers, and, like bookmakers, they come in all shapes and sizes.

The best beards/partners were sports bettors who were well known within the industry as losers and could bet large sums of money. They lived the RFB life—casino parlance for free "room, food, and beverage" granted to high rollers (aka big losers).

In the early days, I did well with my boys from Kentucky coming into town impersonating high rollers. That is, until some bookies stopped taking action from anyone with a driver's license from the Bluegrass State!

I was forced to diversify my crew—a United Nations of partners and beards—who were compensated through a revenue-sharing arrangement. They were paid based on the success of the bets they placed. In most cases, I put up almost all the money and took the majority of the risk until we were on the winning side of the ledger, which was rather often. Or I would allow them to invest up to 50 percent of their money, and we'd bet through their book or books, sharing profits and losses.

Unbeaten former world champion boxer Floyd Mayweather was one of my partners—for one whole day. The problem I had with him was that Little Floyd wanted to expand beyond our agreed-upon territory. He was among the highest of high rollers, and used two casinos, where he had limits as high as $500,000. We agreed that he wouldn't bet my picks anywhere else. But Little Floyd couldn't resist jumping the fence and going to four or five other casinos where I bet. I had to quit partnering with him because he was undermining my strategy.

Human nature being what it is, I'd say most of the people I dealt with over my career have succumbed one way or another to the age-old allure of greed and temptation. They believed they could bet on the side, sell my information, slip a few hundred out of a bundle of ten thousand, or just outright steal my money, hoping I wouldn't notice.

Believe me, I noticed.

You have to hold people accountable in this game. If beards got a sense that you were not atop your game, they would steal from you every chance they could.

For example, a partner I'll call "Johnny" was stopped by federal agents coming off a first-class flight carrying $200,000 he owed me. The feds were curious about the source of all that cash. It took hours of explanation, but Johnny finally persuaded the agents that he was a professional gambler before they let him leave.

The next morning, I got my money and Johnny, after telling me his story, got a reminder. The money was mine. If I didn't get the money, then he was responsible for it.

Without these unwritten rules, can you imagine how many times I would have been stiffed by dishonest gamblers? More times than I could count.

If I identified certain games where the line moved suspiciously after our team placed stealth bets, I would run tests to verify which one of my beards had gone rogue on me. When I found dishonesty—and I always did—I'd punish the perp by giving him the wrong side on the next game, then I would circle back and bet on the right side of the same game. By doing that, I accomplished two things: I taught somebody a lesson, smacking the thief's hand so to speak, and I got a better price on the team I was betting on.

We kept score on a daily basis. I had longtime employees like Bobby Ward, whose job was to do the counts every day. He matched winning and losing tickets with money on hand down to the dollar. If a partner crossed the line, one of two things happened: I gave that person a warning and a second chance, with the understanding that if they did it again, they were done. Or I might sever the agreement then and there.

On one notable occasion, I called the police and reported a theft by a certain Ezekiel Rubalcada, whom I had originally pegged as an honest guy. He'd been a superintendent for a Las Vegas builder who went belly-up during the 2008 financial crisis. Zeke was married with a child, and unemployed when Josh Hill, who ran our internet golf marketing division, recommended him to me. Josh and Ezekiel were neighbors.

"This is the first and last time you'll ever see me," I told him upon our introduction. "If the bookies or their employees see us together, you're no good to me."

I set Zeke up at the M Resort Spa Casino by giving him $500,000 in cash to deposit into an account in his name. His job was to punch in bets on a casino-issued tablet. When the season ended, I sent Bobby Ward over to the resort for a final collection. Upon arriving outside the casino, Bobby saw a man banging on the driver's window of Zeke's car. The window came down and a bag was passed out.

Later, we learned that Zeke, who had become accustomed to the RFB life of a partner, decided to boost his income by staging a carjacking. Trouble was, Bobby wasn't the only one who saw Zeke hand off the bag of cash to the supposed thieves, who then high-tailed it to the freeway. The hotel security cameras captured the entire scene as well.

I pressed charges, and in August 2011, Zeke was indicted on thirty-three theft and burglary counts for stealing $482,883 in a span of five months. Rubalcada pleaded guilty to two felony counts and was sentenced to three years probation. The court ordered him to pay me $364,634 in restitution, but I never saw a nickel.

To understand how I worked, you need to understand that smart bookmakers are on the lookout for lines that consistently move in favor of a specific bettor. If you're just a recreational player, some lines will move your way, some not at all, and others will move against you. Theoretically, it should even out over time. The vast majority of people bet on favorites. Some bookies don't want to deal with a gambler where the line consistently moves in his direction. In their world, that's a smart guy. Good bookmakers see things differently. They couldn't care less; they take the bets and move their line accordingly, writing as much business as they possibly can.

How did I throw suspicious bookies off my scent? I got creative. I opened as many as twenty accounts with one bookmaker instead of just one account, like most people. Why did I need twenty? If I had one account and was making fifty to one hundred bets a week I couldn't disguise the fact that the line would move substantially in the same direction of that account. By opening twenty accounts, the results looked more like those of a random bettor who had a varied impact on the lines.

To further protect my most valued assets, I came up with a color-coded system based on your average traffic light—Green, Yellow, and Red. For educational purposes, let's pretend you are a beard fronting one of my accounts and the first week I give you three bets. You win two of three. You had no previous betting history with the bookie, but in all three games the line moved in your direction. In my world, your account would be marked Red. As a result, for the next week I would make sure that on at least two of the next three bets the line is not going to move at all, or it's going to move against you.

How do I accomplish that?

Here is an example: I have a play on an underdog, and I can take plus 6½. But, naturally, the number I'd like to have is the far more valuable 7. Well, now I can accomplish two things at once. I'm going to take the hot accounts (Red) and use those accounts to bet the "wrong" side of the game. I'm going to lay the 6½, meaning bet the favorite. The game goes to 7. I then send an open order out plus seven, and make as much noise as possible by making sure people know it's me betting. I want everybody and their mother to know Billy Walters bet on this game at plus seven. In the meantime, I've done two things: First, the Red accounts I used to lay the 6½ are cooled off; the bookmaker no longer suspects my beard is a wise guy because he knows Billy Walters came in and took seven. And second, I got the number I wanted at a better price.

Now, let's say I have my beard make three bets the first week and we lose two. One line moved our way, one stayed neutral, the other went against us. In my mind, that beard is Green and good to go the next week. As for Yellow, let's say the beard made three bets and two of the lines moved his way. The beard won one game and lost two, but broke even because he bet twice as much on the winner as the losers. The beard is good to go—but with a caution light.

Each and every week, we had our associates go through every single account, upward of 1,600 accounts total, and rate them Green, Yellow, or Red. Was it a pain in the ass? You'd better believe it. But that's what I needed, and what I lived for, because I was motivated to outsmart bookmakers, whose sole purpose in life was to put me out of business.

It was, as one might imagine, a monumental, multilevel cat-and-mouse game. A game I still live to play.

16

Turning Pleasure into Business

I've played hundreds of rounds of golf around the world and I have seen how many courses are poorly managed. Back in the late 1980s most public courses in this country were run by local municipalities. As a result, conditions often were sketchy, and so was the level of customer service. Food and beverage options usually boiled down to a choice between a cold hot dog and a cold hot dog. Moreover, most head golf professionals were focused on two things: giving lessons and playing golf themselves.

Most private clubs were not much better. They typically were run by well-meaning member-volunteers more interested in hosting parties and staging events than operating a business. The complexities of managing three challenging operations—food and beverage, course maintenance, and retail—were overwhelming. All too frequently, golf course managers let their biggest potential revenue streams go untapped.

And so, as demand for recreational golf began to outpace supply I spotted a business opportunity.

By now I'd established that I could bring a disciplined approach to sports betting, and accumulated the funds to pursue other business interests. Since I prefer to invest in things I enjoy, venturing into the golf industry certainly qualified. When I learned that Paradise Hills, a semiprivate club in Albuquerque, New Mexico, was in default, I couldn't resist making a move.

Mark Tenner, a poker friend, filled me in about the project and its challenges. He was considering acquiring the course, but needed capital to buy the note and secure the property out of foreclosure. He offered me part of the deal. In exchange for putting up the money, I would receive a preferred rate of return and a majority share of any profits.

I did my due diligence and ordered a competitive market analysis of the city and its golf climate. I did not see this as a long-term play. Our objective was to bring distressed properties back to life and sell them for a profit.

I derive a great deal of pleasure in overcoming obstacles to create something special. In the case of Paradise Hills, the club was mature, surrounded by well-kept homes in one of the most active golf markets in the country. It was not luxurious by any means, but I felt it was undervalued with tremendous upside.

On the downside, club members were not happy. The property had gone to hell due to poor management. The clubhouse was falling apart. The fairways resembled cow pastures. The value of homes surrounding Paradise Hills had plummeted.

I had been successful buying, renovating, and flipping commercial real estate in the wake of the savings and loan crisis, so in 1991 I bought my first fixer-upper golf course. Then I turned to a real pro, Jim Colbert, one of my oldest and dearest friends. Jim once said he would trust me with his life, and I feel the same way. He had earned a good living playing golf for the better part of twenty-three years on the PGA Tour before essentially retiring in 1987, largely due to bad knees and a balky back.

He returned to Las Vegas and started Jim Colbert Golf, which at its peak owned or operated some two dozen public courses around the country. His company employed hundreds of people and had annual gross revenues of nearly $50 million.

Our friendship began in the early eighties when I helped Jim bring a PGA Tour event to Las Vegas, the city's first pro golf tournament. In its inaugural year in 1983, the event paid a then-record $750,000 in prize money. Jim and I also worked together to start the city's First Tee program, which introduces golf to young people and teaches them good values. It became one of the largest and most successful chapters in the country.

In 1991, Jim and his partners sold the company. By then, his knees and back had healed, and he was eager to take his custom Callaway clubs to the Senior Tour. Jim won three times in his first year on his way to twenty wins overall. He was named Player of the Year twice during twenty-two successful years on the Senior Tour.

After the sale of Jim's company, several of his top managers became available. I hired a handful of his best guys to take prominent positions at Southwest Golf, the new company I created. I put Dick Campbell in charge of development, capital improvements, operations, hiring and recruitment, and marketing.

I'd like to report we were welcomed at Paradise Hills, but that would be like saying the Chicago Bears are greeted warmly at Lambeau Field. The membership had been burned before, and they had sued the previous owners.

My first meeting with the homeowners association was a testy affair. The head of the HOA was Jim Knight, the father of Dwaine Knight, who later would become the legendary head golf coach at the University of Nevada, Las Vegas, and a good personal friend.

"Mr. Knight, we want to be good partners," I said at the initial meeting. "I understand your frustrations with the former owners, but our plan is to renovate the clubhouse and make serious capital improvements. Just give us a chance."

There was no buzz of approval. No cheering. Not a smile on a single face. Tough crowd, even tougher than I first thought. We had just started to improve the course when someone sabotaged a new piece of construction equipment.

I called another meeting. This time I wasn't so cordial.

"Let me explain how this is going to work," I began. "If this happens again, I will put up a six-foot fence around this golf course, and it won't come down until we're finished."

From that day forward, our problems disappeared. Jim Knight and his wife became our biggest supporters. The lawsuit against the previous owners was dropped. We rebuilt the course, renovated the clubhouse, implemented a high level of customer service, and installed a first-class food and beverage operation. We were cash-flow positive after the first month. Two years later, Paradise Hills was making a million dollars in annual profit. *Golf Digest* ranked it as the top semiprivate course in Albuquerque.

I sold the club to American Golf Corporation for $4.5 million in 1996. I made $2 million on top of my initial investment five years earlier. Everybody seemed happy with our involvement. This success got me to thinking: *This formula might work, and I get to work in golf—a game I love.*

With aces and kings falling our way, Southwest Golf scooped up another failing golf property—Mesa del Sol Country Club in Yuma, Arizona. We applied the same formula that worked so well at Paradise Hills and achieved the same results.

By then, our business strategy had evolved. Our goal was to become a dominant force in daily-fee golf by creating themed courses for guests that delivered a "Country Club for a Day" experience. That meant I needed to expand my executive team.

I found one key player in a pizza joint, of all places. For years, Susan and I ate at the California Pizza Kitchen in Solana Beach near San Diego. Mitch Epstein, the manager of the restaurant, had caught my eye with his attention to detail and customer service.

"Mitchell Lee," as I came to call him, was only thirty years old when we first met in '91.

"How'd you like to do something different?" I asked him a few years later.

"Mr. Walters, I don't know how to do anything else," he said.

I explained what I had in mind—a change of venue where Mitch could apply his same set of skills.

"How about becoming the national food and beverage director for Southwest Golf?"

Mitchell Lee had never set foot outside Southern California when we hopped on a plane and flew to Chicago in 1994 for his first rehab assignment. I put him to the test at the Golf Club of Illinois, another failing club, this one in Algonquin, an hour northwest of the Windy City.

After a tour of the club, I told Mitch he had two days to put together a coming-out party for 150 invitees, with Jim Colbert as the drawing card. He asked where we planned to host the event.

"That's why I hired you," I said. "You'll figure it out."

Mitch scrambled and put up a tent in the parking lot almost overnight. Then he delivered a knockout event. A few days later, he removed the husband-and-wife team that was running food and beverage along with certain employees who viewed "hard" and "work" as four-letter words. We renovated the course and upgraded the staff and service. Susan later remodeled the clubhouse. Before long, we were turning a profit of a million dollars annually.

Eagle Brook in suburban Geneva, Illinois, was another club run amok. The members were irate at the previous owners for failing to deliver on promises, including a new clubhouse.

We agreed to acquire the club with one contingency: I had to get a buy-in from the riled-up members. I held meetings for two weeks, morning and evenings, with twenty members at a time. No alcohol was allowed. We were all business.

When the round of meetings ended, most members emerged as

excited about the project as we were. So we built a forty-one-thousand-square-foot clubhouse, added two swimming pools and new tennis courts, and transformed Eagle Brook into an exclusive private club.

To add some star power, I brought in Ken "Hawk" Harrelson, the revered, longtime announcer for the Chicago White Sox. I offered Hawk a membership and appointed him chairman of our board. When the mood struck, Hawk would wax poetic about Eagle Brook on the White Sox broadcasts, which sent interest and membership soaring.

Our next project was Burr Hill, a down-and-out municipal course in St. Charles, Illinois. We renamed it Black Hawk Golf Club after the great Native American chief (and Chicago's professional hockey team) and turned it around.

With this line of business going well, I needed to be more mobile. I purchased a private plane, a Learjet 35 with a range of about 3,000 miles. This made it much easier to fly back and forth between Las Vegas and Chicago and other places in our growing golf course business.

By October 1995, our company had bagged a high-end public course (Golf Club of Illinois), a private club (Eagle Brook), and a solid everyday municipal course (Black Hawk). Eventually, we sold them all for a profit of $5 million.

My fractured life was starting to come together. In the fall of '95, I was approaching fifty years old. I had not had a drink of alcohol in seven years, and I was no longer hanging out in casinos. Most important, I had settled down as a reliable husband and partner to a woman who deserved my best.

I was running the largest and most successful sports-betting operation in the world. And with my newfound financial stability, I began to diversify. We had acquired, improved, and sold five golf courses in New Mexico, Arizona, and Illinois, while successfully developing and selling residential and commercial real estate in Arizona and California.

What began in the 1980s as Berkley Enterprises, the parent company of Southwest Golf and other business assets, had morphed into The Walters Group, a sprawling set of companies that included mortgage banking, venture capital, biotech investments, golf course operations, and real estate development. Some men my age might have rested on their laurels, played one of their golf courses every day of the week, and cruised around the world with their wife and friends. Not me. Instead, I doubled down on risk, this time in the ultimate garden of gaming.

I never had much interest in politics. But like it or not, politics will take an interest in you, especially if you are a developer in the roaring '90s in Nevada—the fastest-growing state in the union.

The region's population was exploding; family-friendly hotels and gleaming theme parks had displaced honky-tonks and strip joints, and 40 million tourists were pouring into Las Vegas every year. As a businessman, I needed access to decision-makers. Democrat or Republican, their party affiliations never much mattered to me. I wanted to work with politicians who cared about development, public safety, and fiscal accountability.

I knew the golden rule: money equals access. The more you donated, the more access you were likely to gain to people in positions of power. This did not mean I owned a public official's vote. Not one bit. For me, campaign contributions translated into nothing more than an opportunity to state your case.

As I would soon discover, politics and golf went hand in hand in Vegas. Visitors seeking a little sun and sin were welcomed by everyone from pit bosses to VIP hosts to escort services. Want to enjoy a round or two of golf? Well, that was a different story back then in Vegas.

There were simply not enough golf courses and tee times to meet the soaring demand. Consequently, operators of daily-fee courses treated even the finest hotels and casinos like they were doing them a favor by booking tee times for their guests. On top of that, greens fees were astronomical.

Again, I sensed a business opportunity. I looked for properties to develop closer to the Strip and discovered that open land was in short supply. Most of the big tracts belonged to the federal Bureau of Land Management. I felt a bit like Indiana Jones during my search for hidden treasures, poring over zoning maps until I found a small parcel of undeveloped land—a park just under one hundred acres—that was owned by the city.

The property had gone undeveloped for good reason. It was in the highest crime area of the city, an east Las Vegas neighborhood that was called "Nature Park" on the maps, but was known as "Needle Park" by the police department. The land was crawling with drug dealers and dope addicts, murder and mayhem.

Cleaning up the area was not the least of our challenges. Architects will tell you that you need at least 160 acres to build eighteen holes, a parking lot, practice range, clubhouse, and maintenance facility. We were sixty acres short.

Our research said a course could be built on a smaller site, but we needed someone with special skills to pull it off. Perry Dye, the first-born son of the brilliant golf course designer Pete Dye, had shoehorned several courses in Japan onto postage stamp–sized properties. So I hired him and his design team, which included family members Cynthia Dye McGarey and Matt Dye, to work their magic.

My next stop was the office of Jan Jones, the city's first female mayor, a Stanford University grad with an extensive business background. I pitched the mayor on my proposal to replace "Needle Park" with Desert Pines Golf Club. I explained that it would follow my "Country Club for a Day" concept by providing pay-to-play golfers the same level of high-end services and surroundings enjoyed by members at exclusive country clubs.

I pitched a public-private partnership that promised to clean up crime, provide needed jobs, and create a beautiful environment—without costing the city a dime.

Mayor Jones was likely thinking: *If some idiot businessman is willing to take that big of a risk, who am I to say no?* She then told me the city would require me to jump through a few procedural hoops. The first involved the city putting out a request for proposal, which meant it would be a competitive process.

Signature operators such as American Golf, National Golf Properties, and Family Golf would have jumped at most opportunities to build a course in the city. But not for a property in Needle Park. I was the lone bidder. The city council gave its stamp of approval. If they had added, *Good luck, you fool*, I wouldn't have blamed them.

Still, given our experience with golf course development and management in New Mexico, Arizona, and Illinois, I believed we could make Desert Pines work as a business and as a golf tourist attraction. Once we broke ground, I told my team we couldn't afford to just hit a home run. We needed a grand slam. We tailored Desert Pines after the top-rated Raven Golf Club in Phoenix, and I spent $19 million creating it.

To generate some local excitement, we made plans for a major public announcement. I invited the mayor, city council members, the sheriff, the media, and a few of my associates and friends. I gave them my best pitch, selling the theme of Desert Pines as a veritable Pinehurst Resort, right down to the four thousand pine trees and truckloads of pine needles lining the fairways.

I was selling, but nobody was buying. The poker player in me could see that no one in the crowd, and I mean *nobody*, believed a word I was saying. We had a big job on our hands, and it seemed like every few months, we were hit with one daunting challenge after another.

Six weeks into development, a pregnant woman was murdered during a robbery at the 7-Eleven across from our property. Six months after that, a little girl was sexually assaulted on the opposite corner.

At that point, I began to question my own sanity. Playing casino slots was beginning to look like a more lucrative sideline.

To win city approval, I had made—and kept—a lot of promises. We held a job fair and hired sixty-five people from the neighborhood to work maintenance, food, and beverage. We started a GED program and hired an English tutor to help residents advance their education and improve their language skills. In addition, we instituted a kids' program so that area schoolchildren who made passing grades received free golf and instruction.

Despite all of our good intentions and hard work, the project was haunted by unrelated but horrible events. Just three days after our December 1996 grand opening, a rookie police officer celebrated his birthday with another off-duty cop by getting drunk and taking a joyride around east Las Vegas in the early-morning hours. News accounts reported that Officer Ron Mortensen fired several gunshots at a group of people just blocks away from Nature Park, killing twenty-one-year-old Daniel Mendoza. Both officers resigned after the shooting. Mortensen was sentenced to life in prison without the possibility of parole; the other officer received a sentence of nine years in prison.

Members of the Mendoza family were devastated. They couldn't afford to bury Daniel next to his mother in Mexico, so they held a car wash to raise the three thousand dollars needed to send his body there. After I read the story in the *Las Vegas Sun*, I met with Daniel's family and quietly handed them the necessary funds.

That donation and other outreach efforts helped breathe life into Desert Pines. The golf course slowly came together as a source of civic pride, off-limits to drug dealers, gangs, and graffiti artists. Eventually, crime subsided and community leaders gave their support. More than $200 million in development money poured into the area, part of which went to build a new high school two years later.

In 1997, *Golf Digest* named Desert Pines a "Best New Upscale Golf Course" in the country. Six years later, it received a coveted state Tourism Development Award.

From a pure financial standpoint, Desert Pines was one of my worst-performing investments. But it still stands as one of my proudest accomplishments.

After overcoming the Needle Park challenge, I dreamed up something even bigger to tackle. I drafted an aggressive business proposal for several Vegas casinos. My first call was to J. Terrence Lanni—JTL to his pals—then CEO of the MGM Grand and a true giant in the industry. At first, Terry was reluctant to meet with me, and he didn't mind telling me why.

Terry made clear he was still upset about the $2 million I'd won playing roulette at Caesars Tahoe in '86 when he was president and CEO of its parent company, Caesars World Inc.

I explained to him that I'd won that money fairly, based on nothing more than hours of research into roulette wheel biases. Once he understood that I hadn't been cheating his casino, Terry let it go. We forged a friendship that continued until he died of cancer in July 2011, at the age of sixty-eight.

I pitched him with a presentation I had practiced dozens of times along with Mike Luce, the president of The Walters Group. We stressed that Walters Golf was not in competition with the MGM on any level. Rather, we wanted to be a partner by providing a service that didn't exist—to help fill vacant rooms during dead periods with stay-and-play golf packages. And, more important, pay the hotel a commission on every golf booking.

"Do you want business from Travelocity and Expedia, or do you want a golfer whose average income is much higher and likes to gamble?" I asked.

Before Terry could respond, I answered my own question: "You want the golfer. He's a better customer."

I came prepared with charts detailing the average incomes of golfers, along with their disposable incomes. I explained that, in many cases, hotel guests were playing at courses owned by rival casinos. I also pointed out that most golfers happened to be gamblers. In addition, I offered discounted rounds for groups staying at his resort, and I agreed to hold annual tournaments for his employees free of charge.

My vision was to turn Las Vegas into a first-class golf destination similar to Scottsdale, Arizona, or Hilton Head, South Carolina. I wanted to create a Las Vegas *golf experience* and I wanted to do it by outthinking, outsmarting, and outworking the competition.

It didn't take Terry long to decide. We shook hands and I walked out the door with an exclusive deal for MGM's golf business.

17

Betting Big

While turning around failing golf courses was fun, I found myself yearning for even more action, especially the kind that involved my other favorite endeavor—gambling.

In 1996, I decided to take a run at a sports start-up of a different sort. I wanted to become *the* sports bookmaker for Vegas casinos. Sports betting was a growth industry, in my view, but most casinos were not taking it seriously enough. They provided in-house books mostly as a minor annoyance or necessary evil, preferring that their guests wagered on more profitable table games.

I knew better.

Since I'd had success bringing a more professional business approach to golf, I thought I'd try the same with casino bookmaking, which often suffered from sketchy management practices.

My plan was ambitious. I set up meetings with the likes of Terry Lanni, who controlled the MGM empire, and Mike Ensign, CEO and chairman of the Mandalay Resort Group. I told them I'd offer the highest betting limits in the United States and produce a show for ESPN devoted to sports wagering to promote the city and its casinos. In short, I'd market and promote Las Vegas as the sports-betting capital of the country.

The idea was a hit. Within weeks, I had verbal commitments to lease and operate sportsbooks at the MGM and Mandalay group.

At that point, all I needed was a gaming license. I knew that obtaining one would not be easy given my previous run-ins with the law and my reputation as a professional gambler. So I did what any serious candidate for a license did in those days: I hired Bob Faiss, one of the most respected gaming attorneys in the state.

Bob was a senior partner at Lionel Sawyer & Collins, the largest law firm in Nevada at the time. He suggested that we prepare for my gaming license application with a "defensive" investigation into my personal, professional, and financial backgrounds. The idea was to dig up any dirt before the Nevada Gaming Control Board uncovered it.

Bob brought in his wife, Linda, and her partner Helen Foley, who ran a powerhouse PR firm, to help. They advised me to bolster my public image in the belief that it would help if I publicized the community philanthropy that Susan and I had been doing for years. We had been low-key in supporting the United Way, Boys & Girls Clubs, Boy Scouts, and Girl Scouts and working with the city of Henderson's welfare department, giving away holiday turkeys, toys, and clothing for needy families.

We agreed to let Linda launch a subtle PR campaign to elevate our public profile. At the same time, her husband worked the regulatory side, setting up one-on-one meetings with members of the Gaming Control Board, including Chairman Bill Bible. I promised the gaming commissioners that, if they approved me for a license, I would quit betting sports altogether and devote my time to operating the books. It took some convincing, but eventually they gave me their informal, verbal approval.

At the end of 1996, we were *this close* to getting licensed and gaining control of sportsbook operations at the MGM Grand, Mandalay Bay, Excalibur, Circus Circus, Luxor, and the newly constructed Monte Carlo. It was an audacious play that would have been worth billions today.

Instead, on the morning of December 7, 1996, the Las Vegas

Metro Police Department conducted a surprise raid at our Sierra Sports headquarters. The cops seized computer records and documents detailing more than twelve thousand long-distance calls each month and $970,000 in wire transfers to a local bank account under my name. (It's called winnings!) They also targeted some $5 million in cash that we held in safety-deposit boxes at eight different casinos. The only way you could bet on sports in Las Vegas was with cash or chips back then.

The media trumpeted the raids as part of a yearlong investigation by the New York Police Department into an alleged four-hundred-million-dollar-a-year illegal bookmaking operation with ties to the Bonanno and Genovese crime families.

Not again, I thought. *Not after everything we went through with the Computer Group trial. Not after I dotted every "i" and crossed ever "t" to legally set up Sierra Sports. Not after all of the work we put in to take control of casino sportsbooks.*

We were slapped with the same old bogus charges—transferring wagering information across state lines, possessing "illegal gaming winnings," and alleged ties to organized crime. To top things off, the cops had dragged into the mix my software guru, Daniel Pray, and my security chief, Arky Handley, a retired Metro police officer.

Right after the raid went down, Arky called to remind me that we had $2.8 million in cash on deposit at the Horseshoe.

"What do you want to do with that money?" he asked.

If we take that money out, I said, it will look like we've done something wrong. I told Arky to leave the cash right where it was.

It took us some time to unravel the mystery of why we'd been targeted yet again. Here's what I learned: A New York bookie was overheard on a wiretap laying off bets with a Las Vegas bookmaker. Because of the frequency of our calls to that same New York bookie along with the size and scope of our bets, the cops assumed—wrongly again—that we must be bookmakers, too.

The naive lawmen relied on the same flawed "one-plus-one-equals-three" formula that had been used to indict the Computer Group. Only, this time, our antagonists were not the FBI but the Las Vegas Metro PD Intelligence Unit.

Thankfully, local district attorney Stewart Bell (who went on to become a senior judge in the state of Nevada) declined to file any charges after taking a hard look at the bookmaking raid and the legality of my operation.

The same could *not* be said for Attorney General Frankie Sue Del Papa. As the first woman elected secretary of state in Nevada, Frankie Sue was no political novice. She also had an elephantine memory against those who crossed her—including yours truly. In the previous election for state attorney general, I had backed her opponent to the tune of $10,000, which earned me a spot on Frankie Sue's political shit list.

At the same time, state prosecutors were turning up the heat through the use—and abuse—of civil forfeiture statutes that allowed law enforcement to seize assets from people suspected of criminal activity without necessarily charging them with any wrongdoing. When it came to that kind of mindset, certain officers in the Las Vegas Intelligence Unit proved a breed apart—more interested in seizing assets than putting criminals behind bars. Their operation had its own budget and an "ultra-aggressive" style, according to a former deputy police chief.

We discovered that, in one year alone, the intelligence unit had detained more than five hundred "suspicious" people—including unsuspecting tourists strolling through the airport. If cops came across jewelry or cash and if, in their opinion, you started fumbling for an explanation, they seized the property. Then it was Let's Make a Deal time. God forbid that someone flew into the gambling capital of the world and carried some cash through the Las Vegas airport!

We did some digging and found out that two high-ranking officials inside Intelligence had set up a private company that sold surveillance equipment back to the same intelligence unit they worked for. Talk about organized crime!

After raiding our operation, these rogue cops, who apparently had watched too many *Miami Vice* episodes, seized $2.8 million of my money—and they weren't going to give it back without getting part of it. A few days after the raid, Rick Wright received a call from one of the crooked cops.

"We think the money is the product of illegal gambling, possible money laundering," he said. "You want to settle right now?"

This was a blatant holdup. And the cop was asking for a half million dollars. The message was loud and clear: *Pay up or get indicted.*

"I don't think you understand who you're dealing with," Rick replied. "Bill Walters hasn't done anything wrong, and he's not going to give you a dime of his money."

I didn't. And my distaste for these tactics ran so deep that I later testified about my experience with Metro Intelligence before the Nevada Senate Judiciary Committee in Carson City. The ensuing legislation reformed state law and tightened the requirements for confiscating money from the public.

Even with another grand jury indictment hanging over my head, I kept my head, and my money, in the golf course game. I went on a buying spree, spending $34 million in June of '97 to purchase the Sunrise Country Club in Las Vegas from Jim Colbert and his partners.

We renamed the property Stallion Mountain Golf Club and renovated all three of its courses as well as the clubhouse. We then built a second members-only clubhouse next door called Squire, which had its own entrance and white-glove concierge service. In addition, we added a second floor to Squire that became the corporate headquarters for Walters Golf.

Our strategy was to attract tens of thousands of conventioneers and well-heeled out-of-state golfers by leveraging our casino partners. With a new fifty-four-hole facility and Desert Pines, we had an abundance of inventory.

The ground rules were simple: we expected word to spread from the executive ranks to frontline workers—the concierge desk, bellmen, valets, and sales staff—that any guest who walked into the lobby with a golf bag was to be referred exclusively to our courses.

In exchange, we rewarded those employees with either a 10 percent cash commission or free rounds of golf. We also installed golf desks at the airport and in several hotels, including the MGM, the world's largest.

I had no interest in the Dale Carnegie school of winning friends and influencing people. We were at war—nothing more, nothing less—against every other golf course operator in the city. And we didn't operate on the honor system. I held people accountable.

We organized constant "mystery shopping" to make sure that employees at the casinos were honoring their end of our agreement. Every day, I had sales reps masquerade as guests by calling or showing up at the concierge desk, bell stand, and valet desk at partner hotels.

"Hey, I'm in town for a few days and would like to play some golf. Where should I play?"

If the only answer wasn't our name and number, then I'd hop on the phone with the hotel president.

We also held weekly sales meetings to review the numbers of tee times each hotel booked and where they originated. If the valet stand at the Tropicana only produced one round in a particular week, I wanted to know why. There wasn't a single day where we didn't find someone violating our agreement.

When we ran into resistance, we confronted it head-on. Such as the time the chef (French for chief) concierge at the Bellagio (we'll call him Ted) stopped sending hotel guests to our properties. I asked Joe Dahlstrom, my director of golf who had given lessons to Ted and his family, to find out why.

As Joe later recounted, the conversation went like this:

"Ted, let's be straight. I like you. We've had a good relationship.

We pay better commissions than anyone else. We know you're refer-ring people to other places. What's going on? How can I help you?"

"Well," Ted responded, "you tell Bill Walters that I will send peo-ple wherever I want. I'm the chef concierge."

"I get that," Joe said. "But do you really want to pick a fight here? Forget Mr. Walters. We have an agreement with your hotel. I'm here to work with you. Because when I walk out of here, my Nextel is going to go off and it's going to be Bill Walters asking, 'How did things go?' So, are we going to work together or not?"

Well, Joe's Nextel did go off the minute he stepped out of the Bellagio. He told me that Ted had no interest in working with us.

"What did he exactly say?" I asked.

"Fuck you and fuck Billy Walters."

"All right, Joe," I said, "I've got it from here."

I called up Chef Ted's boss to remind him once again that our agreement was being violated by Chef Ted. This time the hotel man-agement decided to act. An hour later, Chef Ted was out of a job.

Walters Golf was on a roll in 1998 when Clark County issued a pro-posal to lease 155 acres located one block south of Mandalay Bay.

Las Vegas was exploding with the rapid growth of housing and tourism, but there was still a shortage of golf courses; the county owned only one public golf course and the city had five. The prop-erty up for lease on the south end of the Strip was undeveloped for a reason—it was a takeoff and landing zone for nearby McCarran International Airport. It also had a very large wash and a power line that ran through the middle of it. The north end of the property was owned by the federal Bureau of Land Management and available to the county to develop.

Competition for the lease was intense. Andre Agassi, the home-town tennis hero, and his longtime agent, Perry Rogers, put together a heavyweight group. So did Sig Rogich, at the time the most powerful political kingmaker in the state.

In 1973, Sig had founded R&R Advertising and built it into the largest advertising and consulting firm in Nevada (now known as R&R Partners). From 1984 to '92, he was a communications and campaign advisor to Presidents Ronald Reagan and George H. W. Bush and Senator John McCain.

When it came to political juice, Sig had his hands on every orange in the state and knew exactly how hard to squeeze. I originally had planned to partner with Sig in my bid for the county land, but we had a disagreement and went separate ways.

Before our split, we had envisioned building a Formula One racetrack with a golf course around it, similar to the four-hole layout called Brickyard Crossing inside the Indianapolis Motor Speedway. But that plan crashed and burned after Sig and I clashed over a Canadian partner he wanted to bring in.

The first time the project came up for a vote it was delayed, which meant that Sig knew he didn't have the votes. Twice more the Board of County Commissioners scheduled a vote, only to postpone. I saw this as yet another Sig tactic. Finally, in September, the commission set a final vote.

Sig wasn't giving up without a fight. Right before that vote, he appeared in front of the board and gave a passionate speech that ended with him saying, as I recall, "Any money my group makes from this we'll give to local charities."

After the audience stopped laughing, four of the seven commissioners abstained from voting, citing various conflicts of interest. It was the first time in the history of the county commission that four members abstained from a vote. The board would later require a minimum of five commissioners to vote on any matter.

We won by a single vote, two to one. That outcome marked the birth of a wonderful project we called Bali Hai Golf Club—a "Tropical Paradise on the Las Vegas Strip," complete with a South Seas theme to complement nearby Mandalay Bay resort.

Bali Hai would become the crown jewel of Walters Golf. And it remains one of the most successful public golf clubs in the United States.

My Bali Hai high was short-lived. A month later, on October 16, 1998, Metro Intelligence and the Attorney General's Office kept their promise after I refused to forfeit $500,000 of the $2.8 million seized nearly two years prior. I was indicted on two felony counts and one gross misdemeanor for misuse of monetary instruments (essentially money laundering). The AG's office accused me of betting with bookies in New York and bringing my winnings back to Nevada illegally.

When the members of Intelligence learned of my indictments, they held a party at Philips Supper House on West Sahara to celebrate. They raised another toast after my case was assigned to Judge Donald Mosley, who had a well-earned reputation as a tough, pro–law enforcement judge. How did I know about the party? Owner Phil Diel, called to offer a blow-by-blow account.

Everyone figured that I was officially screwed when it came to ever getting a Nevada gaming license. But Judge Mosley, to his credit, did the right thing. In December he dismissed the indictments, citing "textual problems"—legalese for get this circumstantial crap out of my courtroom.

One year after Judge Mosley tossed out the bookmaking charges, the state Attorney General's Office and the Intelligence Unit were back at it again. They filed a second money-laundering indictment in November 1999, which was thrown out the following year. They indicted me a third time only to see those charges tossed.

Finally, on October 1, 2002, Chief District Court Judge Mark Gibbons put an end to six years of nonsense and nonstop harassment with a ruling that left no room for appeal. He blasted the Attorney General's Office and Metro police for filing indictments based largely on, in his words, "prejudicial and irrelevant evidence."

A month after Judge Gibbons called them out, a new sheriff arrived in town. The official title is Sheriff of Clark County but, as the only elected law enforcement officer within city and county limits, the sheriff answers to nobody in Vegas, while overseeing nearly 3,500 law enforcement officers.

The new top gun was Bill Young, who had replaced his backstabbing predecessor Sheriff Jerry Keller. The same Sheriff Keller who had allowed his Metro cops to try to shake me down.

Sheriff Young assumed office insisting that he wanted to take the politics out of policing. A classic crime fighter in a city where crime was spinning out of control, Bill Young was a cop's cop. He had no interest in pursuing political agendas.

On the heels of Judge Gibbons's decision, I was in the mood for revenge and considering filing a lawsuit against the police department and the city for malicious prosecution. Sheriff Young had a better idea.

"Billy, I know what they did to you," he told me. "We're going to give you back your $2.8 million plus interest, along with your seized property. If you aren't breaking the law, no one is going to bother you again."

Fair and square was all I could ask for. I was done fighting. I agreed to drop any future litigation. Then, I welcomed back my $4.6 million, including $1.8 million in interest.

The six years of hell cost me a shot at creating a chain of quality sportsbooks. But I felt vindicated, and ready to tee up my next big project.

18

Dodging the Vampires

After dodging four indictments in the state of Nevada, I was tired of being a punching bag for overzealous cops and ambitious prosecutors.

Fighting off their baseless charges had cost me a bundle, and it was a distraction from my business expansion efforts. I had replaced my unhealthy drinking, smoking, and casino habits with a fierce entrepreneurial drive, but I had this nagging sense that successful enterprises like Sierra Sports were making me a bigger and bigger target.

Exhibit A: In 1997, the Nevada Gaming Control Board adopted a statute that reinforced the regulation against "messenger" betting—making it illegal for a person to use a cell phone or pager to place a bet or to place a bet above $10,000 for another person at a sportsbook for compensation. This new rule was instigated by a pack of shortsighted sportsbook operators who were trying to put pro handicappers like me out of business.

I needed to ensure that we were complying with the new regulation. To that end, I retained the two best gaming lawyers in the state, Frank Schreck and Bob Faiss, who between them represented every major gaming company in Nevada.

They advised me to make "partners" of each person betting on my behalf. From that point on, we created separate corporate entities and awarded ownership shares to each partner. Under the new arrangement, they were now making bets for themselves and for me. In turn, they would receive compensation in the form of profit sharing to better address the messenger betting law. At the end of the year, they received a separate 1099 tax form.

The attorneys also advised me to split my betting business into two separate operations—one in Nevada and the other in a foreign country. To avoid any issues, every bet beyond state lines had to be done by employees operating outside of the United States. With that advice in mind, we headed south to Tijuana, Mexico. I rented a home in an upscale neighborhood for our team led by Carl Boblitt and his crew of seasoned vets. But it wasn't long before the banditos came calling.

Like the Metro cops in Vegas, the Mexican police must have figured the cash-heavy Americans were easy marks. No sooner had we set up shop than some *federales* stopped our drivers and issued a series of fictitious speeding tickets. Their ultimatum: pay a fine (the equivalent of $50 in pesos) on the spot or get booked downtown.

We paid up.

Then, the "neighborhood watch" squad showed up at our office selling extra security. We signed up, figuring we had no other choice. I hoped that would be the end of the holdups. But more trouble arrived on the last day of the NBA regular season, in April of 2001.

A gang of off-duty cops broke into our compound, stole $38,000 in cash, and kidnapped two of my key American employees.

When the first ransom call came in, the demand was $300,000 for the release of my men. That's when the negotiations began.

I decided to call their bluff.

"Keep them," I told the kidnappers. "I don't want 'em back anyway."

Then I hung up the phone.

The haggling went back and forth for three more hours, while the dirty cops kept my employees in unmarked police cars parked behind a police station. The ransom demand trended downward and bottomed out at $30,000 in exchange for both snatched employees.

Let's not forget these greedy cops had just stolen $38,000 from me, along with kidnapping my employees. I was outraged, but not enough to argue or have my people mistreated any further.

I arranged for the ransom to be paid, then pulled the plug on the entire Mexican operation.

With Tijuana in my rearview mirror, I cast my eyes across the pond in search of a safer working environment. Wagering on sports is embedded in the culture in Europe. Better yet, gambling earnings are not subject to taxes there, unlike in the United States.

I flew to Zurich and then Amsterdam to meet with Swiss and Dutch bankers, hoping to open dozens of bank accounts to handle millions of dollars in legal offshore betting activity.

Let's take a moment to consider some context: It's late October 2001, shortly after the 9/11 terrorist attacks and the passage by Congress of the Patriot Act, which gave federal authorities wide-ranging power to place court-approved wiretaps and obtain bank and business records of individuals suspected of financing terrorism.

I can tell you from personal experience that European banks, particularly those in Switzerland and the Netherlands, took the Patriot Act far more seriously than U.S. banks. The last thing they wanted was to do business with an American citizen, especially a professional gambler with a slew of indictments to his name, who wanted to wire millions of dollars in and out of offshore accounts. Before bankers would even consider opening an account for me, we were required to produce reams of personal and financial records. You name it, they wanted it: corporate bios, bank statements, tax records, personal and professional references. Every document was scrutinized by humorless, no-nonsense Swiss and Dutch bankers. In the end, we passed muster, allowing us to create a variety of shell companies in the British Virgin Islands, Gibraltar, and Cyprus

with names like Lucy Worldwide LLC (named after my late grandmother) and Action Man LLC. In each case, we were following the
advice provided by our attorneys.

This arrangement marked the beginning of a sixteen-year international odyssey. We moved our legal office to Zurich and our
central offshore headquarters from Tijuana to Camberley, England, on the outskirts of London, then to Freeport in the Bahamas, before our final stop, Panama City, Panama. Once again,
I sent Carl Boblitt and my top people to England. We installed
Vonage Boxes, which provided phone communications via the internet. Each Vonage Box had two phone lines that could be programmed for any area code. Our strategy was to make the calls
to bookmakers look like local calls regardless of their origin. No
bookmaker wanted to see an incoming call from a different area
code than where a bettor resided. This would set off alarms and
raise suspicions that the caller was fronting for someone else. To
further disguise our operation, we hired several Englishmen with
proper accents to make bets. With the help of a friend in Ireland,
we dipped into the Emerald Isle for roughly a dozen partners to
further expand our international base.

There was only one problem: the clocks in Camberley were
eight hours ahead of those in Las Vegas. The time difference forced
my team to work from seven thirty at night until at least five in the
morning. The long hours and intense work environment prompted
my decision to leave England after just one season and move to a
warmer climate and the Eastern time zone in the Bahamas.

We put down stakes in a walled compound that consisted of a
trio of three-bedroom condos in Freeport equipped with the fastest
technology in the form of high-speed T1 internet lines dug halfway
across the island by our Bahamian friends. We had nine bedrooms
filled with employees; the main floor of one condo served as our
base of operations. We also had a huge generator that enabled us to
wager our way through a couple of hurricanes.

Here, I would like to honor someone whose personal strength and support for me in the face of adversity was unyielding.

Kenneth F. Hense showed his friendship to me and dedication to the law in a truly selfless fashion at a time I never would have expected him to have anything or anyone on his mind but his wife and children.

The Department of Homeland Security and U.S. Justice Department were throwing billions of dollars into the fight against terrorism, with a particular focus on border cities like San Diego.

In addition to setting up betting operations in Las Vegas, Europe, and the Bahamas in the early 2000s, I had established a satellite office in San Diego, where Bobby Ward worked with a half-dozen partners traveling to and from Las Vegas. Bobby called me one day to report that people were rummaging through his trash.

We got hit with another raid. The feds confiscated a truckload of documents, and the U.S. Attorney's Office started an investigation into alleged money laundering.

I called Rick Wright, who then explained to U.S. Attorney Anne K. Perry that we were doing nothing illegal. We were betting sports, moving money legally based on an opinion written by New Jersey attorney Kenneth Hense, an expert in gambling laws.

Kenny called me as the investigation progressed. I could tell that something was wrong the moment I heard the halting sound of his voice. The diagnosis, he said, was colon cancer.

"I'm in the hospital and I'm not going to get out," he told me. "If there's anything you and Rick need from me, now's the time."

Rick and I jumped on my plane the next day. When we landed at Toms River regional airport it was bitterly cold. As we entered the hospital room at Ocean Medical Center in Brick, New Jersey, Kenny was almost unrecognizable. His gaunt face was a sickly gray, and he'd lost a ton of weight. His wife, Claire, the mother of their two teenage daughters, Marlena and Kayla, was holding vigil.

Prior to our arrival, Kenny had taken himself off morphine to be lucid enough to read and sign a legal opinion that Rick had prepared. Kenny was so weak he could barely sign his name. Rick then contacted U.S. Attorney Perry. Kenny's dying, he said. If you want to come back and interview him, you'd better do it now.

Perry and her team of prosecutors arrived from San Diego the next day. Kenny had taken himself off morphine again. As the interview was filmed, Kenny confirmed he had read the opinion, signed it under his own free will, and answered the prosecutors' questions.

Kenny Hense died the next day, on February 20, 2004. He was sixty-eight.

Based on Kenny's deathbed interview, Anne Perry dropped the money-laundering case.

We stayed in the Bahamas for three years before relocating once again, this time to Panama City in the mid-2000s. By then, I knew it was time for a change in leadership of our operation. Carl Boblitt had burned out and was bickering with everyone in sight. I took a risk and put a kid nicknamed Jbird in charge.

Jbird was pure Long Island, a fast-talking New Yorker from a straight-up Irish family. He was an underdog, a scrapper, my kind of guy. He had spent some time after high school in the Air Force before rising through our company ranks.

His first assignment was to take a bag of cash and put $75,000 down on three totals at the Gold Coast Casino during the college football bowl season. When he passed that test, we sent him to Chicago with $600,000 in cash to post with a major bookie.

Fronting a bet is one thing. Commanding an international sports-betting operation is quite another. Jbird was hungry but naive. Early on in Panama, I asked him how he was doing and the first words out of his mouth were "We're going to . . ."

I stopped him right there.

"There's no *we*," I told him. "It's *I*. A little word like *we* and these guys are going to pick that up. 'Who is *we*? Who's backing you?' will be the next question coming from the bookmakers."

I was tutoring Jbird on how to train his people. To his credit, he understood right away. He even taught the international crew that didn't speak much English to say, *I*—not we—*want to bet Detroit plus seven. I*—not we—*want Alabama minus 10.*

It only takes one wrong word and your bettors are exposed in Denver, Detroit, Miami, or New York.

The Panama office quickly took on the look of a CIA operation. It was filled with Panamanians, Irish, and all sorts of Americans—southerners, New Yorkers, Nevadans—speaking in a dozen different accents. They used two-dozen Vonage Boxes to disguise the location of our operation—every employee an international man of mystery. The sole purpose was to keep our identities secret and keep my markets alive.

To achieve that goal, we had at least twenty men betting twenty different accounts with the same bookmaker. When necessary, we pulled a "head-fake"—bet the opposite side of a game—to either cool off a hot account, teach someone a lesson, or sometimes just get a better number.

Every weekend, I'd get up at 5:00 a.m. in Vegas, slap on a headset, and go to work. I'd watch the real-time odds flash on my computer screens while coordinating our internet and phone bets down to the second—totals, sides, first half, second half, moneylines.

I'd have my team in Vegas and Jbird on the line, and his team had their people on the line, who had their people on the line. This was our version of a phone tree with hundreds of people directly and indirectly ready to pounce. We used partners, who had access to hundreds of their own accounts, plus the 1,600 accounts that we bet ourselves.

On a busy Saturday in the fall, we'd make up to three hundred bets a day—college basketball and football, the NFL, NBA, NHL, and, at times, the PGA Tour—one game after another. It was like staging a fire drill every forty-five seconds, synchronized down to the last second.

In those days, we ran 270 days a year, making the floor of the New York Stock Exchange look like a morgue by comparison. If you had walked in on our frenzied operation, your first thought would have been *These people are crazy.*

And, you know what? We were.

19

Land of Opportunity

My oldest son, Scott, has a huge heart. He has been a sweet, loving, and giving child since before he could walk. I've asked myself a hundred times why this innocent boy was inflicted with a brain tumor and not me. But there's another side that I rarely talk about—how I've come to terms with having a disabled son, and how Scott's journey led Susan and me to help thousands of other children and adults just like him. The catalyst was a Las Vegas nonprofit organization dedicated to providing intellectually and developmentally disabled people with the opportunity to enhance their lives and the lives of the families that love them.

It's called Opportunity Village. OV for short.

Before Scott was diagnosed at the age of seven, I encountered disabled people, but never really *saw* them. I was too obsessed with making money and being successful. The disabled were just not part of my world, and I was unaware of the full range of their challenges.

Scott was in his early twenties when he came to live with us in Las Vegas. Carol was doing her best, but she was burned out. Unlike other young adults, Scott couldn't head off to college at eighteen or find a job or learn a trade. Prior to moving to Las Vegas, his typical day began at 10:00 or 11:00 a.m. His diet consisted mostly of sodas and candy. He showered just twice a week. He had the intellectual capacity of a sixth grader.

Carol needed a break, and Scott needed a change of scenery. Susan and I were elated to have him. The first thing we did was establish a daily routine—up at six, breakfast, a shower, off to work, physical activity, dinner together at home, in bed by nine.

We wanted Scott to feel loved, productive, and supported. We wanted him to have a purpose in life.

Once he got settled, I bought Scott a sporty red Nissan that he drove around town like an old lady. If the speed limit was forty miles per hour, he drove twenty-five and held up traffic. One day, he went to Carl's Jr. for a sandwich. Exiting the drive-through, he cut a turn short and ran into a telephone pole, ripping off a rear quarter panel.

"Scott, what happened?" I asked after he pulled into our driveway.

Tears trickled out of Scott's eyes.

I continued. "You could have hurt someone. You could have hurt yourself." Then I delivered my punch line. *"What are you going to do about this?"*

That's when Scott hit me with a zinger.

"Dad, I've got my good days and I've got my bad days."

Checkmate. You got me.

But still, I was worried. I knew that I wasn't going to be around forever to help him. Scott needed to find a purpose in life.

By the late eighties, our commitment to philanthropy had reached the point where I was quietly serving on a half-dozen charity boards. The more I learned about how these charities worked, the more frustrated I became with heavy administrative costs siphoning off dollars that should have supported the work itself. I also wondered why more wasn't being done in Las Vegas to help people like Scott. That's when Kitty Rodman entered the picture.

Clarine "Kitty" Rodman was someone out of a William Faulkner novel, a grande dame of the South, a tiny woman with an iron will and philanthropic zeal. Kitty had moved west from Virginia to become one of the most influential women in the history of Ne-

vada. Through her fifty years as a director and part owner of the
Sierra Construction Company, the "First Lady of Construction" had
helped build most of the city's marquee properties, including the
Golden Nugget, Binion's Horseshoe, Four Queens, Santa Fe, and
The Mirage. Her company also worked on various phases of the
Dunes, Fremont, Mint, Sahara, Sands, Hacienda, Flamingo, Las
Vegas Hilton, Gold Coast, Tropicana, Stardust, Frontier, Bally's, and
the Las Vegas Visitors and Convention Center.

In other words, she had a hand in virtually everything significant in Las Vegas.

But Kitty did more than reshape the city's skyline. She poured
her heart and soul—and millions of dollars—into building and rebuilding thousands of lives through her support of Easter Seals Nevada, UNLV, women's rights, special education programs and, for
the better part of four decades, Opportunity Village.

OV was founded in 1954 by parents whose baby daughter had
Down syndrome and five individuals or parents of children with
intellectual and related disabilities. The nonprofit specializes in vocational training, community employment, day services, advocacy,
the arts, and social recreation. Its goals are simple: to give clients a
sense of pride, purpose, and a paycheck.

Despite Kitty's best efforts in the late eighties, OV was struggling. It was overshadowed by more prominent and well-connected
charities and operated out of a dark, tiny, downtown warehouse on
South Fourth Street.

That's when Kitty asked if Susan and I would attend a fundraising event and perhaps make a donation.

Live long enough and you'll have three or four awakenings in
life. This event was one of them for me. Susan and I walked away
from the first fundraiser nothing short of amazed. Then I took a
tour of their headquarters. Walking and talking with staff, I learned
that two-thirds of people with intellectual and developmental issues
were simply living the hand they were dealt at birth. The other one-

third simply subjected to the whims of fate—an accident, an illness, or a life-changing brain tumor like Scott.

What touched me then and continues to touch me today is the fact that not one child or adult we met complained to us. Their shared goal was to have an *opportunity* to simply contribute and become a productive member of society.

After that first visit, Susan and I started supporting Opportunity Village in a big way. Then I took Scott for a visit. Within minutes, I realized that my son had found a new home. Scott gravitated to those with the greatest needs, taking on the role of protector and provider. He was everywhere, pushing a wheelchair, comforting another person, or helping with a task at hand.

"Dad," he said, "I like it here."

Scott quickly became a constant presence at OV. His official title was the Walters Family "Ambassador." In his volunteer role, he insisted on working with the most severely handicapped, God bless him.

Kitty was so impressed with Scott's involvement and our interest that she arranged a meeting in 1993 with someone I view as the Mother Teresa of the desert.

Las Vegas is known for high-profile casino owners, poker players, and entertainers, but the city is also home to a large contingent of philanthropists, nonprofit leaders, caring volunteers, and other bighearted individuals who, in my mind, do not get nearly enough credit for all the good work they do.

Linda Smith stands at the top of that list.

When we met, Linda was OV's vice president of philanthropy, one of many senior executive positions she would hold between 1985 and 2016. Over lunch, Linda shared her life story, which turned out to be like mine in many respects.

She was born into poverty, neglect, and abuse in England. Raised in Canada, Linda became a model and actress who taught herself to dance before marrying Glenn Smith, a top Canadian entertainer.

While living north of the border, Linda gave birth to their first child, Christopher, who had profound Down syndrome.

The young family eventually moved to Las Vegas, where Glenn performed as a singer and piano player with Wayne Newton, the town's longtime premier act. Although Linda and Glenn became U.S. citizens, they had to endure an expensive and prolonged battle involving their son's legal status. They ran up against an archaic law within the Immigration and Naturalization Act, Section 212(a), that denied entry in the U.S. for (1) criminals, and (2) retarded people.

You read that right. *Retarded* people. Those exact words. (The language has since been changed.)

"It took us eighteen years to get Christopher legal status to live in the U.S.," Linda told me.

Her story brought tears to my eyes.

"Whatever you need," I told her. "How can we help?"

I decided then and there to donate not just money, but, more important, my time. Linda and I strategized ways to elevate the profile of Opportunity Village within the community. She was brimming with fundraising ideas, burning with passion, and fearless when it came to the "ask"—requesting donations from me or anyone else.

I do not exaggerate about Linda's fearlessness as a fundraiser. Take the time I introduced her to Celine Dion and her husband-manager, René Angélil.

I had come to know René, an avid poker player and gambler, through a mutual friend in the spring of 2003 shortly after Celine began her spectacularly successful residency at Caesars Palace. Celine was at the peak of her vocal powers, the likes of which Vegas had rarely seen.

I asked René if he and Celine would consider holding a concert at Caesars and donating 100 percent of the proceeds to Opportunity Village. He agreed to meet in early 2004 with Linda, who put on quite a performance of her own.

The meeting took place backstage at the 4,100-seat theater that Caesars had custom-built for Celine. René was there with the head of Caesars and AEG Live, the group producing Celine's show.

In the meeting, Linda played her best card—talking about being a mom with a child with Down syndrome and how children with disabilities are the real teachers in life.

René was sitting at the end of the table. As Linda later recalled, he listened and said, "Okay, we'll pick the date, and we'll sell the tickets."

At which point Linda went one step further and asked René if OV could upsell some front-row seats. The guy from Caesars about fell out of his chair. René had already said yes. Why push it? But push it Linda did.

"We have donors who would pay a lot more to sit up front," she said.

"No, we've never done that before," René said. "I don't want to do that."

But the mother in Linda couldn't keep quiet.

"Well, René," she said, "I have donors who will pay a hundred thousand dollars a seat."

"Somebody would pay a hundred thousand dollars?" René replied.

"Oh, I think several people might. We could raise up to a million dollars in one afternoon."

Linda later told me there was a long pause; she was sure by this time everyone in the room had pretty much stopped breathing.

"Okay," René said. "The charity will have to pay the production cost—a hundred and forty thousand dollars. And then Celine and I will write a check to cover it."

Celine ended up performing two incredible concerts and we raised the million dollars Linda had promised. Celine and René fell in love with Opportunity Village and became loyal champions of the cause. Each year, they brought their first son and their twins to the Magical Forest. And Linda became lifelong friends with Celine and René.

René, rest his soul, died of cancer in 2016.

Our initial fundraising project focused on moving Opportunity Village out of its dismal downtown location, which had opened in 1964, and into a larger and more welcoming facility. That dream came true in 1990 with the completion of its West Oakey Campus.

Linda then came up with the brilliant idea of turning the campus into a Magical Forest, a winter wonderland, for the holiday season. She envisioned a joyful Santa Claus storybook outdoor attraction in glittering Christmas lights with food, drink, and holiday cheer. In 1992, our first year, we raised a total of $3,000. Three decades later, Magical Forest remains a cherished southern Nevada tradition drawing thousands of families and children. Except now it raises more than $2 million a year.

On any given night, it takes more than one hundred volunteers to run the show. Right from the start, I decided The Walters Group would work Christmas Eve, the most difficult night to staff. Susan and I handled the cash register, counting crumpled dollar bills in the entry booth, and, along with our other ninety-eight volunteer employees, doing whatever else was needed.

As you might imagine, I was not shy about asking the biggest movers and shakers in the state to support OV. I have been a major donor to every Nevada governor since Kenny Guinn in 1999, in part to make sure they knew that Opportunity Village provided a better return on the taxpayers' money than any other charity in Las Vegas. I have tapped the shoulders and wallets of governors, senators, casino executives, celebrities, entertainers, and, most recently, Mark Davis, the controlling owner and managing general partner of the NFL's Las Vegas Raiders and owner of the WNBA's Las Vegas Aces. I conducted tours so potential donors could witness for themselves the innovative programs, services, and miracles that make Opportunity Village a one-of-a-kind place.

Sometimes deep financial commitments come straight out of the blue. One year, we had friends from Little Rock, Arkansas, Craig and Elizabeth Campbell, visiting for the Christmas holidays at a time when I run advertisements in local newspapers soliciting contributions to OV.

Unbeknownst to me, Elizabeth picked up the *Review-Journal*, which their family owned, and spotted one of the ads. On their way home, they wrote a pledge on the back of a paper plate. Part of their request was that the check had to be a surprise to me.

Sure enough, I got a call from my friend Terry Lanni, the CEO of MGM Resorts. "Bill, I'm down at Opportunity Village and I need you here right away." Given it was Terry, I didn't question the request, I just rushed down to the administrative office.

Mr. Lanni is out back in the work area, I was told.

I opened the door to see about a hundred of our clients on their feet, cheering. Terry and Linda Smith were holding a supersize check. I found myself blinking back tears as I read the last name Campbell and saw the size of their family donation: one million dollars.

In 2020, the OV's Walters Family Campus in Henderson, Nevada, celebrated its twentieth anniversary. Susan and I agreed to lead a campaign to raise an additional $8 million.

Today, the red-brick building on East Lake Mead Parkway bustles with activity. Clients who work there do everything from document sorting to imaging for Paper Pros, one of the largest media management operations in Nevada. The door to their workroom is decorated with a plaque that reads "In honor of Scott Walters."

Inside, a dozen young men and women with varying degrees of disabilities separate, sort, and scan hundreds of thousands of pieces of paper from Nevada public agencies such as the Department of Transportation and Welfare. In addition, non-gaming receipts from

Caesars Entertainment account for roughly one million pieces of paper per month.

In an adjacent area, a gigantic quarter-million-dollar shredding machine hums eight hours every day recycling eight tons of paper from casinos and law and medical offices—just a few of the six-hundred-plus businesses that OV serves around the state. That's not counting the culinary, printing, mailing, packaging, cleaning, promotional, and thrift store side of the business.

In all my years supporting OV programs, nobody has touched my heart more than a young man I met the first day I stepped inside the Employment Training Center on the West Oakey Campus. His name is Alonzo Allred.

Alonzo was born a healthy child. At the age of twelve, he fell down a flight of stairs. His injuries left him paralyzed from the waist down, and the trauma to his brain resulted in Alonzo losing sight in one eye.

He was destined to spend the rest of his life in a wheelchair, but nonetheless maintained an upbeat and positive attitude. Whenever I saw Alonzo, I made a point of asking him how he was doing. He always gave me the same reply as he clutched his constant companion Barney, the purple dinosaur: "I'm Super D Duper."

Alonzo's parents were in their seventies when I first met them. It took Alonzo three hours to quietly dress himself every morning, because he didn't want to wake up his parents. They naturally worried about what would happen to their son after they were gone. That concern got me thinking: What would become of Alonzo and our other disabled clients after they lost their parents?

So we joined a group of Opportunity Village supporters to kick off a $35 million campaign to build a long-term housing facility for high-need and highly functional adults who otherwise might not have a place to call home. In June of 2021, we staged the grand opening of Betty's Village, an eighty-one-bed residential facility named in honor of the founding donors, Ralph and Betty Engelstad.

Opportunity Village is Nevada's largest employer of disabled people—more than eight hundred employees. They are proud, tax-paying residents who earned a combined $4 million in 2022. There are now four primary campuses to serve some one thousand adults and two thousand children.

Like countless nonprofits and companies, my favorite charity was affected by the pandemic. For the first time in its history, we had to cancel several key fundraising events and were faced with laying off hundreds of staff members. I learned of these problems shortly after I was released from prison. Susan and I made a $1 million matching contribution to kick off a larger fundraising campaign that eventually doubled our gift, in large part thanks to a $250,000 donation from Mark Davis.

Whenever I felt depressed during my time in prison, I thought of our clients at Opportunity Village and how they never complained about having a bad day. I will continue to support this wonderful place.

I came to see my son in a new light there. He became my hero, the most compassionate and bravest person I know.

A quick story about Scott: Through our friends Bion Wilcox, who worked for Bobby Jones apparel, and his wife, Judy, we learned of a school in Rexburg, Idaho, called Ricks College. Their daughter Jenny was a student there. Scott had always dreamed of being a chef, and we learned that Ricks had a program for intellectually challenged students that included cooking courses. A wonderful couple named Dave and Nancy Richards agreed to host Scott at their home while he attended Ricks.

The school was run by the Mormon Church and, while I paid for Scott's tuition and room and board, no one ever asked for any donations while Scott was there.

I was so impressed with Scott's experience that I called Nancy Richards to see if I could help. To my surprise, she told me that her husband, Dave, was in charge of fundraising for the school. Dave and the school's president, Steve Bennion, flew to Las Vegas, stayed at the Horseshoe Hotel and Casino, and had dinner with me and Susan. We subsequently funded the creation of a new kitchen at the school, which now is part of Brigham Young University.

In 1995, two years after arriving in Rexburg, Scott graduated and received a diploma. We were there as he walked across the stage. That day, he joyfully told me: "Dad, I'm the first person in our family to get a college degree." It was one of the proudest days of my life.

Scott's experience at Ricks College would not have happened without the support he received leading up to it. Opportunity Village changed Scott's life, and in the process he changed mine, making me a better man. This special place continues to enrich my life every time I visit. No matter how much we contribute, this is a debt I will never be able to fully repay.

I have no memories of my father, Thurman Walters, who died at age 41 when I was eighteen months old. This is from 1944 in Kentucky.

My mother, Aileen "Dale" Quesenberry Walters, and the family dog, Fluffy, outside our house in Munfordville in 1945, one year before I was born.

My grandmother Lucy Quesenberry instilled in me the principles I still live by today. This photo was taken in 1960.

A veteran of World War II and the Korean War, Uncle Harry served as a role model and father figure to me. He may have inspired my love of cars in this photo from 1949.

At the grave of our father with my sisters, Martha and Barbara Ann, along with cousin, Francis, in 1948.

A school photo from 1955.

Susan and me at Caesar's Palace in 1977 with her brother, Johnny, who introduced me to the game of golf.

Poker great Chip Reese, Las Vegas Realtor Ken Gragson, and I help Las Vegas icon Benny Binion (*in apron*) celebrate his eightieth birthday in 1984. Few people have a history as colorful as Benny.

Kentucky friends Ray "Cabbage" Coy, Luther James, me, Calvin Hash, Sammy Marrillia, and (*standing*) Luther's son, Greg, at Luther's hotel in Indiana.

Christmas 2008. *(Photo by Arica Dorff.)*

For a time, my three children, Tonia, Derin, and Scott, lived with or near us in Las Vegas. This is from 2002.

My daughter Tonia and her husband, Mike Snyder, with Susan and me in 1999. Tonia committed suicide in 2019 while I was in prison.

Freddie Jacobson and our championship trophy at the 2008 AT&T Pebble Beach National Pro-Am.

Susan and I visited the birthplace of golf, St. Andrews, in 1992. She took this photo.

In happier days, Phil Mickelson showing me the Claret Jug outside The Farms Golf Club in Rancho Sante Fe after he won the 2013 British Open.

While the United States and Europe competed for the Ryder Cup at Valhalla Golf Club in Louisville, our band of misfits vied for our "Cider Cup" at nearby Hurstbourne Country Club. Standing with me are my British friends Pat Murphy and Chris Mitchell. Kneeling is Russ Newman. You may not recognize my pal David Feherty, up to his usual antics.

I first knew him as Cassius Clay when we were young Kentuckians. Susan and I had the chance to see him again circa 2005 at a fundraiser in Las Vegas for the Muhammad Ali Center in Louisville.

My close friends Calvin Hash and Jack McClusky at the Cider Cup in 2008.

With financier Carl Icahn on his yacht in 2005.

One of my closest Louisville friends, Ray "Cabbage" Coy, followed me and Susan to Vegas to work in our sports-betting operation. Ray died in 2021.

I made lasting friendships in prison. With my pals and former inmates at a 2022 reunion in Puerto Rico: (*from left*) Pablo Santiago, Ernesto F. Ortiz, me, Antonio Peluzzo, Carlos H. Torres, and Angel Antonio Canchani.

20

Lefty & Me

I am staring at the world's most famous left-handed golfer and can't believe what he is saying. It's a bright spring day in April 2017 and Phil Mickelson is sitting on my patio in Carlsbad, California, over-looking surfers on a sparkling blue Pacific Ocean.

By that point, Phil was a Hall of Fame golfer and winner of forty-three tournaments on the PGA Tour. We had shared an eight-year friendship that featured rollicking rounds of golf and high-stakes sports gambling.

When Phil showed up, he owed me $2.5 million on losing bets that I had placed on his behalf. I had let the debt slide for the better part of three years, and it had continued to grow. Frankly, there were more pressing matters on my mind, specifically a high-profile insider-trading case involving ten counts of wire and securities fraud. The three-week criminal trial had just ended on April 7—badly, for me.

I'd lost the biggest bet of my life in front of twelve Manhattan jurors believing they would see through the government's criminal case. The jury—prevented by the judge from hearing about the illegal actions of government agents—returned guilty verdicts on all charges.

When Phil arrived in his black, tricked-out SUV, I was in my seventieth year of life, under house arrest with an electronic tracking bracelet around my right ankle, and racing to get my business affairs in order. I was awaiting a July hearing, which would deliver another shock to my system when the judge disregarded the official presentencing recommendation of one year and a day in prison. Instead, he hit me with a sentence of five years.

Phil had an opportunity to testify at my trial—to tell the truth about whether he received inside information regarding one of two stocks that I had recommended to him. For reasons I'll describe in detail later, Phil decided not to testify on my behalf. How did I feel? Completely betrayed.

As it turned out, he came to my home not to make amends or offer a mea culpa, as I had anticipated. Instead, he came to finally settle up the money he owed me.

I sat there speechless as he moaned about losing lucrative sponsorships with ExxonMobil and Barclays along with 25 percent of his deal with KPMG. He even whined about the $32 million depreciation he had to take on his precious Gulfstream V jet.

All the while, I was about to go to prison after losing a trial that cost me more than $100 million in legal fees, fines, and restitution.

I thought to myself: *Thousands of people stand in line waiting for Phil's autograph, but if I could buy back my association with him, I'd pay top dollar.*

Phil ended our meeting with a bizarre invitation.

"I'm going to be here for the next two and a half weeks," he told me. "Wanna play some golf?"

Fast-forward four years.

It's May 23, 2021. I've been out of federal prison for a year and am sitting in our living room with Susan. We're watching thousands of screaming fans on the TV overwhelm security guards and charge down the eighteenth fairway of the windswept Ocean Course on picturesque Kiawah Island, South Carolina. Their conquering hero, just three weeks shy of his fifty-first birthday, is about to become the oldest major champion in professional golf history.

The scene playing out on my flat-screen is nothing short of sur-real. Phil emerges from the roiling sea of fans, putter in hand, about to wrap up an epic victory. And to be brutally honest, I'm having a hard time wrapping my head around it. Not Phil's glorious moment. I'm absolutely thrilled for the golfer and the game I deeply love.

No, I am reflecting on our now-fractured friendship. I play out what happened between us, deconstructing my feelings bit by bit:

What would I have done if I were in Phil's shoes?

What if I had to choose between helping gain the freedom of a good friend or refusing to answer questions in court?

Would I have abandoned that friend in his ultimate hour of need?

Would I have helped the feds convict a friend to save my own skin?

After the final putt falls and Phil gets swept away in joyful cele-bration, I think to myself that people would never shower this man with so much affection, if they knew him the way I did.

Fast-forward nine months.

It's February 2022 and Phil has gone from prince to pariah fol-lowing his move to join the Saudi-backed LIV Golf league in ex-change for a reported $200 million payout. But Phil didn't just join the LIV league: he was actively recruiting other pros to leave the PGA Tour.

In an interview with author Alan Shipnuck, Phil portrayed the Saudis as "scary motherfuckers to get involved with." And he didn't stop there.

"We know they killed [*Washington Post* reporter and U.S. resi-dent Jamal] Khashoggi and have a horrible record on human rights. They execute people over there for being gay. Knowing all this, why would I even consider it? Because this is a once-in-a-lifetime oppor-tunity to reshape how the PGA Tour operates."

Phil went on to blast the Tour's "strong-arm" tactics as "manipulative" and "coercive." In an earlier interview with *Golf Digest*, Phil complained about the PGA Tour's "obnoxious greed." This would be the same PGA Tour that had paid Phil $96.4 million in prize money through 2022—more than anyone in the sport except Tiger Woods. Not to mention more than $800 million in endorsements, sponsorships, and off-the-course earnings.

The public was starting to see a side of Phil Mickelson that many of his fellow competitors on the PGA Tour and other insiders had known for years.

Phil went on a self-imposed exile from golf for several months. He returned to public life in June 2022, on the eve of his commitment to play the inaugural LIV event outside of London. Two months later, Phil revealed in court papers he had been suspended by the Tour through March of 2024. (In a shocker, the Tour announced in June 2023 that it plans to merge with LIV Golf.)

After his suspension, Phil's first act of contrition was to speak with Bob Harig of *Sports Illustrated*. In a phone interview, Phil expressed "regret" about the "mistakes" he had made in his life, including an "addiction off the course that I really needed to address."

He added: "I hurt a lot of people and I'm really sorry. My gambling got to a point of being reckless and embarrassing. I had to address it. And I've been addressing it for a number of years . . . for hundreds of hours of therapy."

Phil didn't share any details about his "reckless and embarrassing" gambling habits, so I'll offer one example here.

In September 2012, Phil was at the Medinah Country Club just outside Chicago, site of the 39th Ryder Cup between the United States and Europe. He called to tell me that he was feeling supremely confident that the American squad led by Tiger Woods and Phil himself would reclaim the Cup from the Euros. He was so confident that he asked me to place a $400,000 bet for him on the U.S. team to win.

Once again, I could not believe what I was hearing.

"Have you lost your fucking mind?" I told him. "Don't you re-member what happened to Pete Rose?" The former Cincinnati Reds manager was banned from baseball for betting on his own team. "You're seen as a modern-day Arnold Palmer. You'd risk all that for this? I want no part of it."

"All right, all right," he replied before hanging up.

I have no idea whether Phil placed the bet elsewhere. Hopefully, he came to his senses, especially considering the "Miracle at Medi-nah." Trailing, 10–6, going into the final day of singles matches, the Europeans pulled off the greatest comeback in Ryder Cup history. They won eight matches, tied one, and lost only three to beat the Americans by a single point, 14½ to 13½.

Phil's 1-up loss to Justin Rose that Sunday contributed to the stunning defeat.

As you can see, my gambling and golfing relationship with Phil is a complicated saga. I was a mentor, a confidant, a loyal friend, a golfing buddy, and a betting partner. I am twenty-four years and one month older than Phil, but we were virtually the same age when it came to gambling, golf, and life.

There has been speculation in the media, the golf world, on Twitter, and beyond about what I will have to say in this book about Phil. Much of it has centered on the assumption that I will settle old scores and that Phil has a lot to worry about.

After a great deal of introspection, I have decided to set the record straight and let the facts speak for themselves. I am not here to deni-grate Phil for his gambling. My only motivation is to share the truth about what happened between the two of us, regarding our gambling partnership and the stock trading that sent me to prison. Up until now, the full story has not been told. You can decide for yourself what to make of the man. That said, I'm not going to share any details about his personal life. I will leave that to others if they so choose.

•   •   •

We first met in 2006 at the AT&T Pebble Beach Pro-Am in Northern California. Swedish pro Freddie Jacobson and I made the cut and, as fate would have it, we were paired with Phil and his amateur partner, Steve Lyons, the vice president of North America marketing for Ford Motor Company, one of his corporate sponsors.

Phil and Freddie were on their way to a pair of 77's and a tie for thirty-eighth place. Throughout the final round, Phil and I talked nothing but sports, oblivious to the beguiling beauty of the Monterey Peninsula and one of my favorite courses in the world. It was evident that he knew of my sports-gambling success and was trying to connect on that level.

Despite his bloated score that day, Phil's brilliance as a golfer was in full bloom. Throughout the years, I have played with many PGA Tour pros and, frankly, Phil had another gear that most others don't have. He was also willing to put it all on the line and risk losing a golf tournament to hit one miraculous shot. A man after my own heart!

Over the years, Phil and I played a few dozen rounds of golf together, most of them in Southern California at La Jolla Country Club, the Grand Del Mar, the Del Mar Country Club, Rancho Santa Fe, The Farms, The Bridges, the Plantation Club, and The Madison Club.

Tour legend Jim Colbert joined us once; we played with Phil's likable brother, Tim, on a couple of occasions. Dustin Johnson and Ben Crane joined us at The Madison Club. But most of the time it was just Phil and me. While we played, we would discuss a range of topics—sports, business, gambling, and life in general.

We usually had a bet, but that was just to keep it interesting. It was an eighteen-hole match-play bet, not medal. The bet was small, generally $10,000. If the match ended early, we'd allow one press for half the bet.

Mostly we played the same tees and I'd get anywhere from six to seven shots a side. We were grinding the whole time.

Overall, I'm sure I didn't beat Phil out of any money on the course. I'd say we about broke even, but the matches weren't about money. They were about two hypercompetitive guys trying to beat each other. We could have played for nothing and we'd still have battled as hard as possible. During the time we spent on those golf courses, we became what I thought were friends.

In May 2008, I was invited to play in another Pro-Am at the Wachovia Championship in Charlotte, North Carolina, as a guest of the bank. I bumped into Phil in the locker room. This time, he was more direct.

"I hear you do partnerships," he said.

"I do," I said. "But only if someone has access to places I can't bet. Or places where they can bet more money than me."

Phil had both. After the Wachovia meeting, we kept in touch and eventually entered into a gambling partnership that lasted five years. During that time, I saw a lot of things in Phil that reminded me of my younger self, when I was consumed by gambling and used my automobile business to fund that addiction. I loved his energy and his personality.

More than once throughout our betting partnership, I found myself compelled to offer some quiet counsel to help Phil avoid some of the same issues that plagued me as a younger man.

From the start, our betting agreement—one we verbally negotiated—called for us to split everything fifty-fifty. Phil put up half the money; I put up the other half. That way, we shared an equal amount of risk and reward.

Phil said he had two offshore accounts that would take big action from him. In all the decades I've worked with partners and beards, Phil had accounts as large as anyone I'd seen. And you don't get those types of accounts without betting millions of dollars.

My reason for partnering with him was simple. Given my reputation in the gambling world, my limits with Phil's two bookmakers were roughly $20,000 a game on college and $50,000 on the pros. Even after our fifty-fifty split, Phil's limits of $400,000 on college at offshore sportsbooks and another $400,000 on the NFL enabled me to at least double my limits. Phil also had a $100,000 limit on college over/under bets with each book, twenty times my maximum.

By his own admission, Phil was worth an estimated $250 million during our time betting together (he collected a reported $50 million annually in endorsements alone). We agreed that anytime our winnings or losses reached $3 million, we would settle up. In truth, I was no more worried about Phil paying me $3 million than an average person owing me a thousand bucks.

In the beginning, I didn't know Phil's betting habits or background, so I did some research. My strategy was to emulate his betting patterns to disguise the fact that it was Billy Walters, not Phil Mickelson, placing the bets. I followed his patterns, betting at the same time, in similar amounts, dogs or favorites, riding his horses as long as we could.

The first six months of our agreement ran like Secretariat. The offshore bookies failed to detect anything different in the pattern of Phil's bets other than that he was winning far more often. Despite our best efforts to keep the two accounts alive, it wasn't long before the offshore bookies closed them. They told Phil the bets were far more disciplined than usual, so they knew they weren't solely his. He could resume betting, they said, but only if it was on his own. This led Phil to activate a formerly dormant account for our partnership.

Under our original agreement, I made clear to Phil that our betting had to be legal and that a vital part of our partnership was discretion. We were not to discuss our arrangement with anyone and he couldn't use my information to bet someplace else.

I was virtually certain that the way Phil had previously conducted his sports-betting activity violated the law and I was not about to be a party to it. Because I had employed the top legal minds of sports betting, I knew how to bet legally. And I told Phil that would be the only way we could be partners.

Phil, however, wanted more action for himself. We agreed that I would place bets on his behalf on games on which I was either neutral or had no interest. My thinking was that Phil's action would help me camouflage our plays and expand my market.

Within a month, I caught Phil going behind my back and violating our agreement when I bet a Monday night football game for the partnership. Unknown to me, Phil had seen the pick and, without my permission, made his own separate bet with the two bookmakers who had closed our joint account. His wager caused those bookmakers to immediately move their line on the game, and other books immediately followed. With the line moving a full point, my bet was no longer a play for me.

With one quick phone call, I learned the culprit was Phil. I confronted Phil and told him of my concerns about the legality of the way he was conducting his betting. If he wanted to continue that way, he was free to do so, but I would stop being his partner. He needed to make a choice. Phil apologized to me and promised that he would never do business with them again.

My betting partnership with Phil ended in the spring of 2014 when we learned of a government investigation into my stock trading, which I'll describe in detail in a future chapter.

After my business relationship with Phil ended, I learned a lot more about his betting from two very reliable sources in sports gambling. They said it was nothing for Phil to bet $20,000 a game on long-shot, five-team NBA parlays. Or wager $100,000 or $200,000 a game on football, basketball, and baseball. Based upon my detailed betting records and additional records provided by the sources, here is a snapshot of Phil's gambling habit between 2010 and 2014:

- He bet $110,000 to win $100,000 a total of 1,115 times.

- On 858 occasions, he bet $220,000 to win $200,000. (The sum of those 1,973 gross wagers came to more than $311 million.)

- In 2011 alone, he made 3,154 bets—an average of nearly nine per day.

- On one day in 2011 (June 22), he made forty-three bets on major-league baseball games, resulting in $143,500 in losses.

- He made a staggering 7,065 wagers on football, basketball, and baseball.

Phil didn't let his playing in PGA tournaments get in the way of betting. Indeed, according to the 2010–2014 betting records, he made 1,734 wagers on games during twenty-nine events. This included seventy separate bets on baseball and preseason pro football during The Barclays tournament in August 2011 where he shot 8-under and tied for 43rd (he won $415,000 in bets that weekend).

On February 11, 2012, a busy college basketball Saturday, Phil blew himself up by running his betting losses to nearly $4 million, according to the gambling sources familiar with Phil's other bets. Even so, he displayed an incredible ability to compartmentalize. He shot 64 the following day to win the AT&T Pro-Am at Pebble Beach while playing with, and demolishing, Tiger Woods, by eleven strokes.

The same gambling sources also said that Phil was so slow to settle his debts that several offshore books refused to take his action. Documents in a money-laundering case show that, when Phil finally did pay up, money was wired on at least two occasions from his management company to a real estate company with a memo listing the payments as an "initial investment" or "additional funding"—an effort to conceal his gambling losses.

Based on our relationship and what I've since learned from others, Phil wagered a total of more than $1 billion during the past three decades. The only other person I know who surpassed that kind of volume is me. During a twenty-year period beginning in the mid-nineties, Phil's losses approached $100 million. That amount is two-and-a-half times higher than the $40 million reported by Alan Shipnuck in his bestselling unauthorized biography of Phil.

Frankly, given Phil's annual income and net worth, I had no problems with his betting—and still don't. He's a big-time gambler, and big-time gamblers make big bets. It's his money to spend how he wants.

On Tuesday, February 11, 2014, I met Phil to settle a $2.2 million debt he owed me from his personal betting losses. We had lunch at The Bridges, one of several private country clubs in San Diego County that he belongs to. The meeting turned comically cloak-and-dagger when Phil instructed me to leave my cell phone on the table and follow him back to the men's locker room.

I was thinking: *What the hell is going on?*

After being friends for years, all of a sudden Phil was making like Tony Soprano. I had recently learned the IRS was looking into Phil and two other gamblers as part of a money-laundering investigation, so I thought he might be concerned that *his* phone was being tapped.

In the locker room, Phil began by informing me that two FBI agents had surprised him several months earlier after he competed in a FedEx Cup tournament in Boston. When the agents boarded his private aircraft, Phil told me, he thought some fellow golf pros were pulling a prank on him.

"But then they started asking me questions about you and others," Phil said. He didn't say who the "others" were, but I assumed they must have been the two guys involved with him in the separate money-laundering investigation.

Phil then warned me not to say a word to anyone about this because the FBI agents said he'd get in trouble if he told me.

Specifically, Phil said, the FBI questioned him about some stock trades and wire transfers. He said he answered their questions truthfully, but worried that the agents were investigating him for possible money laundering.

Regarding the $2.2 million he owed me, Phil asked, "Can I just pay someone other than you?"

"Hell no!" I told him. "If you wire that money to another account, *that* is money laundering. You and I have never done one thing illegal. You need to wire that money to the exact same account you have been sending it to. We're not going to do it any other way."

After our conversation ended, I retrieved my phone and left the club. When I reached the parking lot, I called my attorney, Rick Wright, and told him verbatim what had just transpired. Rick made notes of our call.

During a round of golf eleven days later, Phil shared more details about the FBI interviews. He said he told the agents that he could not think of a single conversation with me that would make him uncomfortable, that I did not provide any "material nonpublic information," and that I never suggested Phil could pay off the gambling debts he owed me by trading on stock tips.

He said the agents asked him the following: If he knew that I had made $25 million on specific stock trades, what would he think?

Phil said he responded: "Good for Bill. He's an honest and honorable guy—as honest as anyone I know."

I reminded Phil that all of the betting I do—and the betting we'd done together—was entirely legal. I also reassured him that I had legal opinions in writing to support that position.

"If you ever have to talk about me, tell the truth," I told Phil. "You and I have nothing to hide."

Had I known that Phil was making payments to offshore books through certain business entities that subjected him to possible charges of money laundering, I never would have entered into any kind of a betting agreement with him.

I was already in the government's frying pan and didn't need any more heat. I had been indicted five times before meeting Phil. As explained previously, I'd gone to great lengths to comply with U.S. laws, including paying millions of dollars to attorneys and moving much of my sports-betting operation offshore.

What I find downright hysterical is Phil's portrayal of our gambling arrangement. Two weeks after I was indicted on insider-trading charges in New York, Phil spoke out on the eve of the Memorial Tournament, which is hosted each year by founder Jack Nicklaus at his Muirfield Village Golf Club in Dublin, Ohio. Phil began the press conference on June 1, 2016, by saying he was "disappointed to have been a part of that whole thing." He added: "I'm pleased it's behind me, that it's over, that it's behind me."

Asked about his association with gamblers (meaning me), Phil told the media:

"Well, I have to be responsible for the people I associate with. Going forward, I'll make the best effort I can to make sure I represent myself, as well as my family, as well as my companies, in a way that I want to and they deserve."

In June 2022—six years after making those remarks—Phil had no qualms about associating with the "scary motherfuckers" who killed journalist Jamal Khashoggi and paid Phil the reported 200 million in Saudi petro dollars.

Looking back, it's easy to see the blatant hypocrisy in Phil's remarks. Fact is, he has a track record of associating with dubious characters.

One year before he partnered with the Saudis, Phil was linked to "Dandy" Don DeSeranno. Citing previously unreported court records, the *Detroit News* published an article on June 21, 2021, under the headline "Lefty and Dandy Don: How a Grosse Pointe Bookie Allegedly Cheated Phil Mickelson."

The story described DeSeranno as "one of the biggest gamblers in Detroit history . . . who also handled bets for big shots as a Las Vegas casino host and bookie from 1994–2002." The court records revealed that a "mob-connected bookie . . . was accused of bilking Phil out of $500,000."

The names of DeSeranno and Mickelson were uncovered by the *News* in a trial transcript related to the 2007 federal racketeering trial of Jack "Jackie the Kid" Giacalone. Jackie the Kid is the nephew of Anthony "Tony Jack" Giacalone, the late Detroit mob boss who was set to meet Jimmy Hoffa the day the labor leader disappeared in 1975.

Phil is also good pals with Bryan Zuriff, the former executive producer of the Showtime hit *Ray Donovan*.

Working with Zuriff, Phil helped create and produce *The Match*, a made-for-TV golf series for Turner Sports featuring top pros competing with celebrities such as Tom Brady, Aaron Rodgers, Charles Barkley, and Peyton Manning. Phil starred in the inaugural event by defeating Tiger Woods in a twenty-two-hole match at the Shadow Creek Golf Course in Las Vegas and taking home $9 million in prize money.

Before he conceived *The Match*, Zuriff pleaded guilty to a felony in July 2013 in connection with his role in the operation of a high-stakes illegal gambling ring on the East and West Coasts with ties to a Russian American mob. Zuriff was one of thirty-four defendants named in a federal indictment charging members and associates of two organized-crime enterprises with racketeering, money laundering, extortion, and gambling-related offenses.

As part of his plea agreement Zuriff admitted he "operated his own illegal gambling enterprise in Los Angeles," booking several million dollars of bets through accounts on unlawful internet gambling sites and "assisted" a "vast" high-stakes illegal sportsbook in New York that "catered to millionaires and billionaires."

Zuriff was later sentenced to six months of home confinement, two years of probation, 300 hours of community service, 300 hours of community service, and a $20,000 fine.

. . .

In June 2022, I had finished hitting balls on the driving range at my club in Rancho Santa Fe and was walking back to my golf cart when I saw Phil approaching. At that point, we hadn't spoken in five years. He had never so much as written a note to me during my prison term.

"How are you doing?" Phil asked. "Great to see you out golfing. I'm glad to see you back."

A dozen or so club members milling nearby spotted Phil and me together and knew the score between us. You would have thought someone set off a stink bomb; nobody came within thirty feet of us. Our conversation lasted fewer than ten minutes.

We engaged in small talk before Phil tried to justify his decision not to testify at my trial. He said his lawyers didn't want him to face questions on the stand.

I cut him off right there. It was the same lame excuse he offered when we last met at my home in Carlsbad in the spring of 2017.

"Stop the bullshit," I told him. "Please don't insult my intelligence. All anyone wanted to know about was the relationship between you and me. All I wanted was for you to testify to the truth."

Phil stumbled and stammered a bit before simply saying, "I'm sorry."

The timing of his overdue apology was not lost on me. Phil had gone out of his way to publish two press statements to distance himself from me. The most recent was in January 2021, when he felt compelled to state publicly—and correctly—that he had not supported my commutation, contrary to a statement issued by the White House.

I suspect Phil was only apologizing because he was becoming an international outcast as part of the LIV Golf fiasco. He knew that he had betrayed our friendship. And he knew I was writing this book.

Sorry indeed.

21

Master Class

I didn't realize it then, but when I went broke the first time in my life—betting on the 1955 World Series at the age of nine with the Munfordville town grocer—I was taking the first step toward preparing me to write this chapter. Welcome to my master class for sports betting.

From that moment until now, I have been through more trials and tribulations than anyone could ever imagine. It's safe to say that, over the course of my sixty-plus years of betting, I have wagered billions of dollars (yes, billions).

I also have spent countless millions of dollars trying to stay ahead of the game. If we had not updated our computer models and I hadn't reinvented how I think about sports at least fifty different times, I would have been out of business way back during the Reagan administration.

The truth is, until I decided to write this book, I would not have taken $20 million to share the details of my system. Friends ask me why I'd want to give away my secrets now. The simple answer is I'm not getting any younger and I want to give something back to sports fans. I could write entire books about strategies and variables and databases and percentages, but I've tried to distill everything that I've learned into the next two chapters.

This chapter outlines my core principles and discusses the three key elements of successful sports betting: handicapping, betting strategy, and money management.

The following chapter dives deep into each of those elements. It includes charts and numbers that I've never shared before.

I want to say up front: I'm sharing details about *my* system. Your model can be what you want it to be. But there are bedrock principles of sports wagering that are important to know regardless of the specific system you use or the size of your wagers.

Also, while the next two chapters focus on the NFL, the methods outlined here can be applied to any sport. Over the course of my career, I've handicapped and bet nearly every sport. And I've been successful at it by following the guidelines that follow.

The Basics

It wasn't long ago that Nevada was the only place in America where you could make a legal sports wager. Now the sports-betting world is more competitive and complicated than ever, thanks to the emergence of BetMGM, DraftKings, FanDuel, Caesars, Circa, Pinnacle, and a host of other sites and mobile apps—none of which, I can assure you, exist to help you win.

And winning isn't easy: the odds are stacked against you from the start.

Let me start out with the absolute basics: there generally are many ways to bet, but the main one is spread betting.

In a spread bet, the score matters. For example, the Tampa Bay Bucs are favored by 7.5 points against the New Orleans Saints. You can either take Tampa Bay at –7.5 (which means they have to win by 8 points or more for you to win the bet) or New Orleans at +7.5 (which means they have to either lose by 7 points or fewer, or win the game, for you to win the bet). In either case, you generally must pay an additional 10 percent to make the bet. So a $100 wager will cost you $110. This is called the "juice" or the "vig," from the Russian/Yiddish word *vigorish*.

Because you have to pay that extra $10, it means you'll need to win 52.38 percent of the time to break even.

Here's another way of putting it: even if you pick winners half the time after laying $110 to win $100, you will only get back 95.4 percent of your money—because you have to pay the bookmaker. Consider you place two bets, laying $110/$100 for a total investment of $220. With one loss and one win, you get back $210 on your winning bet (your bet plus the winning of $100) and you lose $110 on the losing bet. Bottom line: you win $210 on a $220 investment, which is 95.4 percent. This is worse than most slot machines, which on average return about 96 percent of the money played. The odds are even worse if you're playing parlays and teasers, which we'll explain later.

In a moneyline bet, you're simply wagering on who will win. Moneyline bets are common in baseball, tennis, soccer, and other events where the scores tend to be smaller numbers, but you can bet the moneyline for any event.

Favorites in a moneyline bet are denoted with a minus sign. Underdogs are a plus sign. Let's say, for example, the Tampa Bay Bucs are playing the New Orleans Saints and Tampa is a −180 favorite and New Orleans is a +160 underdog. If you like Tampa to win, you must bet $180 to win $100. If you like New Orleans, you bet $100 to win $160. The final score doesn't matter—you win if your team wins. The bookmaker's fee is baked into the numbers.

My primary message is that the average Joe or Jane faces an almost insurmountable set of disadvantages that virtually guarantee a significant loss over the long term unless you can flip the odds in your favor. I did that for thirty-six consecutive years, and I've developed a set of core principles for sports wagering that I'll share with you now:

- Everything begins and ends with identifying value.

- Maintain an investment fund approach to betting.

- Only make big bets when the opportunity presents itself. Keep your bets to 1 to 3 percent of your bankroll.

- Time equals money—the more time you invest to analyze teams and opportunities, the better your chances of finding value.

- Stick to the facts. Avoid being a fan driven by emotion and loyalty.

- Understand the value of points. In football, the value of 3, 6, 7, and 14 outweigh other numbers—with 3 and 7 being the most important, simply because of the way football scores touchdowns and field goals.

- Understand the value of a half point in football. It's been the second-most important factor in my success. (Handicapping being first.) A significant number of NFL games are decided by 2 to 8 points. If you can bet a spread with an extra half point, it can make all the difference in the world. Our team has mathematical formulas that show the actual values of these numbers, which I'll share with you in the next chapter.

- Shop around to get the best prices. Set up betting accounts at different venues. Compare odds and prices. This is a must! Every cent matters, especially over the course of a season. The difference between winning and losing is razor-thin; make sure you're getting the best prices/odds before you make your bets.

- Keep learning. I've been betting for more than six decades, and I learn new things all the time.

Handicapping

Being a good handicapper is, of course, essential to being a winning sports bettor. I have teams of handicappers that develop power ratings for every NFL team—and ratings on every single player, in addition to keeping statistics on all of the important factors that go into a game. We make outcome predictions for every NFL game, just like the Las Vegas bookmakers. And I bet my opinion against those bookmakers' opinion. My track record speaks for itself.

Many sports bettors do not have the time or expertise for in-depth handicapping, which is understandable. So use the resources that are publicly available, from ESPN to local newspapers. But here are a few key tips that every sports bettor should know.

Home Field Advantage

The standard NFL home field advantage, taking fanfare, folklore, and conventional wisdom into consideration, is generally thought to be worth 3 points. Well, not so fast. The actual average home field advantage, taking into account every NFL game from 1974 to 2022, is closer to 2.5 points. In addition, the home field advantage over the last four years of NFL football is actually less than 1 point (thanks largely to COVID).

If you had made the mistake of using 3 points for the average home field advantage over the last three years, you certainly would have lost. This is a variable that needs constant updating to keep up with trends. I do a lot of reading and examining scoring trends over time to determine exactly what advantage home field affords.

Also, the average home field advantage is different based on specific cities. Some teams enjoy extra special advantages due to geography (think the Denver Broncos) or weather (think teams built for the cold or hot weather such as the Green Bay Packers or Miami Dolphins). Overall attendance, the presence of rabid fans, the comforts of home, home field familiarity, and travel issues for the visitors are other factors that may also affect home field advantage.

Prevent

Prevent is the tendency to relax defensively when holding the lead late in a half or in the game.

It is important to understand each team's tendencies. Do they play soft with a lead or not? Does the coaching staff rest key players when the lead is big? Do they play prevent defenses when they're ahead by double digits?

These are crucial things to study and understand. If you learn these tendencies, you will see that some teams are much better to bet on, regardless of whether they are a favorite or an underdog.

Injuries

Injuries and illness can significantly affect a team's performance. To me, this is a hugely important factor in gaining a handicapping advantage. It is absolutely critical to know who is playing in each game, who is not playing, and who is playing hurt.

We closely monitor NFL injury reports and look at media and other sources for key information about the extent of injuries.

It's also important to understand the terminology. Nothing is set in stone, but here are the NFL guidelines:

- Out: They won't play.

- Doubtful: Unlikely to play. Significantly less than 50 percent chance they'll suit up. This has changed with time; teams are more cautious about playing doubtful players these days.

- Questionable: You'll hear this a lot. It's viewed as a fifty-fifty proposition that a player will be on the field. And this is where you need to pay very close attention, especially if it involves a key player.

When handicapping for injuries, you must have a good sense of the quality of the backup. Will the team or the opponent adjust its strategy because of the injured player? If so, adjust your thinking accordingly.

You also have to factor in cluster or stack injuries. If more than one player at key positions are injured, it can have an exponential effect. I'll discuss this more fully in the next chapter.

Game Factors

We also consider many other factors that could affect an individual game situation. They include:

- Turf: Is the visitor playing on different turf than its home field?

- Divisional play: Visitors tend to play tougher in divisional matchups.

- Teams coming off Thursday night: The extra rest time often helps.

- Teams traveling and the distance traveled: Long trips have an effect.

- Consecutive weeks on the road: The second consecutive road game is more difficult than the first, and the third is more difficult than the second.

- Teams coming off byes: Again, a week's rest may or may not help. It depends on the team.

- Teams changing time zones.

- Temperature differences: Warm weather team to cold.

- Rain, snow: Some teams do much better than others in adverse conditions.

All of these factors are listed and ranked in the next chapter. Remember, good handicapping is essential to successful sports wagering. But handicapping alone won't guarantee maximum success. It's only part of my three-pronged plan; betting strategy and money management also are essential.

Betting Strategy

After you've developed a handicapping strategy, it's time to think about betting. But before you start betting, you must develop a betting strategy. The goal is simple: to get the best price. But getting the best price is not easy or simple. It requires some work. Here are some key elements of any successful betting strategy.

- Know all your options. There are multiple places to make bets—more legal places than ever before. And the number of bookmakers just seems to keep growing, with television networks and sports leagues working in tandem with gaming companies to promote sports betting.

- Don't just bet with one casino or betting site—you're a chump if you do. You need to shop around to get the best price. To be successful, you must be fully informed.

- Set up as many accounts as you can. Don't be wed to the same bookmaker. Just be sure it's legal and you are confident you can get paid.

- Familiarize yourself with betting resources. There are a few sites that aggregate information, pulling from hundreds of sportsbooks. I recommend five key sportsbooks every bettor should monitor, whether you bet with them or not. These market leaders—they post odds the earliest and take the biggest bets—provide a very strong indicator of how betting lines are moving, and knowing how the lines are moving is an absolute must in a betting strategy. They are: Circa, MGM, Caesars, Sports411, and Pinnacle.

- DonBest.com, Vegas Insider, and SpankOdds.com are industry aggregators, chock-full of resources for shopping prices. At these sites, you'll see the opening lines, current lines, and differences in odds and pricing by different books, and you'll easily see how the lines move during the day and week.

- Bet favorites early and dogs late. This is a general rule of thumb. There are exceptions, which I will explore later.

- Specific numbers matter far more than other numbers, and small percentages will make or break you over time. Bookmakers allow you to buy points, in half-point increments, to increase your chances of winning a game. You must know how and when to buy onto and off of points to increase the odds in your favor, but only if you can buy them at the right price. I have a few charts and some examples in the following chapter to help guide you.

- Understand the value of half points. The NFL season has 272 games. If you could use a half point for all those games, that would be 136 points over the course of a season. Getting (or buying only at the right price) that extra half point can make the difference between winning and losing. I'll explain the strategy behind half points in the next chapter.

- Know when to bet the point spread and when to bet the moneyline. Always bet the one that includes the most value. I've included a very helpful chart in the betting strategy section of the next chapter that compares the moneyline to the spread.

- Be disciplined. Have a plan and stick to it. Don't try to recover losses by making bets that are not in your plan. Chasing losses on Sunday and Monday night games is a recipe for disaster, just as betting the long shot in the last race at the racetrack to get even is usually a sucker's bet.

- If the difference between your line and the sportsbook's line is significant enough, this becomes a play for you. However, before you bet, you must determine how much to bet. That will depend on the point differential and the value of the points involved. I've also provided charts in the next chapter that will show the value of each point, and the value of buying half points.

- I bet at different times during the week. I bet early when I think I'm getting the best number and I bet late if I think I'm getting a better number. I'm always watching the key sportsbooks to see how the lines are moving, and I pay attention to key numbers and the value of those numbers. You'll read more about that in the next chapter.

I cannot stress enough that, when betting, search not just for the best number, but also the best price. The industry standard is $110/$100, but you may find bookmakers with better prices. Pinnacle, an offshore, regulated bookmaker that is not available to U.S. citizens, offers $105/$100 on some bets. Over time, that lower price matters greatly. In a $110/$100 bet, you have to win 52.38 percent of the time. With a $105/$100, you have to win 51.2 percent of the time. That difference is significant.

Teasers and Parlays

Parlays and teasers are popular wagers, especially among football bettors. They're a little bit like the lottery—they offer a bigger payday, but they're not easy to win. And the house loves them for one reason: they are much more profitable than a straight bet.

Because the house has the advantage, every bettor starts out at a disadvantage—that disadvantage is the expected loss, which is the amount a bettor would be expected to lose if placing a bet at the same odds multiple times, without the benefit of any smart handicapping.

In a straight bet laying $110 to win $100, the expected loss is 4.6 percent. Under the current rules in which a tie is a non-bet, a two-team parlay has an expected loss of 9.8 percent—more than twice the expected loss of a straight bet laying $110/$100. A three-team parlay has an expected loss of 12.4 percent, almost three times the expected loss of a straight bet.

My message: relative to a $110/$100 straight bet, two-team and three-team parlays are not smart options at current prices—period, exclamation point. I'll provide more detail about parlays and teasers in the next chapter.

Money Management

Properly managing your money is almost as important as handicapping and betting strategy.

The first order of business: sit down and decide what you want to risk. Start with the assumption that you'll lose it all. The simple fact is you can't play without a bankroll, so the top priority should be to do everything possible to protect the money you decide to risk.

With that thought in mind, I recommend that you set specific limits on how much you wager. Ideally, you should not risk any more than 1 to 3 percent of your bankroll on any single bet. This allows you to spread the risk and limit significant losses.

I like to bet in units. For purely illustrative purposes, let's say you have a $10,000 bankroll and want to bet in units of $100, or 1 percent. So you've got one hundred units to start with.

I also recommend you bet in half units ranging from 0.5 to 3 units and the number of units you wager is based on your handicap analysis. For instance, you could assign a star value to each game— the higher your confidence in the bet, the more stars you'll assign. Some games may be between numbers, so you should make a 1.5- or 2.5-unit bet rather than a 2- or 3-unit bet.

Most important: be disciplined.

Taxes

Last and certainly not least, there's Uncle Sam.

As sports betting expands across the United States, we need Congress to start looking at some issues regarding taxation and sports wagering.

It's my experience that some serious investors in the stock market want to bet—and bet big—on sports. But these people are not stupid. They're used to paying 20 percent tax on long-term gains. In sports betting, you're taxed as if your earnings are ordinary income. In 2023, that's as high as 37 percent for a couple filing jointly, plus another 3.8 percent for a net investment tax. Add in state taxes and you're at or above 50 percent in some states.

Also, you can't carry forward any of your wagering losses. Under the current IRS tax code, losses sustained in real estate, stocks, bonds, or business can be carried over from one year to the next. Not so with legalized gambling,

One of the great advantages of betting in Europe is any money you win gambling, if you're a European citizen, is tax-free. Countries like England have long realized that bettors, or punters as they are called in England, almost never win and betting on sports is as much a part of their culture as soccer. Legalized gaming promotes jobs and creates other forms of tax. They know the average recreational bettor has no chance of winning over time, yet they encourage gambling because it employs thousands of people, generates taxes, and provides recreation to citizens that is free of crime. They regulate it to make sure it's honest.

As sports wagering becomes more and more mainstream, I certainly hope we see a more concerted effort to improve the tax laws for gaming. At least make it fair. Currently it isn't treated that way because industry leaders have not done anything about it. State and federal governments will make their money by expanding customer participation and creating jobs and taxes on income from the industry.

Unfortunately, I do not believe the U.S. betting public is aware of this and I'm concerned there are thousands of bettors who are going to be getting surprise tax bills. The sports-betting industry needs to be more proactive in protecting its customers.

As I wrap up this chapter, let me make one thing abundantly clear: no system is foolproof. There is no magic formula to guarantee wins. You could follow every last bit of my advice and still lose.

Above all, know your limits. As a former degenerate gambler, I cannot stress this enough. Hunt for value and be disciplined with your betting. I promise you this: if you don't run out of money, you won't run out of things to bet on.

22

Advanced Master Class

In the last chapter, I shared the basics of sports betting. In this chapter, I'm going to give you a deeper look at how I handicap sports. In doing so, I'll reveal the secrets to my success, such as the value of certain numbers and everything that goes into creating a power rating. (We will again use the NFL as an example.) This chapter is not for the faint of heart—there's a lot of math and statistics involved. You'll see how much work we do to stay ahead of the game.

First off, I've been successful because I've worked with some of the brightest minds in the business, true geniuses when it comes to computer modeling and probability theory. For years, my proprietary betting models were built by teams of best-in-class handicappers, quants, and statisticians.

Over the years, my brain trust of more than twenty-five people has included a guy who was number one in his class at Caltech, a department chair of economics at a major U.S. university, mathematical savants, computer wizards, PhDs, and quantitative and database handicappers who live and breathe algorithms and theoretical angles not found in your average textbook.

Our team members act like hedge fund analysts, assigning a numerical value to every conceivable factor or variable capable of affecting sporting events to within a tenth of a point.

In the NFL alone, I have several teams of experts working independently. They have never met each other, even though most have worked with me for more than thirty years, funneling their information to one common denominator: me.

After more than six decades of sports wagering, I know the strengths and weaknesses of every player on my team, which allows me to weigh their numbers and ratings. Then, and only then, do I decide whether or not to make a bet.

Power Ratings

Because of the abundance of information on sports these days—and the ease of access to it—nearly anyone can develop a handicapping system. This would have been extremely difficult just twenty years ago.

The flowchart below outlines the specific steps for how my system works. You start out each season with power ratings for each

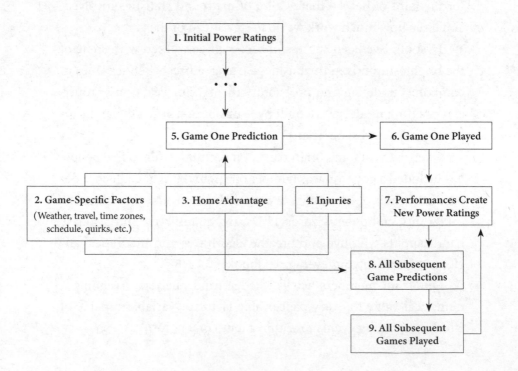

team (step 1, labeled "Initial Power Ratings" in the chart), with game-specific factors (step 2), home field advantage (step 3), and an assessment of injuries (step 4).

Once you arrive at a game score prediction, you compare the prediction to the posted point spread (step 5) and act accordingly. Then the game is actually played (step 6).

After the game ends, you need to prepare for the next week's games. This starts with creating new power ratings for each team (step 7). The repeat cycle is then in place—the new power ratings are combined with game-specific factors (step 2), home field advantage (step 3), and an assessment of injuries (step 4) to determine the next game prediction (step 5). This is shown in step 8.

Then the next game is played (step 9), and that information is used for the subsequent power rating. Repeat, repeat, repeat until the season ends.

To begin, you can easily find some very good sources for power ratings in the NFL, college football, and other sports. In no particular order, they are ESPN, Sagarin, GoldSheet, Massey Ratings, Sonny Moore's Computer Power Ratings, and Kenny White Sports. Again, these ratings must be in point-spread equivalent units. Most professional handicappers, including me and my team, assemble a new season rating by starting with each team's rating at the end of the previous season. We then have databases that include values for each player, each coach, each draft choice. We use an addition/subtraction system—essentially a bookkeeping approach—to create a preseason rating.

Remember: in this system, everything must be in a point-spread equivalent value. We assign a point-spread equivalent value to every coach, every player, every division rivalry, etc. We then use basic math to arrive at a power rating. The power ratings then determine how we think teams will perform against each other.

Our power ratings generally range between +10 (think Kansas City Chiefs of 2022) and –10 (think Houston in 2022). The average team has a rating of 0. Good teams have positive ratings, weak teams have negative ratings.

Here's a specific example: the New York Giants ended the 2021 season with a −7 rating (negative values are bad, positive values are good). The 2021 Giants were not very good. During the off-season, the franchise drafted well (+2.0 points), employed a new coaching staff (+1.6 points), had some acquisitions (+1.8 points), and we expected key players to improve in the 2022 season (QB Daniel Jones and RB Saquon Barkley). On the negative side, the Giants lost players via free agency, trade, and waivers that amounted to −3.9 points.

On the plus side: $2 + 1.6 + 1.8 + 2.2 = 7.6$. On the negative side: −3.9. Net change: +3.7. So the −7 Giants gain a net +3.7 points in the off-season to start the season at −3.3. As you'll read below, we then adjust that power rating every week throughout the season—for every team.

Each element of a successful handicapping system is important, and the smallest factors can make the difference between success and failure. These factors can play small, medium, or large roles, but they all play a role.

- Relative strength or power of the competing teams, which establishes strength differential on a neutral field. These relative power ratings will change over the season and from end of season to the beginning of the next season.

- Each team's previous performances.

- Home field advantage, which could vary by each home and away team.

- Individual values for each player on each team.

- Presence of injuries or illnesses that affect a team's relative power. Note that injuries/illnesses will subtract from a team's relative power. Not only do you need to adjust based on players out for the week, but you also must adjust based on active players who are playing with an injury.

- Game factors such as weather, each team's previous schedule (e.g., byes, multiple away games in a row, etc.), travel distance/difficulty, stadium quirks, and turf types.

- Motivational factors such as revenge, rivalries, coaching changes, etc.

Only after we quantify and weigh each of these factors do we arrive at a predicted outcome for each game—what we see as the competitive difference between two opposing teams. The magnitude of any differential between the two lines—the bookmaker's and ours—offers an initial indication of the size of the bet. Remember, the final determination on the size of the bet will depend on the price you get.

Relative Power of Teams

The first variable to consider when creating a game prediction is the relative strength or power of the opposing teams, aka the power rating. You need to develop or find a power rating that is enumerated in point-spreads/game-equivalent values. ESPN's NFL rating, for example, is called FPI, Football Power Index.

Two important conclusions can be drawn from this type of system. First, understanding the relative importance of past performance will be essential to predicting performance going forward. Second, it is essential to start with a good power rating for each team and that rating must be in points.

Most handicappers use similar logic to predict future performance based on past performances. The key assumption of this type of model is that more recent games are more important than games that happened in previous weeks. We calculate power ratings every week for every NFL team, using a formula that I'll outline below.

These expected power ratings are numerical values and are directly transferable into point-spread differentials. Say the Chicago Bears have an expected performance (or power rating) of 10, and the Minnesota Vikings have an expected performance of 7. The Bears would be a three-point favorite. But you must adjust your raw power rating to account for the specific factors that will affect this particular game. Every game will have different factors that only apply to that matchup.

In the last chapter, I outlined most of those key factors. I'll expand upon some of them in more detail below.

Player Rankings

You need to assign numerical values for all key players—offense and defense. In the NFL, that means keeping values for approximately 1,700 active roster players. It's not as difficult as it sounds because at least 60 percent of NFL players have a near-zero value. That leaves approximately six hundred players with significant non-zero numerical values.

There are several potential systems for valuing players. For example, you could use the ESPN player ranking or the Madden player rankings. But, remember, a rank order does not produce a point-spread-relevant numerical value. You need to convert these rankings to be compatible with point spreads and power ratings.

Consider one such point-spread-consistent system. You could start by estimating the numerical worth of "star" players, identified by your own rankings or from published reports on top-tier players. Quarterbacks, for instance, are worth an average of a little more than a touchdown, with the best worth more. The best non-QB players generally rank between 2.5 and 3 points.

Injuries and illnesses can significantly affect a team's performance. To me, this is the second-most important factor in gaining a handicapping advantage in sports. Therefore, as noted in the previous chapter, it is absolutely critical to know who is playing in each game, who is not playing, and who is playing hurt. If a player is injured, but still playing, you would reduce his point value based on the extent of the injury. If the player is out, you remove his point value, but add back in a point value for his replacement, if that player has a point value.

Also be aware of stack or cluster injuries. Multiple injuries at key positions can have an exponential impact—and it varies by position and team. The most important non-quarterback positions for stack injuries are pass receivers (wideouts, slot receivers, and tight ends), defensive line, offensive line, defensive backs, linebackers, and running backs.

Let's say the two top receivers on a team are injured. One is valued at 2.5 points; the other is 1.5. We don't assume that their loss equals 4 points; because they are the top two receivers, the combination may be worth 50 percent more, or 6 points. If it's a defensive lineman, you might only add 40 percent to it. And so on.

Regarding the importance of injuries and their effect on overall team performance, here's a great example from the NFL: Tampa Bay's offensive tackle Tristan Wirfs usually wouldn't be considered a high-impact player. But when Tampa Bay met the Los Angeles Rams in the 2022 playoffs, Wirfs was injured and, because of the unique set of circumstances involving that game, his absence had a major impact.

The Rams, led by all-world defensive tackle Aaron Donald, had a ferocious pass rush, and Tom Brady was not the most mobile of quarterbacks. Wirfs, who we normally graded at 1.3 points or so in the regular season, suddenly became a lot more valuable because of his injury—maybe worth as many as 6 points.

Here's why. With Wirfs out, his backup (normally worth 0.3 points) was also injured, but playing. Therefore, with an injury, he was worth no points. We knew the cumulative totals of that injury, along with Wirfs's absence, were going to have a significant impact on the Bucs' performance and the outcome of the game. Add the disappearance of wide receiver Antonio Brown, who had left the team weeks earlier, the loss of wide receiver Chris Godwin, and, therefore, the need for tight end Rob Gronkowski to stay inside to help block the pass rush, and I knew the Bucs were in trouble.

I wagered accordingly and won the bet, largely because I knew that an injured offensive line was going to change the dynamics of this game. I would have acted differently in the same scenario if the team had a more mobile quarterback or a stronger running attack. Again, these are the special situations in which you have to understand the value of each player, the quality of the opponent, and the overall impact on the score of the game.

We closely monitor NFL injury reports and look at media and other sources for key information about the extent of injuries. We have a software program that electronically scrapes social media accounts of key journalists and bloggers to know that information instantaneously.

For example, we monitor social media accounts of NFL beat writers; we pay attention to pro football medical experts Dr. David Chao (@profootballdoc) and director of physical therapy Edwin Porras (@FBInjuryDoc), who provide real-time injury analysis on Twitter. We closely monitor who participates in practices, Wednesday through Friday. If they're practicing Wednesday, it's almost a lock that they'll play Sunday unless they're injured in practice.

Some coaches have hard-and-fast rules, such as you don't play if you don't practice on Friday. You need to pay attention to the player and the injury as well as the coach. Know a coach's tendencies when it comes to reporting injuries—there's gamesmanship by coaches in revealing a team's game-day lineup. We assign percentage values to injuries; a wide receiver with a foot injury is more likely to be affected than, say, an offensive lineman with a pulled hamstring.

Once you have a good sense of injuries, then you'll need to adjust your player ratings accordingly. I provide a formula for doing so later in the chapter. These ratings may adjust by tenths of a point or full points, but cumulatively, they are going to have an impact on the score.

Joey Bosa, a six-foot-five, 280-pound, game-changing outside linebacker for the Los Angeles Chargers, is a good example. When he's healthy, Bosa is worth 2.5 points a game in our rankings. That can be worth changing a big bet to no bet or vice versa.

So how *questionable* is Bosa when he's injured? We investigate all the sources above and then and only then do we start asking: Is his knee injury a full point downgrade? A half a point? A point and three-quarters? Is there a significant drop in his backup? These are essential decisions for handicappers.

Remember: quarterbacks are different, in that they are much more valuable than other position players. Therefore, it is important to create a quarterback-only ratings system. Both long-term and short-term performances metrics need to be analyzed.

Long-term variables that should be considered for each season, and career prior to that season, are:

- The NFL quarterback rating

- The quarterback's total pass attempts

- The average yards per pass attempt

- Total interceptions thrown

- Total yards gained rushing by the quarterback

- Total times sacked

- Total fumbles by the quarterback

Other potential considerations when evaluating quarterbacks are the quality of the supporting offensive players, the strength of schedule, and the strength of each opponent.

What does this look like in real terms?

In our system, there are currently 991 non-QB players who have values that equal or exceed 0.10—this would be my group of non-zero players. The average value for these non-zero players is 0.63. Of those 991 non-QB players, only 612 players have values that exceed 0.25, which are meaningful values.

We have sixty-seven ranked quarterbacks in our current database. These QBs have an average value of 7.74, with a minimum value of 6.0 and a maximum value of 9.5 (with Kansas City QB Patrick Mahomes at the top).

Bottom line: About 40 percent of the players in the league have meaningful values. That's why it's important to understand injuries and player status.

Game Factors

Okay, let's summarize. We are trying to develop a scientifically accurate prediction of an NFL football game. To this point, we have considered each team's power rating (which includes player and coach values), home field advantage, and injuries/illness (which adjust player values depending on the injury and replacement).

Next, as outlined briefly in the last chapter, there are other factors that could affect an individual game situation: the expected weather, each team's previous schedule (e.g., byes, multiple away games in a row, etc.), travel distance/difficulty, stadium quirks, and turf types.

For every one of these factors, we have analyzed historical data from 1974 to 2023 and created a point-spread consistent value. Each number in these factors is worth one-fifth of a point. So if the factors add up to 5, you will adjust your power ranking by 1 point. If it's 10, then it's worth 2 points.

Game factors are very important. These factors include S-factors (special situations), W-factors (weather), and E-factors (emotional).

All these game factors are based on long-term statistical analysis and are defined below.

One important note: the numbers here are from the end of the 2022–23 season. These are not necessarily the exact numbers we'll use in the future because we always reevaluate from year to year, upgrading, downgrading, or even eliminating some factors based on trends.

Most of these factors should be self-explanatory, with either the home team or visiting team benefitting from that specific factor. In those cases where you see "Variable," you will need to know more about each particular team's strengths and weaknesses to assess the value of the factors for that matchup. For example, very high winds in an open, outdoor stadium will hurt a passing team and favor a running team. High winds also are likely to reduce the total score.

S and W Factors for 2022 NFL Season

S-Factors (0.20/S)

Turf

Home and Visitor have Same Turf	+1 Visitor
Home and Visitor have Opposite Turf	+1 Home

Division

Home and Visitor are in Same Division	+1 Visitor

Conference

Home and Visitor from Different Conferences	+1 Home

Schedule

Home Team Thursday Night	+2 Home
Teams Coming off Thursday Night	0
Home Team Sunday Night	+4 Home
Home Team Monday Night	+2 Home
Home Team Coming off Monday Night and Home	0

Home Team Coming off Monday Night and Away	+4 Opponent
Away Team Coming off Monday Night and Home	+6 Opponent
Away Team Coming off Monday Night and Away	+8 Opponent
Home Team Saturday Night	0
3rd Away Game in Four Games	+2 Home
Team Coming off Home Over-time Game	+4 Opponent
Team Coming off Away Over-time Game	+2 Opponent

Bye

Below Average Team Coming off Bye	+4 Team
Below Average Team Coming off Bye and Away	+5 Team
Average Team Coming off Bye	+5 Team
Average Team Coming off Bye and Away	+6 Team
Great Team Coming off Bye	+7 Team
Great Team Coming off Bye and Away	+8 Team

Playoffs

Bye in the Playoffs	+1 Home

Super Bowl Teams

Winner of Super Bowl— First Game of Next Season	+4 Team
Winner of Super Bowl— First Four Games of Next Season	+2 Team
Loser of Super Bowl— First Game of Next Season	+4 Opponent
Loser of Super Bowl— First Four Games of Next Season	+2 Opponent

Travel Distance

2000 plus miles	+1 Home
TB/Jac/Mia	+1 Visitor
Dal/Hou	+1 Visitor
Atl/Car	+1 Visitor

LAR/LAC	+2 Visitor
LV/LA	+1 Visitor
Ind/Cin	+1 Visitor
Phl/NYG, NYJ, WAS, NE, Bal, Buf	
(any combination except)	+1 Visitor
NYG/NYJ	+2 Visitor
Bal/Was	+2 Visitor
Chc/GB	+1 Visitor

Time Zones

10:00 a.m. Games	Penalize West teams	+2 Opponent
	Penalize Mountain teams	+1 Opponent
Night Games	Penalize East teams	+6 Opponent
	Penalize Central teams	+3 Opponent
	Penalize Mountain teams	+1 Opponent
Teams Playing Second Consecutive Game		
at Least 2 Time Zones Away		+2 Home

Bounce Back

Team Lost Previous Game by 19+ Points	+2 Team
Team Lost Previous Game by 29+ Points	+4 Team

Matchup Situations

Offensive and Defensive Matchups, Injuries	Variable

W-Factors (0.20/W)

Warm Team to a Cold Outdoor Environment

If Temperature is 35 Degrees Fahrenheit	+0.25 Home
If Temperature is 30 Degrees Fahrenheit	+0.50 Home
If Temperature is 25 Degrees Fahrenheit	+0.75 Home
If Temperature is 20 Degrees Fahrenheit	+1.00 Home
If Temperature is 15 Degrees Fahrenheit	+1.25 Home
If Temperature is 10 or below Degrees Fahrenheit	+1.75 Home

Cold Dome Team to a Cold Outdoor Environment

30–20 Degrees Fahrenheit	+0.25 Home
20–10 Degrees Fahrenheit	+0.50 Home
10–5 Degrees Fahrenheit	+0.75 Home
Rain	+0.25 Visitor
Hard Rain	+0.75 Visitor
Snow	Variable
Heavy Wind	Variable

These W-factors can also be dependent on quarterback performance. Each quarterback in the league is evaluated in a variety of situations (home, away, day, night, turf types, and weather conditions—presence of precipitation, wind conditions, and temperature).

These performances are evaluated at the end of the season and periodically throughout the season. W-factors are assessed where warranted. For example, Josh Allen of Buffalo gets +1 W for hot temperatures and dome games. Surprisingly, he loses –1 W for cold-weather games. Aaron Rodgers is the exact opposite; he tends to perform better in cold weather than hot. Each of the quarterback W-factors is worth 0.15 points.

E-Factors—These are emotional factors related to recent previous performance or unique playoff situations. For example, one team has lost two games in a row, or one team has playoff possibilities, and the other team does not. Each E-factor is worth 0.2 points. In addition to the examples above, the list of the relevant situations that receive E-factor consideration include: (1) coaching movements; (2) player movements; (3) the relative importance of the game for each specific team, as determined through an examination of the schedule meaning or as indicated by coaches/players; and (4) results history.

Creating/Updating Power Ratings

Each week, you will need to update your power ratings based on all the factors above. We use a relatively simple mathematical formula.

The new power rating is 90 percent of the old power rating plus 10 percent of what I call the True Game Performance Level. You arrive at the True Game Performance Level by calculating the net score of the last game and adding or subtracting that opponent's old power rating and the net injury differential.

This may seem complicated, but it's not. To help, I'll share the following example. Let's use the Bears and Vikings.

The Bears played the Vikings on a neutral field (i.e., no home field advantage):

(1) Going into the game, the Bears had a power rating of 10 and the Vikings had a power rating of 4;

(2) The Bears had an injury level of 3.5 and the Vikings had an injury level of 1.7;

(3) The Bears win the game, 27–20.

Before we figure out the Bears' new power rating, we must determine the True Game Performance Level. It is calculated this way:

Net Score = Bears +7

Add Opponent's (Vikings) old power rating = +4

Add Differential of Injuries (Bears injury number minus Vikings injury number): (3.5 –1.7) = 1.8

So the True Game Performance Level for the Bears is:
7 + 4 + 1.8 = 12.8

Now, go back to our Power Rating Formula: 90 percent of the old power rating + 10 percent of the True Game Performance Level. It looks like this: 90% of 10 + 10% of 12.8 is 9.0 + 1.28 = 10.28

By beating the Vikings, 27–20, and accounting for injuries to both teams, the Bears' power rating goes from 10 to 10.28.

Now let's calculate the Vikings' new power rating.

The True Game Performance Level for the Vikings is calculated as follows:

Net Score = –7

Bears' power rating = +10

Net Injury Differential (Vikings minus Bears injuries [1.7 – 3.5]) = –1.8

True Game Performance Level: –7 + 10 + (–1.8) = 1.2

So the Vikings' Power Rating Formula is 90% of 4 + 10% of 1.2, which is 3.60 + 0.12 = 3.72

By losing, 27–20, to the Bears, the Vikings' power rating has dropped from 4 to 3.72.

The table below provides some additional examples. The key thing to remember is that, when creating a new power rating for a specific team, all relevant values must be from the perspective of that team. That is, the team's True Game Performance Level receives positive credit for its own injuries, its opponent's rating, and its net score. The team's True Game Performance Level receives a debit for its opponent's injuries. Once the True Game Performance Level is determined, then the team's new power rating is a combination of the old rating and the True Game Performance Level.

Let's look at the first example in the table. Remember, my formula is 90 percent of the old team rating + 10 percent of the True Game Performance Level. In that example, the True Game Perfor-

TABLE 1 Updating Power Ratings Examples

TEAM RATING	TEAM INJURIES	OPPONENT RATING	OPPONENT INJURIES	NET SCORE	TRUE GAME PERFORMANCE LEVEL	NEW TEAM RATING
8	4.7	−4.2	6.5	14	8.0	8.0
6.2	3.5	9.0	1.8	−10	0.70	5.65
−4.5	3.8	11	5.1	−8	1.7	−3.88
7.6	4.1	2.1	3.8	7	9.4	7.78
−2.8	1.9	6.4	2.8	−21	−15.5	−4.07
5.0	5.4	7.6	2.9	11	21.1	6.61

mance Level is 14 (the net score) + the old power rating of the opponent (−4.2), and the net injuries (4.7 − 6.5 = −1.8). So the formula for the True Game Performance Level is 14 −4.2 − 1.8 = 8.

Thus, the new power rating is 90 percent of 8 (7.2) + 10 percent of 8 (0.8) for a new power rating of 8.

Over time, you'll get the hang of doing this.

For those still with me, let's add in one more complicating factor. The earlier example (Bears vs. Vikings) was somewhat contrived because the game was played on a neutral field.

In actual practice, very few NFL games are played on neutral fields, with games in London, Mexico City, and now Germany being notable exceptions. This implies that for almost every game there is a home field advantage that must be accounted for in the True Game Performance Level. For purposes of these calculations, assume that home field advantage = 2.0. If the Bears are the home team and win, 27–20, then you subtract 2.0 from the True Game Performance Level to account for home field advantage. Similarly, if the Vikings are the away team and lose, 27–20, then you add 2.0 to the Vikings' True Game Performance Level.

It looks like this:

True Game Performance Level for home team Bears = 7 (score differential) + 4 (opponent's power rating) + 1.8 (injury differential) –2.0 (home field disadvantage) = 10.8

The True Game Performance Level for visiting Vikings = –7 (score differential) + 10 (opponent's power rating) + (–1.8) (injury differential) +2.0 (home field advantage) = 3.2

The resulting new team ratings would be:

Bears: 90% of 10 + 10% of 10.8 is 9.0 + 1.08 = 10.08

Vikings: 90% of 4 + 10% of 3.2 is 3.60 + 0.32 = 3.92

Once you have updated the power ratings, you need to start thinking about home/away and other game factors that are likely to influence the next week's score. Just as you did with home/away results, you should deduct game factors and injuries from each team's power ratings as you head into the weekend.

The number of factors assigned in a matchup can vary greatly. In the 2022–23 season, we assigned as many as 18 S-factor points to a team in one week. We also had matchups in which no factors were assigned. On average, we assigned 3.2 S-factors per team per week—which equate to an average power rating adjustment of 0.64 points per team for that specific matchup.

S-Factors in 2022–23:
Smallest Value = 0
Largest Value = 18
Average Value = 3.2

Your final step is to adjust your power rating by adding or subtracting the point-spread equivalent game factors (5 factor points equal 1 point-spread point).

Then you compare the two power ratings. If Team A has a power rating of +3 and Team B has a rating of –2, Team A is a 5-point favorite in your system.

Betting Strategy

After you've done your calculations and arrived at a predicted score, it's time to think about wagering. I bet anywhere from five to ten games per week in the NFL season. But I bet only those games when there's a large enough difference in our predicted spread and the quoted line. The bigger the spread between our prediction and the established line, the more I bet.

You'll also want to watch how other money is coming in—if it's coming in for your team, you may want to increase your bet (by no more than a half star), or if the line moves significantly against you (watch the key bookmakers), you may want to reduce the size of your bet. Especially if there are a lot of injuries or morale concerns.

It is critical you remain disciplined about managing your bankroll. As your bankroll grows, so does your unit price. Because unit sizes are in percentages (1 percent of bankroll, for instance), your unit sizes will automatically adjust based on winning and losing—that takes the guesswork out of determining how much to bet.

Again, remain disciplined.

The Value of Numbers

As I mentioned earlier, certain numbers are more valuable than other numbers when you're betting football. We investigated number values for every game in the National Football League since 1974 and created the chart below.

These numbers can change over time. For instance, if game rules change—extra points are now kicked from the thirty-two-yard line, and more coaches go for two after touchdowns—then some numbers will become more important, some less important over time. As you can see in the chart below, the number 3 has the highest relative value—by far. It carries a weighted value of 8 percent.

Think about that for a second. In mathematical terms, it means *8 percent of the time* when the spread is 3, the favorite is going to win by three points. That's more than any other number, so 3 is far and away the single most valuable number in NFL football betting. As you'll see in the chart, 3 is relatively more valuable than 11, 12, and 13 combined, which are only worth 6 percent total.

It's important to understand the relative value of points, particularly as the spread moves during the week.

If the underdog is getting 6.5 and you like the underdog, it's best to wait to see if more money comes in for the favorite. The line might move to 7 or you may be able to buy 7 at an attractive

The Relative Value of Each Point, NFL

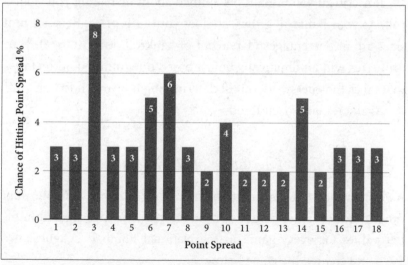

* The values in the table above are rounded for presentation purposes. Numbers above a half or more are rounded up; half or less is rounded down. For example, the percentage 3.5 gets rounded to 4; 3.4 would be rounded down to 3.

price—and that's a big percentage advantage for you (6 = 5 percent, while 7 is 6 percent). If the line goes the other way, say from 6.5 to 6, it's not as big of a disadvantage, so the risk-reward remains in your favor. And if you're betting the dog and the number is 7.5, grab it as fast as you can—you don't want the line to drop to 7. If it goes to 8, it's not all that significant (8 is worth 3 percent, compared to 6 percent for 7).

The opposite applies if you're betting the favorite. Lay the 6.5 as soon as you can because if it goes to 6, you gain a small competitive advantage compared to what you have to lose if it goes to 7. Thus, the adage: bet favorites early and dogs late. Always pay attention to the value of the numbers as the line moves.

Buying Points

You can buy points before the game to increase or decrease the margin your team must win or lose by. It's a strategy I use, but only when I know I'm getting a fair price for those points.

Here's how it works: Most bookmakers will sell half points for an additional ten cents for every dollar bet, with the exception in football of 3 and 7. Some bookmakers charge twenty-five cents or more to increase the spread from +2.5 to 3. However, twenty-five cents extra to buy a half point to get to or get off of 3 is too high of a price. The table below shows you the right price for buying each number. If you can buy a half point for the amount in the table, or less than this amount, do it.

Remember, one of the most important issues in buying points is to shop around—see who is offering the best price. If the price is not right—and this chart outlines the values—do not buy the half point. Stick with the original number. And choose the bet that provides the best value.

The Value of Points*

POINT SPREAD	CHANCE OF HITTING POINT SPREAD (%) (ROUNDED)	DOLLAR VALUE OF BUYING HALF POINT TO GET ON OR OFF KEY NUMBERS ($100 WAGER)	GAUGING BET SIZE: VALUE OF EACH SPECIFIC NUMBER WHEN COMPARING YOUR MARGIN TO POINT SPREAD
1	3	6	3
2	3	6	3
3	8	20 off tie, 22 on to tie	8
4	3	6	3
5	3	6	3
6	5	10	5
7	6	13	6
8	3	6	3
9	2	3	2
10	4	9	4
11	2	5	2
12	2	4	2
13	2	5	2
14	5	11	5
15	2	5	2
16	3	6	3
17	3	6	3
18	3	6	3
21			
24			

*The values in the table above are rounded for presentation purposes. Numbers above a half or more are rounded up; half or less is rounded down. For example, the percentage 3.5 gets rounded to 4; 3.4 would be rounded down to 3.

Deciding Strength/Size of Bet

Now that you've seen the value of points and buying half points, you need to decide how much to bet. I use a star system: the more stars, the more I bet.

First, you identify your spread and the posted spread, then apply percentage values to each number contained in that spread.

Consider the following example. Your handicapped spread is 7.5 and the posted spread is 4.5. Each point within that spread—5, 6, and 7 in this example—has value. From our table above, you see that the number 5 is worth 3 percent, 6 is worth 5 percent, and 7 is worth 6 percent. So 3 + 5 + 6 = 14%. In the table below, you'll see that a 14 percent spread is nearly a three-star bet.

If your projected spread or the posted spread is a whole number, you only count half of the value of that specific number. For example, let's say you project a 4-point spread and the line is 2.5. In this example, you include the full value of the number 3 (8 percent) and half of the value of the number 4 (1.5). So you have a 9.5 percent spread, which equates to a 1.5-star bet.

If the point values between your prediction and the posted spread don't add up to at least 5.5 percent, then the bet does not qualify for a play.

Another thing to remember: If you predict an upset and you have to cross the number 0, you need to deduct the value of a point. For example, if your predicted spread is +1.5 and the bookmakers have a line of –1.5, you do not include the value of +1. The values of the differential are   1 (3%) and +1 (3%), which would be 6% and worth a play. But because you crossed 0, you must deduct the value of one of the points (3%). So the actual value is 3 + 3 – 3 = 3%. That's not worth a play.

Here's the table that shows our star system.

TABLE 2 Strength of Play Guidelines

PICK MINUS SPREAD	PLAY STRENGTH
5.5%	0.5 Star
7%	1.0 Star
9%	1.5 Star
11%	2.0 Star
13%	2.5 Star
15%	3.0 Star

Understanding Line Changes

Some bookmakers, instead of moving the point spread, will move the money on a game. For instance, rather than move the posted spread off of 3, they may charge $1.20 to win $1 for the 3-point spread.

When they do, you need to be aware of the implications. An example: let's say you think your team will win by 4.5 and the posted spread is 3. At $1.10/$1, the value of the differential is 7% - (half of 3 is worth 4% and 4 is worth 3%). A differential of 7% is worth a play

But what if the bookmaker decides to charge $1.20 for the 3-point spread? As you can see from the chart below, a 3-point spread at -120 really is equivalent to 3.25. When you calculate the differential between the posted spread and your line, you no longer can count the number 3 because it's really 3.25. In our system, 3.25 is worth one-quarter of the value of 3, or 2%. Then include the number 4, which is worth 3%, and you're at 5% and and not worth a play.

The opposite occurs if the bookmaker charges less than $1.10/100. At even money or $1.05/$1, certain spreads may have a larger differential and become worth a bigger play.

In general terms, in the price is above par ($1.10/$1) for key numbers, you should reduce the size of the play. If price is below par, increase the size of the bet.

How changes in bet price affect implicit spread

This chart shows the implicit odds when the bookmaker charges a price other than $1.10 to win $1. Even though the spread is listed at a certain number, it equates to a different number based on the price of the bet. Use the implicit spread when you're calculating the strength of your play.

POSTED SPREAD	BET PRICE	EQUATES TO THIS SPREAD AT 110/100
2.5	−115	2.625
3	+105	
2.5	−120	2.75
3	100 (even money)	
2.5	−125	2.875
3	−105	
3	−110	3
3	−115	3.125
3.5	+105	
3	−120	3.25
3.5	100 (even money)	
3	−125	3.375
3.5	−105	
7	100 (even money)	6.75
6.5	−115	
7	−105	6.875
6.5	−120	
7	−110	7
7.5	100 (even money)	7.25
7	−115	
7.5	−105	7.375
7	−120	

Moneyline vs. the Spread

Another huge consideration in betting is a simple one: Do you bet the spread or play the moneyline?

The moneyline allows you to simply bet on the winner of the game and take moneyline odds rather than a point spread. Let's say the Bears are playing the Vikings. The Bears are –158 and the Vikings are +120. That means the Bears are favored and you need to bet $158 to win $100. If you like the Vikings, a $100 bet will get you $120 if the Vikings win. The point spread doesn't matter; if you're betting the favorite, you are risking more money to win. By betting the dog, you're not getting points, just wagering less money to win more.

The table below shows how the moneyline correlates to the point spread if you're laying $110/$100.

To explain: If I like the underdog and I'm getting two points, that's the moneyline equivalent of taking no points and getting $108 for a $100 bet. If I can get more than +108, that's better than betting the spread and getting 2 points:

TABLE 3 Moneyline Conversion Table

POINT SPREAD	MONEYLINE		
	Favorite	/	Dog
1	+116	/	–104
1.5	123	/	102
2	130	/	108
2.5	137	/	113
3	170	/	141
3.5	197	/	163
4	210	/	174
4.5	222	/	184
5	237	/	196

5.5	252	/	208
6	277	/	229
6.5	299	/	247
7	335	/	277
7.5	368	/	305
8	397	/	328
8.5	427	/	353
9	441	/	365
9.5	456	/	377
10	510	/	422
10.5	561	/	464
11	595	/	492
11.5	631	/	522
12	657	/	543
12.5	681	/	564
13	730	/	604
13.5	781	/	646
14	904	/	748
14.5	1024	/	847
15	1086	/	898
15.5	1147	/	949
16	1223	/	1012
16.5	1300	/	1076
17	1418	/	1173
17.5	1520	/	1257
18	1664	/	1377
18.5	1803	/	1492
19	1985	/	1642
19.5	2182	/	1805
20	2390	/	1977

Another example: Take our favorite football number: 3. If I like the favorite, anything better than –170 would be better than laying 3 at $110/$100. For the underdog, anything better than +140 is better than taking the 3 at a price of $110/$100.

Parlays and Teasers

Now let's look at parlays and teasers. Under current rules, "ties" are considered non-bets. That is, a two-team parlay in which one of the games results in a tie reverts to a single one-team bet. The bookies/casinos pay $90.90 for a winning $100 bet in those situations. In non-tie, two-team parlay situations a player must win both games (win/win) to cash a ticket. (The four non-tie possibilities are win/win, win/loss, loss/win, and loss/loss.) In this case, you are expected to win 25 percent of the time and a two-team parlay pays 13-5, so a $100 winning ticket means a positive $260. Under the current rules, a two-team parlay has an expected loss of 9.8 percent, significantly worse than a straight bet laying $110/$100, which has an expected loss of 4.6 percent.

A three-team parlay has an even worse payoff structure. In that situation, one tie means the three-team parlay reverts to a two-team parlay, and two ties means the three-team parlay reverts to a single-game bet that pays $90.90 for every $100 wagered. Under current rules, the expected loss from a three-team parlay is 12.4 percent, significantly worse than a straight bet laying $110/$100, which has an expected loss of 4.6 percent.

	WIN %	PRICE	BET	EXPECTED LOSS (%)
Straight Bets	0.5	110	100	–4.6
Two-Team Parlays	0.25	260	100	–9.8
Three-Team Parlays	0.125	600	100	–12.4

Teasers are parlay-type bets that allow you to move the spread by a certain number of points, thus the "tease." They come in a variety of forms—two teams, three teams, 6-point, 6.5-point, 7-point. The bettor must win both games (i.e., win/win) to be successful and there are four non-tie possibilities (win/win, win/loss, loss/win, and loss/loss), so the bettor is expected to win about one-quarter of the time.

There is a perceived advantage in the 6-point (or 6.5-point or 7-point) teaser in that you get to "move" the spread by the teaser points (i.e., 6, 6.5, or 7 points). For example, in a 6-point teaser if the spread is 9.5, then you can bet the favorite and win if the favorite wins by any value greater than 3.5. Or, if you take the underdog and the underdog loses by less than 15.5, your bet is a winner.

Consider a standard 6-point two-team teaser with the generally accepted rule that ties are "no bets." In other words, a tie in one of the games means that bet is no longer in play. No blood, as they say in the industry.

Being able to move the spread obviously increases the chance of winning a specific game. Each additional point increases the probability of winning the game by approximately three percentage points. A 6-point move increases the probability of winning from 50 percent to 68 percent. This is great, except that you have to win both games and you have to play the quoted spread in the second game. This compares to a straight bet, where you would have to lay $1.23 to win $1.

If you lay $120 on a 6-point, two-team teaser, the expected loss is 14.8 percent. That's the same as laying $129.60. If you lay $130 on a two-team, 6-point teaser, the expected loss is 17.7 percent, which is the same as laying $134.60. As you can see, at current prices, the odds are stacked against you.

In the table below, I list examples of recent prices for teasers from a variety of betting locations. Note that there are no situations in which the bettor can lay $110/$100 for a two-team teaser, regardless of the points involved. In fact, every one of these bets has a significant negative expected value for the bettor.

Two-Team Teaser Prices, Various Outlets
All Prices Are Relative to a $100 Bet

TWO TEAMS	6 POINTS	6.5 POINTS	7 POINTS
Caesars	–$120	–$130	–$140
MGM	–$130	–$140	–$150
Circa	–$120	–$140	–$150

Wrapping Up

I've provided a lot of information in the last two chapters. I hope you'll find it useful. No one, I believe, has worked harder to build and cultivate a system designed to provide an edge in an increasingly complex game of man versus machine. If you're committed to sports betting, put your mind to it and work hard at it. And good luck.

23

War Stories

How do we put this information into play?

Let's look at the 2009 Super Bowl. In the run-up to the big game, I spent a week with my team of experts analyzing every aspect of the contest between the favored Pittsburgh Steelers (6.5 points) and the underdog Arizona Cardinals.

Our power ratings had Arizona at +7.6 and Pittsburgh at +10.5. Pittsburgh had a few more injuries (–1.6 points vs. –1.2 points for Arizona). Because the game was on a neutral field in Tampa, we had no real game factors.

Our raw pick was Ratings Differential (10.5 – 7.6 = 2.9 in Pittsburgh's favor) + Injury Differential (1.6 – 1.2 = 0.4 in Arizona's favor) for a predicted spread of 2.5 points for Pittsburgh.

With the betting line favoring Pittsburgh by 6.5 points, we saw a big opportunity to bet the underdog, believing the game would be much closer. The difference between our line (2.5) and the posted spread (6.5) covered the numbers 3, 4, 5, and 6. The value of those numbers is nineteen percentage points, which exceeds the 15 percent required for a three-star play.

I made a big bet on Arizona. I broke it up into different bets to spread some of the risk.

Normally, I avoid gimmicky "prop" bets such as which team will win the coin toss, what player will catch the first pass, or how long it will take to sing the national anthem. The Super Bowl is a smorgas-bord of such sucker plays, but we identified three other bets that we believed offered us an edge.

Our research showed that, when the Cardinals won the coin toss, they occasionally deferred to their opponent, but not nearly as often as the Steelers, who elected to play defense on the opening kickoff most of the time. Given our numbers, we believed the team that received the kickoff was the favorite to pick up the initial first down, to score the first points, and to win the first quarter. We be-lieved that all three things were related.

I made a small play ($50,000 at even money) on the Cardinals to get the game's initial first down and placed bigger bets ($100,000 each at even money) on the Cardinals to score the first points and to win the first quarter.

Well, what do you know, the Cardinals won the coin toss and—going against the trend lines we researched—elected to defer and kick off to the Steelers to start the game. On the second play, Pitts-burgh quarterback Ben Roethlisberger hit wide receiver Hines Ward for thirty-eight yards and a first down. Just like that, I was down $50,000. The Steelers finished the opening drive with a chip-shot field goal (a hundred grand down the drain) to grab a 3–0 lead that somehow held up through the entire first quarter (another $100,000 out the window).

For those scoring at home, I'd lost all three bets and $250,000 before my first trip to the bathroom.

I could feel the sweat with eighteen seconds left in the first half and the Cardinals trailing by the score of 10–7 with the ball on the Steelers' one-yard line. I had bet $850,000 at $11/$10 on underdog Arizona (plus 4 points) to win the first half. If the Cardinals did nothing, I stood to win $600,000 ($850,000 minus the $250,000 in losses). If they scored a touchdown or a field goal, I'd still be up $600,000.

There I was on the verge of moving into the black when one

of the most memorable plays in Super Bowl history scrambled the molecules in my brain. You may remember it. James Harrison, a beast of an outside linebacker, intercepted a Kurt Warner pass on the goal line and started to rumble up the field, weaving his way along the right sideline, picking up speed and blockers as the voice of announcer Al Michaels rose another octave with every yard marker.

Harrison past mid-field!... Harrison still on his feet!... Harrison is going to go all the way!

As the record-setting one-hundred-yard interception return for a touchdown unfolded on the TV screen in our Las Vegas home, Susan and I could not believe that a 243-pound linebacker was traversing the entire length of a football field *with my pretty money in his arms.*

Halftime score: Steelers 17, Cardinals 7. Now I was down $1.185 million.

Fortunately, I had bet $1.5 million on the final outcome, so I had a chance to recover. And as expected, the Steelers pulled out the victory, but only by four points, 27–23. I won the $1.5 million on the game, leaving me up $315,000 for the day.

(The year after the Harrison interception, I won my biggest Super Bowl bet to date—$3.5 million betting on the New Orleans Saints, 31–17 winners over the Indianapolis Colts [–4.5]. I also won another $2 million—before the season started, I'd made two futures bets that New Orleans would win the NFC and the Super Bowl that year. When the Saints came marching in, I found myself $5.5 million richer.)

As Lady Luck would have it, in another Super Bowl, I found myself staring straight into a seven-figure hole ... only to crawl out alive at the very last minute.

The 2015 Super Bowl will be remembered for as long as the game is played. It opened with the Seattle Seahawks as –2.5 favorites over the Tom Brady–led New England Patriots.

We had New England with a +9.3 power rating compared to Seattle's +7.6 for a 1.7 differential in favor of New England. Seattle had −2.3 deducted for injuries, while New England had −1.0 for injuries—a 1.3-point advantage for New England.

With no home field advantage and game factors even, we had New England favored by 3 (1.7 + 1.3).

I had bet $2 million on New England, taking the points. By game time, the betting line had gone to pick 'em, no doubt aided at least in part by the size of my bet.

New England was down by 10 going into the fourth quarter when Brady, true to his MVP form, kicked into high gear, putting the Pats ahead, 28–24, with two minutes left on a touchdown pass to wide receiver Julian Edelman. At that point I wasn't counting my money, but I was feeling pretty darned good.

Then, with the clock ticking down, Seahawks QB Russell Wilson heaved a pass downfield to Jermaine Kearse, who made a miraculous sideline catch while lying on his back at New England's five-yard line. The clock read 1:05 left in the game.

Well, I'm in serious trouble now, I thought. A really bad beat was just fifteen feet away.

Sure enough, on the next play, Wilson handed off to Marshawn "Beast Mode" Lynch, who bulled his way down to the one-yard line. *Now I'm screwed.* But then, as the clock ticked down to inside thirty seconds, a little voice in my head reminded me that the Patriots had a strong defensive line anchored by defensive tackle Vince Wilfork. I knew what Seattle head coach Pete Carroll knew: it wasn't a cinch they could run the ball in. Seattle was also having clock-management issues.

In a decision that will be debated by Monday morning quarterbacks from here to eternity, Carroll made the fateful decision to put the ball in the air, calling a slant pass to wide receiver Ricardo Lockette. A millisecond after Wilson fired a dart toward Lockette,

Pats cornerback Malcolm Butler sliced in to intercept it. Nothing less than a play for the ages.

As time ran out, Brady took a knee and the Pats captured their fourth Super Bowl.

Luckily, I'd jerked one out of the fire. I went from losing $2.2 million to winning $2 million—a $4.2 million swing—on a single play.

What a way to make a living.

Now, for one final Super Bowl story.

Despite a ton of early money coming in on the Philadelphia Eagles (−1.5) in their 2023 matchup against the Kansas City Chiefs in Super Bowl LVII, I liked KC with this caveat: the game depended heavily on the health of the Chiefs' receiving corps, particularly wide receiver JuJu Smith-Schuster (knee) and tight end Travis Kelce (back). Both Patrick Mahomes and Jalen Hurts were banged up at quarterback, but I knew the more-experienced Mahomes needed healthy receivers. As the game drew near I liked what I heard and read—neither Smith-Schuster nor Kelce showed up on injury reports—leaning into the Chiefs' ability to score against the Eagles' defense.

Going into the game, we had Kansas City's power rating at +10.6, with Philly at just +6.4, for a differential of 4.2 for Kansas City. But the Chiefs had more injuries than the Eagles (2.3 vs. 1.1), so we deducted 1.2 from the 4.2 advantage. Using our formula, that put Kansas City as a three-point favorite.

Most of the books had Philly as a 1.5-point favorite, so it created a good opportunity. We were covering the numbers −1, 0, 1, 2, and half of 3, so it added up to ten percentage points, or a two-star play.

Wouldn't you know it, Kelce grabbed six receptions for eighty-one yards and a touchdown, Smith-Schuster caught a total of seven balls for fifty-three yards, and eventual Super Bowl MVP Mahomes rallied his team from a ten-point halftime deficit, driving down the field at the end of the game, draining the clock, and getting help from an entirely legitimate defensive-holding call. Mahomes set up Harrison Butker for the game-winning twenty-seven-yard field goal with just eight seconds left to put the Chiefs up by the exact three points I'd predicted. My phone lit up with texts. I'd won $880,000.

24

Market Play

I did not get smart about investing in the stock market until I met the Master of the Universe.

Time magazine bestowed that title on Carl Icahn in 2013 after he made his bones and billions in the 1980s as—depending on your perspective—a corporate raider, vulture capitalist, or activist investor.

Carl was both loved and loathed for taking big positions in what he saw as undervalued public companies before launching highly publicized and mostly hostile takeover attempts on major targets. These were marquee brands including Tappan, TWA, Texaco, AOL Time Warner, and RJR Nabisco, to name a few.

His image as a predator was burnished by his open contempt for the senior management of his takeover targets. Carl unleashed so much drama in the staid world of high finance that he inspired the character Gordon Gekko, played by Michael Douglas in the hit movie *Wall Street*. In the film, director Oliver Stone used a classic Carl quote: "If you need a friend, get a dog."

In 2022, the HBO documentary *Icahn: The Restless Billionaire* portrayed Carl as "the great white shark in a sea of capitalism" for his propensity to torch negotiations in high-stakes proxy fights. In other words, not a man you want to trifle with.

Carl parachuted into Las Vegas in 1997 when he purchased the mortgage debt of Arizona Charlie's, a value-conscious casino and hotel chain. He sold it—in typical Icahn fashion—less than a year later to Station Casinos at a huge profit. Then he scooped up the bankrupt Stratosphere hotel and casino, marked by its iconic 1,149-foot tower.

Around that time, I met Carl at the Hilton hotel for an early dinner arranged by a mutual friend. There was Carl, the only person seated in the back of the restaurant, dressed in a pair of old khakis and an off-the-rack shirt—not for a second exuding the air of a man with a personal net worth north of $11 billion.

We bonded quickly because, strange as it may seem, we had a lot in common. Except for our education, that is. I barely scraped by high school, while Carl graduated with a degree in philosophy from Princeton. He wrote a senior thesis with a title that I can barely pronounce, let alone comprehend: "The Problem of Formulating an Adequate Explication of the Empiricist Criterion of Meaning."

Still, we found common ground in our backgrounds. Carl is a New York Jew from the mean streets of Far Rockaway, Queens. My roots are planted in the hardscrabble Kentucky countryside. Neither of us was particularly close to our parents, but we each had uncles who were role models. I had Uncle Harry. Carl had Uncle Elliot, a real man-about-town figure who loaned his young nephew $400,000 to help purchase a seat on the New York Stock Exchange.

Most of all, Carl and I were bonded by the belief that to win big, you needed to risk big. We connected that day over our brittle backstories, contrarian beliefs, and the little-known fact that Carl is one funny guy in the right setting. (See YouTube, Carl Icahn, Caroline's, 2003.)

Carl is an avid sports fan and is infatuated with pro football. He peppered me with questions about strategies, teams, and players. We both played it cagey at first, like diplomats protecting national security interests. I wasn't about to give away my gambling secrets, so I spoke in generalities. Carl did the same while fielding my questions about his investment philosophy.

During our dinner, Carl told me that he had big plans for the Strat, which was saddled with a poor location in a crime-ridden area. He wanted to clean up and develop the entire neighborhood, but he was having difficulties with the zoning department. I suggested I could help him there, and eventually spoke to members of the city council on his behalf.

After dinner, Carl was about to walk back to his hotel, when he stopped and asked me, "How exactly do you do what you do in sports?"

"I'll tell you what," I replied. "I'll make a deal with you. I'll tell you how I do sports if you tell me how you do your business."

He laughed, and from that evening a lasting friendship was formed. Over the years, Susan and I socialized with Carl and his wife, Gail, at their homes in the Hamptons and Indian Creek, Florida, near Miami Beach.

While I was driving back from our first dinner, a thought flashed in my head: *This is the Mike Kent of Wall Street. I need to know how he thinks.*

The next day, I called Alan Duncan, the manager of the Dean Witter office in Las Vegas and a former colleague of Rick Chulick, the CEO at The Walters Group at the time. I told Alan I wanted to take a deep dive into Carl's entire portfolio. He had the magic sauce, and I wanted a taste. I quickly became obsessed with Carl's every financial move—scouring SEC disclosure forms, annual reports, analyst reports, newspaper clippings, and earnings calls. I searched for any inkling on why Carl targeted companies, when he invested in the market, and how his stock purchases performed.

Carl quickly became my investment role model. After all, stalking his investments wasn't like trying to find Bigfoot. Carl primarily dealt with publicly traded companies. He also wasn't shooting craps with someone else's money. He was betting his own. His personal philosophy could be summarized like this: "In life and business, there are two cardinal sins. The first is to act precipitously without thought, and the second is to not act at all."

I had been trading stocks for several years before I became a true believer in Carl's investment strategies. Ironically, my first big order with Alan was fifty thousand shares of Wynn Resorts stock, the first step on what I naively believed was a new path to riches for Wild Bill from Louisville.

I must say that in the beginning Wild Bill found it liberating to play in basically an unlimited market. I bought stocks as aggressively as I bet sports. I'd call Alan to buy fifty thousand shares here and five hundred thousand there, risking millions on this exciting little thing called margin, an investment style guaranteed to burn through my bankroll. One minute I was $20 million long (positive) on Hertz, inspired to buy that stock after I'd waited in long lines for car rentals at airports. The next minute I was $25 million short (negative) on USG, the building supply conglomerate, because it faced a string of asbestos lawsuits that threatened to plunge the company into bankruptcy.

Bottom line: I was playing too high for my bankroll, money I didn't exactly have lying around. More than once, I had to call Alan or my company president, Mike Luce, to come up with enough cash to meet tens of millions of dollars in margin calls. I was never a minute late.

By the mid-nineties, those self-inflicted wounds had taught me enough lessons to conclude that I needed to stop investing irresponsibly. Instead, I vowed to apply the same money-management strategies that I had relied on in business and betting. In other words, I needed to manage my bankroll like I was playing no-limit poker— playing with patience, hedging my bets, knowing when to fold, evaluating the risks and rewards of every stock transaction. If I liked a stock, I would not buy all I wanted initially. I would buy 50 to 70 percent of the total amount, keeping some powder dry in case the stock went down so I could buy the balance at a lower price and average my cost. A lesson I learned from watching Carl.

A new pattern took hold: I barraged Alan and his son, Scott, with daily phone calls seeking information on credit markets, interest rates, commodity prices, currencies, performance charts, analyst reports, current earnings, company debt, and cash flow—an unquenchable thirst for public information that has endured for thirty-plus years.

Eventually, I narrowed my investments to a limited number of stocks, six to eight at any given time. I wanted to ensure that I completely understood the investments before taking positions ranging from $5 million to $100 million.

Given the volume and frequency of my trades, I could negotiate institutional rates—50 percent initial margin, but no call on your money until you're down to 30 percent. After over-leveraging myself early on and paying the price for my mistakes, I learned how to wisely use margin to my advantage.

I lived and died on my contrarian streak, buying enormous blocks of stock when prices were falling—often doubling down at a cost of tens of millions of dollars. Sound familiar? I chased Hertz stock all the way down the drain to a $25 million loss. Then again, I shorted MGM stock in the wake of 9/11 and did well, only to lose $48 million in the market in one year alone during the financial downturn.

I was the same boom-or-bust guy, only the stakes were a lot higher than when I was playing pool and poker back in Kentucky. Indeed, the risk-reward of stock trading exceeded anything I had wagered on sports.

And I loved every minute of it.

Despite my losses, I had enough winners in the market to weather the most severe financial downturns. I was among the fortunate few with enough cash on hand—earned through my sports-betting and golf businesses—to take advantage of opportunities in tough economic times. I had learned a lot in the 1980s about buying nonperforming assets; I also liked investing in things I knew, which drew me into the retail automobile business.

In 2004, I bought a passive interest in a Ford dealership in Nicholasville, a suburb of Lexington, Kentucky. I didn't go all in until five years later when the financial crisis of 2007–08 opened opportunities to purchase dealerships across the country. If ever there was a business in which you reap what you sow, it's the car business. My partner was Robert Bayer, who had worked at the Larry Miller Auto Group. We named our company Walters Bayer Auto Group. We initially had dealerships in California, Georgia, and Kentucky. I later bought Bayer out of the stores in Georgia and Kentucky. We remained partners in California with seven dealerships. I then partnered with Jared Gaiennie in the Southeast.

At its peak, our starting lineup of dealerships in California, Georgia, Florida, and Kentucky went like this: Hyundai, Chrysler, Jeep, GMC, Ford, Buick, Infiniti, Nissan, Fiat, Toyota, Dodge, Kia, and Lincoln.

I bought the dealerships as stand-alone businesses, while on the prowl for acquiring the real estate as well. I knew the automobile business inside and out. Simply put, our strategy was to capitalize the dealerships, improve them, and manage them correctly with an emphasis on customer service, because selling and servicing cars is nothing if not a people business. At our peak, we were moving twenty-eight thousand or more new or used cars a year.

One of my lasting memories of the auto business was an unexpected trip to Detroit in September 2009, where I had the privilege to meet Alan Mulally, the CEO of Ford Motor Company.

At the time, the auto business was in a death spiral. General Motors and Chrysler had filed for bankruptcy and had to be bailed out by the U.S. government. Mulally, who had joined Ford in 2006 after a stellar thirty-seven-year career at Boeing, led a major overhaul that positioned Ford for long-term success.

Roger Cleveland and Luke Williams, two executives at Callaway

Golf, were friends of mine. Roger had founded and sold Cleveland Golf, a company that became widely known for its wedges.

Roger and Luke were headed to Detroit to visit Ford for a trip involving Callaway's joint venture with Ford related to metal finishes on cars and golf clubs. I had two Ford dealerships and told them I'd love to tag along. Roger didn't hesitate to invite me. I toured a Ford factory, visited the executive offices, and got a chance to fill out a foursome with Roger, Luke, and, yes, Alan Mulally.

I had never met someone with Alan's background. He was an accomplished engineer and had extraordinary people skills. Morale at Ford seemed terrific, despite the crippling recession. After golf, Mulally invited me back to Ford's offices and we took a photo together. I quickly understood why Ford's board of directors, employees, dealers, and customers were rallying behind him. I believe that we would be in a better place as a nation if someone like Alan Mulally would serve as U.S. president.

I've since sold all but two dealerships to simplify my life. But I remain—and will always remain—a car guy at heart.

In 2009, Alan Duncan retired as my longtime investment advisor. I continued to invest in the stock market through his son, Scott, and other advisors before settling in with Rob Miller, who worked for the private wealth group at Goldman Sachs. Rob later moved on to Barclays, the London-based bank, and is now with Stifel Financial, a multinational investment bank based in St. Louis.

With Rob, I turned up the intensity. We were on the phone six, eight, ten times a day, and I was drinking in a fire hose of data, constantly on the prowl for what I believed to be undervalued companies. One was Dean Foods, a company I started investing in with Alan Duncan in 2004. Dean Foods was the largest milk distributor in the U.S. when I started looking. I developed a keen interest in commodity prices, particularly for raw milk, diesel fuel, and oil, and how one commodity affected another. For example, elevated grain prices drove up the price of feed for dairy cows, which in turned caused a spike in the price of milk.

When I was investing, I thought nothing of buying millions of shares in a single trade if I saw value in a stock I liked.

My gambling and other experience came in handy. I was constantly on the lookout for "tells"—hints of unusual price fluctuations compared to the market. The move might be due to action in the options market, interest rates, currency rates, or savvy investors buying or selling large blocks of stock.

For instance, whenever Carl Icahn bought a significant share of stock and it became public, the price would rise because Carl was an activist investor. Most of the time, the stock would fall back over time, and my strategy was to buy it at about the same price that Carl had paid, or even lower. I was confident that as long as Carl held a significant share of a company's stock, it would go up over time.

At various times, up to 80 percent of my portfolio consisted of an idea or company backed by Carl, but only if his investment reached at least a billion dollars. Just like in sports, I looked for four-star—not one-star—plays.

I also invested heavily in Icahn Enterprises, buying hundreds of thousands of shares in the conglomerate controlled by Carl and his son, Brett. Their investments ranged from energy to automotive to food packaging to real estate. And it paid off: from 2000 to 2022, the value of Icahn Enterprises skyrocketed more than 1,900 percent, three times the S&P.

As I've heard Carl say a thousand times: the only thing he liked better than buying a stock was buying a stock and seeing it go down, so he could buy even more for less money.

Today, that philosophy prevails. And I haven't slowed down at all when it comes to playing the market.

25

60 Minutes to Five Years

Lowell Bergman was a classic *60 Minutes* producer portrayed by Al Pacino in the movie *The Insider*. In the early nineties, Lowell tracked me down to say that *60 Minutes* wanted to do a story on me and the Computer Group.

"I have zero interest in being interviewed by Mike Wallace on *60 Minutes*," I assured him.

Thankfully, I heard nothing more from *60 Minutes* until nearly two decades later, when my good pal David Feherty asked me to reconsider. David had just signed a new contract with CBS Sports as a golf announcer.

"There's not a chance in the world I'm going on *60 Minutes*," I told him. He asked if I would at least call Jeff Fager, the program's executive producer.

I gave Fager the same response. He claimed the top priority of his show was fairness, which sounded to me like more journalistic bull. Fager then asked if I would at least meet with two veteran producers, Tom Anderson and Coleman Cowan, who subsequently came to visit me in Las Vegas.

Their pitch went like this: *The net worth of millions of Americans has plummeted during a financial crisis precipitated by widespread corporate fraud. What about a comparative analysis of risk taking—*

sports betting included—featuring you as one of the few with deep experience in both worlds?

Now they had my ear. I had long grown weary of seeing Las Vegas portrayed as the nation's brothel and sports gamblers cast as degenerates. I thought this could be a chance to demonstrate how, at the highest level, legalized sports betting was no different than buying real estate, a stock, or a bond. It was all about risk versus reward.

The segment was called "The Gambler" and it aired on January 16, 2011—right after a massive NFL playoff game between the New York Jets and New England Patriots.

All said and done, I was treated fairly, just as Fager promised. Lara Logan was the correspondent. Most of my family and friends considered it a perfectly entertaining and amusing feature.

Until the final minute, that is, when I made some comments that I never should have made in front of 17 million viewers, no matter how true.

LOGAN: It was on Wall Street where Walters says he was taken for a ride.

WALTERS: I've been swindled out of quite a bit of money in the stock market. I bought Enron stock once and got swindled. I bought a lot of WorldCom stock and got swindled. I bought quite a lot of Tyco stock and got swindled.

LOGAN: His disdain for Wall Street is one of the reasons Billy Walters decided to talk with us. The chance, he says, to make a point that the gambling world is not as shady as most people think.

WALTERS: I ran into a lot of bad guys, a lot of thieves, I mean they'd steal the Lord's Supper. But I can tell ya, percentage-wise, I ran into many more with suits and ties on than I have with gamblers.

LOGAN: So you would say that the hustler from Vegas got hustled by Wall Street?

WALTERS: No doubt about it.

Tick . . . Tick . . . Tick.

I can tell you the good folks in government who regulate financial markets did not take kindly to the words "swindled" and "thieves."

Unbeknownst to me, in July 2011, seven months after the *60 Minutes* piece aired, the FBI and the U.S. Attorney's Office in the Southern District of New York began investigating me, Carl Icahn, and others for what they believed was "suspicious trading" on Wall Street.

That same month, Carl had bid $10.2 billion for Clorox, which caused the stock of the cleaning-products company to jump. Carl's bid came eight months after he had announced that he had acquired a 9.4 percent stake in the company. When he made that initial announcement, I started watching Clorox closely on my Bloomberg Terminal.

Days before Carl announced his takeover offer, a large volume of trades—primarily options—raised eyebrows among regulators. The options trades, in particular, earned headlines when it was learned that they returned 600 percent in just four days. Speculation was running rampant.

I had not bought any options, but I did buy Clorox stock three days before Carl's public offer after I saw its shares rise nearly $4 on a day the Dow Jones Industrial Average fell some two hundred points. Having followed Icahn's investments and knowing that he already had that 9.4 percent stake in the company, this checked all the boxes for me to invest: Clorox was one of Carl's biggest investments; it was moving differently than the overall market; and it was at an attractive price compared to what Carl had paid for it earlier. In my mind, it was a four-star investment, so I bought.

I didn't know it then, but soon I would have four big, bad agencies of the federal government pursuing me after nearly thirty years of swings and misses. In addition to being investigated by the SEC, the Justice Department, and the FBI, the IRS also began conducting extensive audits of my personal and business tax returns.

As you know, a jury of my peers eventually would convict me of insider trading in 2017—not of trading in Clorox stock, but a completely different company. As bitter as that was, I accept the verdict and do not want to gripe about it. I don't care much for whiners. But I do want to share some facts about the investigation and my subsequent trial, which involved a cast of characters, including Phil Mickelson.

We ultimately learned that, by early 2014, the SEC had concluded its three-year investigation into Clorox with nothing to show for it. The feds still had no case against me, Carl Icahn, or anyone else for that matter. But as we would later discover, Preet Bharara, the publicity-seeking U.S. attorney in the powerful Southern District of New York, and his team of Department of Justice loyalists refused to let die an investigation that the lead FBI agent on the case called "dormant." To that end, on April 22, 2014, the FBI received court authorization to conduct a thirty-day wiretap on my phones. A month later, on May 23, FBI agents received a second authorization for another thirty-day wiretap. They'd already placed pen registers on my phone starting in November 2011, recording all the numbers I'd dialed or received. They put those in place for more than 650 days. Now they could *listen* to all of my calls, too.

On May 30, 2014, *The Wall Street Journal* posted a story headlined: "FBI, SEC Probe Trading of Carl Icahn, Billy Walters, Phil Mickelson; Insider Trading Investigation Began in 2011 with Unusual Trades in Clorox." The *Journal* story, by Susan Pulliam and Michael Rothfeld, might as well have carried a government byline. It read, in part: "Federal investigators are pursuing a major insider-trading probe involving finance, gambling and sports, examining the trading of investor Carl Icahn, golfer Phil Mickelson and Las Vegas bettor William 'Billy' Walters. The Federal Bureau of Investigation and Securities and Exchange Commission are examining whether Mr. Mickelson and Mr. Walters traded illicitly on non-public information from Mr. Icahn about his investments in public companies, people briefed on the probe said."

Later that same day, *The New York Times* published a similar article. Both the *Times* and the *Journal* were dead wrong about Mickelson and the Clorox trades; he had never traded Clorox shares. The *Times* conceded in a follow-up story that it published information that "overstated the scope of an investigation that involved Phil Mickelson." In truth, it was not entirely their fault; the reporters had been fed erroneous information by David Chaves, the FBI Supervisory Special Agent in charge of my case. When *Times* reporter Ben Protess complained to Chaves about having to correct his story, Chaves responded by threatening Protess and the *Times*, saying they were on his "radar."

That resulted in Protess calling Deputy U.S. Attorney Richard Zabel to complain about being threatened by an FBI agent. Zabel, in a follow-up email to Bharara and five other senior members of the U.S. Attorney's Office, called the conversation "astonishing" and said his office would need to speak with the FBI. Tellingly, Zabel wrote: "I don't think this should be discussed generally right now for a number of reasons . . ." Translation: we don't want to rein in the leaking just yet, and we certainly don't want it to become public.

So the FBI leaked secret grand jury information, which is illegal. Agents also listened to my calls for sixty days. What did they get? Nothing.

But that didn't stop them.

On May 18, 2016, the temperature was already pushing ninety degrees by noon in Las Vegas. I'd just finished lunch at Bali Hai with Linda Smith from Opportunity Village when she noticed a couple seated nearby who looked like they missed the memo on how to dress for the desert. I knew instantly they were FBI agents.

My time was nearly up. My attorneys had suspected for weeks that I was about to be indicted. I had tried on multiple occasions through my attorneys to surrender voluntarily, but it appeared as if someone wanted to create a spectacle.

When the FBI agents left Bali Hai, our security people trailed them to the parking lot of a nearby fire station, which was crawling with black SUVs, cheap suits, and mirrored sunglasses. Shortly thereafter, a half-dozen federal agents rushed into my office, handcuffed me, and paraded me out the door in front of my employees. The agents stuffed me in the back of an SUV. I assumed they were taking me to the Henderson Detention Center for fingerprinting and booking—standard practice. Instead, we drove off in the opposite direction.

This seemed strange. Then things got even stranger. The SUV pulled into the parking lot of the JW Marriott Las Vegas Resort & Spa. The agents whisked me past the front desk to a one-bedroom suite on an upper floor.

Five FBI agents stood watch over me in the room. A few minutes passed before one finally spoke up.

"I guess you're trying to figure out why you're here," he said.

"You're right about that."

The agent explained that U.S. Attorney Preet Bharara had scheduled a press conference the next day in New York to announce my arrest and he didn't want to be scooped by the Las Vegas media. So he had to stash me at the Marriott until TV time.

The next morning, Bharara preened in front of a gaggle of cameras crowing about the high-profile insider-trading arrest. "It was all good news for Walters because he had the information before everyone else," Bharara said, playing cute with my life. "He had tomorrow's headlines today."

Bharara's case against me relied on the conduct of two crooks—FBI Agent David Chaves and my one-time friend Thomas C. Davis. I'll share my thoughts on Davis first.

In April 2013, two years after the Clorox news, the Financial Industry Regulatory Authority (FINRA) made a referral to the SEC about the stock I owned in Dean Foods. The FBI and U.S. attorney were still smarting about the time they wasted investigating the Clorox trades. Once they heard about Dean Foods, they were doubly determined to take me down.

For nearly a decade, I had been buying and selling shares of Dean Foods and dozens of other publicly traded companies. Just as I did with my sports betting, I spent hundreds of hours researching stocks, talking with analysts, reviewing past performance, and developing investment strategies.

I had never heard of Dean Foods before I met Davis around 2000, when I was trying to raise capital for a potential acquisition of American Golf and National Golf Properties. A Harvard Business School graduate and Navy veteran, Davis was a managing partner of banking for the investment bank DLJ—Donaldson, Lufkin & Jenrette.

Davis, a close friend of famed Texas investor Tom Hicks, eventually became a minority owner of Hicks's Texas Rangers baseball team and the Dallas Stars hockey team.

I saw Davis as nothing less than a gold-plated member of the Dallas business and social elite. Our first meeting was at Preston Trail, one of the most exclusive golf clubs in the country, where Davis had served as president. We hit it off from the start. Davis was funny and outgoing. He liked to spend time at his residence in San Diego, where he was a member of the La Jolla Country Club.

Every week, Davis would call me to talk about sports, whether it was baseball, basketball, tennis, or golf. He struck me as a small-time bettor, although we never had any kind of a gambling relationship.

Shortly after I met Davis, DLJ was acquired by Credit Suisse for about $12.5 billion. Davis walked away from the transaction with at least $10 million.

As Davis later testified in court, one of his responsibilities as a Dean Foods board member was to promote the stock, including speaking to major investors like me. I did ask him questions now and then about any public information that I might be unaware of, any past or upcoming investor conferences, or any major investors buying or selling large blocks of stock. For example, in 2011, I noticed when David Tepper at Appaloosa Management, a global hedge fund I deeply respect, took a huge position in Dean Foods. That's not inside information. (That's *public* information.)

I thought of Tom Davis as a wealthy guy, so I was shocked in April 2010 when he asked to borrow $625,000 from me. When I asked why, Davis said he was asset-rich and cash-poor. This wasn't all that surprising. When the Great Recession hit a few years earlier and the stock market was down, a lot of people found themselves over-leveraged and short of cash.

I asked Davis why, as a prominent guy, he didn't go to a bank for a loan. He told me he didn't want anyone in Dallas to know that he needed to borrow money. I wanted to help, but I'd long since learned that lending money to friends can cause problems. Unfortunately, that never stopped me. I'm a sucker when it comes to supporting friends and acquaintances. So I referred Davis to Luther James, my friend in Kentucky since I was a teenager. Luther was living on a fifty-two-acre Thoroughbred ranch and had a fortune tucked away in a bank that was drawing very little interest.

Luther agreed to lend Davis $625,000 on a personally guaranteed note and scheduled payments. When the note came due, Davis paid the interest and rolled it over. When it came due again, he paid interest only. By this time, Luther was having heart problems. He was scheduled for surgery and had put all of his money into a trust. He didn't want to roll the loan over. He wanted to get paid.

In January 2012, Davis asked if I would assume the note—now $647,000. He promised to pay it off by year's end. I reluctantly agreed. We put the loan on our corporate books, accepted collateral, and scheduled principal and interest payments. I've made similar arrangements with two dozen others over the years. Sometimes I've been repaid, sometimes not. That's my weakness. I like to help people.

On May 18, 2015, Davis met with the SEC, and insisted we both were innocent of any wrongdoing. "Whatever we discussed was typically available by analysts," he told them, according to court records. "[Bill Walters] never asked me any leading questions about Dean Foods, so I felt like he respected the fact that I was on the board and didn't want to put me in that kind of position, so he never did."

Unbeknownst to me, the feds had uncovered a dark side to Davis. He was leading the classic double life—a prominent business executive revered in the community by day who had become a heavy drinker, gambler, and sex addict by night. Davis, desperate to cover gambling losses—up to $200,000 on a single hand of blackjack—resorted to embezzling funds from a Dallas charity. The nonprofit, Shelter Golf, held an annual charity golf tournament that gave money to a women's shelter that provides services to victims of domestic violence. Davis conveniently served as co-president and trustee of Shelter Golf, flanked by a board of directors drawn from the Dallas business and social elite.

Davis bilked the charity out of tens of thousands of dollars in personal expenses, including a lavish birthday bash for his wife, and he embezzled $100,000 from its account. When the charity's accountant refused to sign a fraudulent tax return, Davis replaced him with one who would.

Davis ultimately repaid Shelter Golf by, essentially, stealing money from me. He asked for a $400,000 line of credit to acquire a failed Dallas bank from the Federal Deposit Insurance Corporation. I agreed to lend him the money. He used it to repay the charity to cover up his embezzling, then gambled away the rest. He never followed through on the bank deal.

But that was just the beginning of Davis's problems. According to court transcripts, he had called twenty-two escort services while "window-shopping" for sex on a business trip. As investigators dug into his sordid behavior and unearthed a lode of lies, Davis faced serious prison time for alleged embezzlement, tax fraud, obstruction of justice, and, yes, insider trading.

It turns out that Davis had passed nonpublic information about Dean Foods to two prominent Dallas jewelers. When Davis learned that federal agents had questioned the jewelers about their suspicious trades, and one immediately cut ties with him, Davis feared that they had snitched. He freaked out and decided to make a deal.

His Dallas attorney was Thomas Melsheimer, who had represented billionaire Mark Cuban in an insider-trading case. Melsheimer knew that the best way to deal with the U.S. Attorney's Office in Manhattan was to hire one of its alums. To help with the Mark Cuban case, Melsheimer had hired New York lawyer Christopher Clark, a former federal prosecutor in the Southern District. Cuban won his insider trading trial in Dallas.

Clark recommended that Melsheimer hire one of his new colleagues, Benjamin Naftalis, to help with Davis. Naftalis had just left the U.S. Attorney's Office in Manhattan after eight years of prosecuting white-collar crimes and working alongside the very people who were after me. Melsheimer knew that Davis would benefit greatly from being represented by someone who had recently worked in Bharara's office. (In 2022, Bharara would go through that same revolving door when he joined fellow former federal prosecutors at the white-shoe law firm of WilmerHale. Three other prosecutors on my case would go on to join big-name white-collar firms. A fourth became a U.S. congressman from New York. Each of their biographies would trumpet the fact that they prosecuted me.)

From his side of the aisle, Naftalis recognized that the feds were using Tom Davis as a pawn. The former prosecutor knew the game. He had played the same game for years in that office, and I was the prize.

We later learned from a private investigator that Davis had driven his ex-wife, Louise, to the quiet of a Dallas cemetery in August 2015.

After asking if she was wearing a wire, he told her: "I don't think they want me. They just wanted me to roll over on Billy Walters."

So it was on May 16, 2016, that Davis finalized his deal to plead guilty to twelve counts of embezzlement, tax fraud, and perjury.

The very next day, I was indicted by a federal grand jury in Manhattan on ten counts of conspiracy, wire fraud, and securities fraud for allegedly earning $32 million in realized and unrealized profits and avoiding approximately $11 million in losses through an alleged insider-trading "scheme" between 2008 and 2014.

Twenty-four hours later came my arrest and overnight stay at the Marriott.

For Davis, the number of felony charges against him hardly mattered. He would have pled guilty to a hundred counts of wrongdoing because he figured there would be no prison term or penalty to pay. Why? The government had rolled out the proverbial red carpet in exchange for his testimony against me. In fact, Davis acknowledged at trial that, on the day he finalized his deal with the government, he arranged a gambling junket to Las Vegas to celebrate with his then-wife and another couple, blowing $50,000 in the process.

The other bad guy who helped convict me, FBI special agent David Chaves, oversaw the most visible securities investigations in the New York office. As we later learned, he was leaking secret grand jury information about my case to the media—for years. It turns out that leaking such information, even if it's true (and some of his was not), is patently illegal.

On September 23, 2016, my attorneys asked for a hearing to explore the unlawful leaking. Predictably, the prosecutors opposed our motion, and in doing so, they lied. As part of their response, Bharara and the DOJ denigrated our request as nothing more than a "fishing expedition" filled with "false and baseless accusations." They knew, of course, that such motions were routinely tossed by courts.

We did not have high hopes. Our case was in lower Manhattan, the judicial equivalent of playing the New York Yankees at Yankee Stadium. The home-team judge was U.S. District Court Judge P. Kevin Castel.

In a shocker—and the one and only major ruling in our favor—Judge Castel granted our motion, setting a court hearing for December 12, 2016. A few days before that hearing, the prosecutors said an issue (which they wouldn't share with us) had arisen and they received continuance to December 21.

Turns out, five days earlier, Bharara quietly had sent a remarkable twelve-page mea culpa letter to Judge Castel. Faced with the prospect of being caught red-handed after lying to the court, the Southern District and DOJ had finally decided to cut their losses in regard to their corrupt and illegal conduct.

In that ex parte letter, which the prosecutors asked to be permanently sealed, Bharara acknowledged what he called "an incontrovertible fact" that a senior supervisory law enforcement official (he did not name Chaves) had repeatedly fed secret grand jury information to as many as four reporters at two of the nation's leading newspapers—*The Wall Street Journal* and *The New York Times*—to revive a stalled investigation. As my lawyers outlined in legal papers, the DOJ "also admitted that senior officials in the United States Attorney's Office in Manhattan had knowledge of the leaks in real time and intentionally chose not to investigate the illegal activity for two and a half years—in derogation of their mandatory duty." Even worse, they had lied to a federal judge about the illicit scheme.

Lawyers for Chaves requested that his name be kept secret because of "psychological problems." They said he was "fragile"—hilarious when you consider that this was the same agent who had threatened the *Times* and sent countless people to prison. Judge Castel told them he wanted to see a doctor's note. After a couple of days and no note, Castel scheduled a call. When the attorneys on the call were discussing the impact of disclosing Chaves's name, Judge Castel told Chaves's lawyer that his client "had better buck up."

Shortly thereafter, Chaves, the agent overseeing all white-collar criminal investigations in the FBI's New York field office, was publicly revealed to be the person illegally leaking grand jury information.

According to Bharara's office, Chaves supposedly had confessed to his bosses that he was the sole architect of a calculated and sustained campaign of leaks, all done to resuscitate a "dormant" investigation into my affairs. Bharara's office admitted that, during its investigation of the leaks, Chaves sometimes gave "vague or contradictory" statements and the U.S. Department of Justice was not "in a position to vouch for his credibility."

Let those words settle in for a moment.

The Department of Justice admitted that the man who headed up major white-collar investigations for three years and targeted me with the Clorox and Dean Foods trades—could not be trusted or believed.

And Preet Bharara, the U.S. attorney for the district that includes Wall Street, the financial center of the world economy, admitted to a federal judge that, in its attempt to nail me, the FBI broke the gold-plated law that protects grand jury secrecy. To top it off, the prosecutors lied, and when caught, they wanted to keep the entire saga secret.

In response to a request by my legal team, the Justice Department had turned over only six of the thousands of emails and texts related to the leaking in my case. Bharara assured the judge—the same judge he'd just been caught lying to—that there was nothing in those emails. He even made up an excuse: the government's illegal grand jury leaking operation could not be fully disclosed because that would violate grand jury secrecy requirements!

I believe the only reason the U.S. Attorney's Office came clean was that prosecutors and the FBI had concluded that too many people were involved in the leaking and cover-up operation to keep it from getting out. But even the admission letter was a classic whitewash. It suggested that Chaves, and Chaves alone, was responsible for the leaks.

Yeah, right.

Initially, Judge Castel was angry at the government's conduct—and rightly so. Here's what he said in court:

> I wasn't cynical enough to think that I was going to learn of deliberate disclosures by a special agent of the FBI and deliberate disclosures after the fact of leaks became known within the bureau and the U.S. Attorney's Office and a warning, a strongly worded warning, was issued by a person within the bureau in a supervisory capacity. Human nature being what it is, I could certainly understand if an agent found themselves in communication with a member of the press and somehow a conversation got out of hand and went beyond where it should have, and the agent, without any real thought ahead of time, misspoke. That is not what happened here. This included dinner meetings and the like. I am a wiser person today for having been exposed to this. To say I was shocked would be an accurate statement . . . I find it truly ironic that Mr. Walters is charged with, among other things, tipping material nonpublic information to another. And to help support that case, the special agent apparently tipped material nonpublic information improperly to another. That's what we have here.

Castel then said that Chaves probably should be prosecuted for criminal contempt and obstruction of justice, and he invited my lawyers to file a motion to dismiss the entire case. As the calendar turned to a new year, my lawyers submitted that very motion, arguing the leaks involved "systematic and pervasive" government misconduct and were so "outrageous" as to violate my civil rights.

Having witnessed Castel's denunciation of Chaves, we believed he would issue a judicial blow to the government and set me free. At the very least, we thought he would schedule an evidentiary hearing so that we could see those government emails and question under oath Chaves and the five other FBI agents about their meetings with journalists.

In March, however, it seems Judge Castel remembered which team he was playing for. He denied our motion and ordered the prosecution to continue.

A month after I was indicted, a federal prosecutor reached out to my attorneys to offer a deal. Without ever mentioning Carl Icahn by name, the prosecution made clear that if I could give them *any* evidence of illegal activity by Carl (who was guilty of absolutely nothing), my problems would essentially go away.

I told them to pound sand.

Based on the facts of my case and my previous experience with law enforcement, I wasn't the least bit concerned about being convicted. The odds of winning at trial, I figured, were better than 10–1 in my favor. I would have bet everything I owned that a jury of my peers would find me not guilty of all charges after reviewing all of the evidence.

I'd been in courts in Nevada, California, and Kentucky and thought I understood the judicial process. In retrospect, I was naive about the Southern District of New York; no wonder they call it the Sovereign District.

As Susan and I flew to New York for the trial in March 2017, it was hard not to think about Phil Mickelson's role in my case.

In July 2012, after playing a round at Rancho Santa Fe Golf Club, Phil asked me over lunch what stocks I liked and I mentioned two. One was Amylin Pharmaceuticals, a San Diego biotech company in the final stage of approval by the FDA for a weekly diabetes drug. The other was Dean Foods. I told Phil I had owned the dairy stock dating back to 2004, and I believed the company's shares were undervalued.

As my team outlined at trial, Dean Foods stock was depressed because of a drought, which caused corn prices to rise, resulting in higher costs to feed dairy cows. The company also had a booming organic food business called WhiteWave that many experts said was undervalued. In 2010, Dean Foods had publicly explored spinning off WhiteWave, but decided against it.

In early May 2012, analysts from both Credit Suisse and Deutsche Bank issued reports suggesting WhiteWave would be an excellent spin-off; it could help Dean Foods pay down its debt and put the company on stronger ground. Then, in a conference call after its May earnings report, Dean CEO Gregg Engles was asked by Deutsche Bank managing director Eric Katzman about a spin-off or sale of WhiteWave. Engles said, "We understand that there is an opportunity to recognize value for our shareholders by separating it," but the company had not made any decision yet. Analysts from Credit Suisse, Deutsche Bank, UBS, and Sanford Bernstein that month were suggesting a spin-off could come soon. Even CNBC's Jim Cramer touted Dean Foods on May 21, saying the possibility of a spin-off could unlock value. I figured the combination of a cyclical drought and the opportunity with WhiteWave made the stock a good value at its current price.

It was simple; if WhiteWave got spun off, the stock should go up 40 to 50 percent. If it didn't, the stock would go up as soon as the drought ended. Either way, I viewed it as a great investment.

After our lunch, we later learned Phil bought $2.4 million in Dean Foods' shares. A month later, on August 7, Dean Foods announced what its CEO had publicly discussed as far back as 2010 and as recently as a May earnings call with analysts: it would spin off WhiteWave, boosting the stock price 40 percent. Bingo.

About the same time, and unknown to the public, Mickelson was involved in a money-laundering investigation. More than a decade before the start of my partnership with Phil, he had been betting big-time through Gregory Silveira, a former San Diego stockbroker and avid golfer who associated with high-profile actors and celebrities. According to two sources with direct knowledge, Silveira acted as a middleman from 1996 through 2013 for thousands of bets by Phil, including more than a dozen plays a day.

In the spring of 2010, Mickelson asked Silveira if he would do him a favor. Mickelson wanted to transfer several million dollars to Silveira and then have Silveira wire it from his personal bank account to the offshore book to pay off Phil's gambling losses. Unfortunately for Silveira, he said yes. The wire transfer quickly caught the attention of the criminal division of the IRS.

The crux of the case, according to court documents, centered on a transfer on March 26, 2010, of $2.75 million into Silveira's Wells Fargo account by "a gambler known to Silveira, who did not want his identity known . . ." That gambler, according to a court document, bore the initials P.M., which stood for Phil Mickelson.

On March 29, Silveira transferred $2.475 million into an account he controlled at Chase Bank to facilitate payment of Phil's offshore debt. Silveira had previously transferred $275,000 into a second account he held at Wells Fargo as part of his 10 percent commission on Phil's losses.

Not surprisingly, given the size and speed of the transfers, Wells Fargo turned a Suspicious Activity Report in to the IRS, which launched a criminal investigation into the transaction. Not long after, Phil was named in newspaper stories related to trading in Clorox stock and, eventually, Dean Foods stock.

With the feds on his heels, Phil told me that his friends at KPMG, his main corporate sponsor at the time, had introduced him to a D.C. attorney named Gregory Craig. He was not just any lawyer; Craig had been chief White House counsel for President Obama. With boyish looks and trademark white tousled hair, Craig had an Ivy League pedigree, having attended Harvard as an undergrad and Yale Law School. Craig also was tight with Bharara, former U.S. attorney general Loretta Lynch, and the director of enforcement at the SEC. Now that's political juice.

With Mickelson in the midst of a money-laundering investigation and a target of an insider-trading investigation, what did super-lawyer Craig do to get the prosecutors off Phil's back? He performed a legal trick so improbable that it was like Harry Houdini pulling a rabbit out of a hat while in chains underwater.

On May 19, 2016, the SEC issued a press release headlined "Pro Golfer Agrees to Repay Trading Profits." The statement, which was related solely to the Dean Foods case, named Phil as a "relief defendant," government-speak for people not accused of any wrongdoing but named in complaints for "purposes of recovering alleged ill-gotten gains in their possession from schemes perpetrated by others."

It went on: "Mickelson neither admitted nor denied the allegations in the SEC's complaint and agreed to pay full disgorgement of his trading profits totaling $931,738.12 plus interest of $105,291.69." It also noted that I had "urged" Mickelson to trade in Dean Foods stock and he later sold almost a million dollars in profits to pay off part of his gambling debt to me.

"Mickelson will repay the money he made from his trading in Dean Foods because he should not be allowed to profit from Walters's illegal conduct," the press release stated.

There was no mention of any money-laundering investigation. Craig chimed in on cue by releasing his own statement claiming that Phil was "an innocent bystander" to any alleged wrongdoing by others.

Phil and Bharara both got what they wanted. Phil's attorneys issued a statement that made it look like Phil was an innocent victim of an insider-trading case that implicated me. And in the process, Phil was off the hook on the money-laundering case. The only person who ended up looking guilty was me.

Then, one month later, Greg Silveira, who had pled guilty to making the ill-fated wire transfer as a favor to Phil, was sentenced to twelve months and one day in prison for laundering $2.75 million.

Phil, the man in the middle of all the alleged wrongdoing, walked away scot-free.

I still was hoping Phil at least would agree to testify at my insider-trading trial. When Susan and I arrived in Manhattan, I learned through our lawyers that Phil intended to invoke his Fifth Amendment right against self-incrimination if we called him to the stand. I reached out to a mutual friend and asked a favor.

"Listen, I hate to put you in the middle of this," I said. "But I need Phil to publicly declare what he told the FBI—that I never gave him inside information. I need you to ask him to do that. Tell him all I want him to do is tell the truth."

A call was made. A meeting set.

According to our mutual friend, here is the message he delivered to Phil: "This is Bill's life at stake. This is his freedom. He could potentially go to prison for a long time. He would like you to just say the truth. That Bill never gave you inside information."

"Okay, I'll do it," Phil told him.

"Are you positive?" our friend asked. "Because when you leave, I'm going to call Bill."

Phil reiterated that he would issue a statement.

But he never did.

To this day, after countless hours of reflection, I still wonder whether I would have walked out of court a free man had Phil testified or spoke out on my behalf. We knew the prosecution would not call Phil to testify because he'd already told FBI agents in two separate interviews that I had never provided him with insider information on Dean Foods or any other stock. The last thing prosecutors wanted to see, given the power of his celebrity and personality, was Phil Mickelson walk into a courtroom and testify on the witness stand under oath that, as far as he knew, I was not guilty of the charges they'd brought against me.

But Phil did not do it.

Looking back, I realize there's a common denominator in many of Phil's long-term relationships—be it thirty years playing on the PGA Tour, twenty-five years working with caddy Jim "Bones" Mackay, seventeen years betting with Greg Silveira, or five years gambling with me.

When push comes to shove, Phil doesn't care about anyone except himself. Time and time and time again. He never stood up for a friend. He refused to simply tell the truth when it could have meant the difference between prison and exoneration.

In his opening statement to the jury in my trial, senior assistant U.S. attorney Michael Ferrara stood tall and spoke a single word.

Greed.

"That's what this case is about," Ferrara told the jury. "It's about this man, William Walters, illegally and unfairly using secret business information to make millions in profits and avoid millions in losses."

Ferrara admitted up front that the government's case would hinge on the credibility of Tom Davis, my former friend and now star prosecution witness.

I believed in my heart there was no way on earth the jury would trust Tom Davis. What I didn't factor in was that my lead lawyer would get his ass kicked. I had hired Barry Berke, a six-foot-four New York attorney who graduated Phi Beta Kappa from Duke and cum laude from Harvard Law. At our first meeting, Berke was a completely engaging guy who sold us on his reputation as the Michael Jordan of white-collar defense. Little did I expect he'd be chucking air balls at my trial.

It began with the first words out of Berke's mouth during his opening statement: an obscure Greek reference that seemed straight out of a *Saturday Night Live* skit.

"A long time ago," Berke told the jury, "a man left a small town in Greece to travel to the capital, Athens, with a plan to steal the riches of others. When he reached the gate of Athens, the guard asked him his business. He falsely said he was there to see old friends because he used to be from Athens. The guard inquired, 'Are you going to visit Piraeus?' The man falsely and confidently replied, 'But of course, he is very close to me, like a cousin.' The guard looked at the man and said, 'Arrest him,' and told the surprised imposter that Piraeus is the oldest port in Athens, and he would have known that if he was telling the truth."

That fractured fairy tale kicked off Berke's long, winding, and mind-numbing opening. I guarantee the jury didn't know if Berke was talking about Bill Walters, Tom Davis, or a bumbling crook from ancient Greece.

Only toward the end of the opening did Berke finally get to the crux of our case.

"I submit to you, you will be persuaded of two things: Tom Davis is lying, and Bill Walters never believed he was doing anything wrong."

Tom Davis and I talked hundreds of times from 2002 onward, about a variety of matters. We talked on our cell phones—and the prosecutors claimed they could tie our phone calls to specific trades I made, even though I did nearly all my trades after public earnings announcements. When they charged me, they claimed they had phone records linked to nine of ten key trades I'd made.

But they didn't have a phone call related to one of my biggest trades.

No problem. Davis made up a story.

Davis told the government, in quite a bit of detail, that I gave him a black prepaid cell phone in the parking lot of the private air terminal at Love Field in Dallas. They called it a "bat phone," claiming I talked to Davis on this phone before making a big trade in July of 2012—a month before the announced spin-off of White-Wave.

Davis couldn't recall the exact date I supposedly gave him a phone, but testified it was "sometime in 2011 . . . I remember the weather was good, so I don't remember exactly the date. I thought it was the summer of 2011."

Not true. And we had proof.

Flight logs and phone records showed that the only time I was with Tom Davis at Love Field on December 18, 2012, months after the supposedly incriminating "bat phone" calls and stock purchase.

Where's the phone? The records? The government solved that sticky little problem by having Davis testify that he had thrown the "bat phone" into Turtle Creek, a meandering body of water in an exclusive area of North Dallas. This tale triggered a two-day search by a team of FBI divers that came up dry.

According to testimony by Davis's second wife, Terie, the couple was watching the FBI search on local TV when Davis smirked, shook his head, and said, "They'll never find the phone."

That's because there was no "bat phone." The government wanted the jury to believe that we talked hundreds of times on our cell phones, but decided to start using a burner phone for one call in July 2012. And then, according to their claims, we went back to using our cell phones in September and October 2012 so I could get "inside information" for other trades in the indictment.

Which makes absolutely no sense.

Based on Davis's false testimony, we filed a motion for a new trial. Prosecutors then claimed Davis "misremembered" or "confabulated" how and when he received the phone.

Once again, Judge Castel made clear his loyalties when he denied our motion for the new trial. In doing so he said, "It is more likely that Davis testified accurately that he received the phone in 2011, and that he misremembered the precise circumstances under which he received the bat phone or mistakenly confused the meeting at which he received the bat phone with a later meeting with Walters at Love Field."

Of course, there was no evidence that I met with Davis in 2011. Moreover, my phone records showed that I had not stepped foot in Texas any time that year.

But, in this case—and with this judge—the facts didn't seem to matter.

My lawyers had conducted a mock trial to prepare me for the real one. They asked me about phone calls surrounding specific trades that took place seven or eight years earlier. I said I couldn't recall. My lawyers said I sounded inconclusive. Of course I sounded inconclusive. I honestly couldn't remember.

If anyone honestly tells you they can remember what they said in a fifteen- or thirty-second phone call seven or eight years earlier (especially if that person is on the phone thousands of times a month), I advise you to hire them to run your company. Yet, on the stand, Davis sounded like a member of Mensa, rattling off precise times, dates, and descriptions of what we discussed, sticking a knife in my back with every false recollection. This was the same guy who had to meet twenty-nine times with the FBI to get his story straight. That's right—*twenty-nine* separate meetings, all while being coached by Ben Naftalis, the attorney who had worked eight years with the same prosecutors looking to nail me.

I do have to give my attorney Barry Berke *some* credit. On cross-examination over four days, he destroyed Davis and exposed him as an adulterer, tax cheat, serial liar, and addicted gambler.

FBI special agent Paul Roberts took the stand a couple of days after Davis. He detailed dozens of calls between Davis and me from 2008 to 2014. Roberts focused on the timing of the calls using charts, graphs, emails, and texts. He noted my collective purchase or sale of

more than 5 million shares of Dean Foods' stock from May 2012 to
February 2013.

But Roberts did not put my trading activity, or the amount of my
research, into context in any of his materials shared with the jury. As
he acknowledged under cross-examination by Paul Schoeman, the
other senior lawyer defending me, Roberts ignored all of my telephone calls with brokers and analysts, and all of my trades in other
stocks at the same time.

Here are excerpts from Roberts's cross-examination, taken directly from the court transcript:

Q: Now, you testified yesterday, and I think at the beginning—at
the very end of the day here, that you chose what calls and trades—
what calls and trades to put on your charts? You selected them?

A: Yes, I did.

Q: It's not every call and it's not every trade?

A: That's correct.

Q: And you testified yesterday that in order to do that, you reviewed the indictment and consulted with the prosecutors, do you
remember saying that?

A: Yes, I do, sir.

Q: So there is nothing on these charts that isn't based on some se-
lection that was done by you in consultation with the prosecutors?

A: That's correct.

And this:

Q: You only put them on your charts when it was around trading
that you believe was connected to the allegations against Mr. Walters?

A: That's correct, sir.

Q: So if the calls did not tie into the allegations that the prosecution is making in this case, you omitted them?

A: I did not include them, correct.

Roberts also did not share this important fact: In February 2013, I sold one million shares of Dean Foods because I was acquiring a property at Bighorn Golf Club in Palm Desert, California. Two weeks later, Dean Foods issued a disappointing earnings report and the stock fell two dollars per share. The government claimed I sold the one million shares because I had inside information to avoid a $2 million loss.

What they didn't share: I did not sell the other 4.3 million shares of Dean Foods that I still owned. So I lost $8.6 million when that earnings report came out.

Obviously, that evidence would have allowed the jury to consider why if I were cheating, would I have willingly taken an $8.6 million loss? Why wouldn't I just sell everything?

Also not shared with the jury: I actively traded another stock of a company where Davis served as a board member. It was Affirmative Insurance Holdings, and I began trading the shares in 2005. Just as with Dean Foods, I never shorted the stock, even as the company was struggling. It eventually filed for insolvency in 2016, and I sold my last five hundred thousand shares for a total of one cent! (Tom Davis with his razor-sharp memory must have forgot to tip me off.) Why would I hold on to those shares until they were worth a penny?

As we neared the end of the prosecution's case, I firmly believed I would be vindicated. Susan, who is very good at reading people, wasn't so sure. She thought Berke had come across to the jury as cocky and condescending, talked too fast, and went so overboard in seeking to destroy Davis that the jury took pity on him. That was the last thing we wanted.

Our lawyers saw it differently. Their consensus was that we had the trial won. They advised that we not run up the score and risk watching the jury's eyes glaze over even more than they already were. We were heading into a holiday weekend, jurors were losing interest (the judge had to stop the trial a few times to wake up some jurors), and all of them seemed eager to go home. One even told the judge he would have to leave the next week to return to work. We did not want to risk angering them by putting on our entire defense.

We decided to scrap the twenty-three defense witnesses scheduled to testify. Including, most regrettably, our renowned expert, who was ready to explain the legitimacy of my trades: Professor R. Glenn Hubbard, then the dean of Columbia University Graduate School of Business and a former chairman of the U.S. Council of Economic Advisers under President George W. Bush.

In the end, we went all-in on our belief that the jury would see Davis as a skillful liar and horrible human being, and recognize that he was just trying to save his skin at my expense.

My lawyers recommended that I not take the stand because they were confident we had the case won. Make no mistake, they left the decision up to me and I went with their recommendation.

In short, I blew it.

As the trial came to a close and Berke finally concluded his two-hour closing argument, the entire jury looked like it needed CPR.

My defense team was in a room at the courthouse when we got word that the jury had reached a verdict after only a few hours of deliberations. Despite all the mistakes and pitfalls, my heart raced when I saw prosecutor Brooke Cucinella get emotional. Lawyers assume that a quick verdict usually favors the defense.

But when the jurors walked into court, not a single one looked at me. Not a good sign.

A hot bolt ran through my body as the foreman rose and uttered the words that sent me reeling: Guilty... Guilty... Guilty... Guilty.

On every count.

Guilty times ten.

The court adjourned. I was still in a daze in the hallway outside the courtroom when a newspaper reporter approached and asked for my reaction.

"I just lost the biggest bet of my life," I said. "Frankly, I'm in total shock."

In retrospect, after spending thirty-one months in prison replaying my trial over and over, I am convinced that I made a monumental miscalculation and a life-altering mistake by not taking the stand. When your life is on the line, jurors want to understand who you are, where you come from, how you were raised. They want to *know you* and hear an explanation for your actions.

In my case, there were things the jurors were not allowed to hear, which, I truly believe, would have swung the case in my favor.

- They never heard that the government wiretapped my phones for sixty days and came up with nothing.

- They never heard from Phil Mickelson, who told the FBI in two separate interviews that I had not given him inside information.

- They never heard about the government's illegal campaign of leaks and false news stories, or its blatant cover-up of wrongdoing by Chaves, the agent who created and managed the entire case against me from day one.

- They never heard that Chaves had been suspended, had hired a criminal lawyer, and was invoking the Fifth Amendment. Bharara himself said Chaves was a man who could not be trusted.

- They never heard that Judge Castel, the same judge the jury looked up to every day with respect, had recommended that Chaves should be investigated for two potential felonies.

I have asked myself hundreds of times if the jury would have convicted me if they had heard those things. Ask yourself: If you knew these facts, would you have convicted me? I keep coming up with the same answer.

Prior to my sentencing, I flew back to New York to spend a day with U.S. probation officer Rebekah Dawson. She did a thorough interview and told me it usually takes a month to six weeks to complete a background investigation and make an official sentencing recommendation to the judge.

Meanwhile, my friends wrote more than one hundred letters of support for delivery to Judge Castel. There were ten from current and former governors, congressmen, and mayors. Among my supporters were former Nevada governor Jim Gibbons and Senate Majority Leader Harry Reid.

In the end, the probation office recommended that I receive a sentence of one year and one day. I was told that 95 percent of the time, judges accept the probation office's recommendation or reduce it—and they rarely increase it.

In late July, Judge Castel imposed a sentence of sixty months in federal prison and a $10 million fine. He later ordered me to pay $34.2 million more in forfeiture and restitution penalties.

"When it comes to the stock market, Billy Walters is a cheater and a criminal and not a very clever one," Judge Castel said. "Money was a way of keeping score."

Well, I have to say that is the one point Judge Castel and I agree on: if I had been involved in an insider-trading scheme and dumb enough to not conceal my calls with Davis and give Mickelson material nonpublic information after being indicted five times, I should go to jail for outright stupidity.

Outside the courthouse, Susan and I hugged, her tearstained cheeks pressed against mine. "Don't worry," I whispered, "we'll get through this just like everything else."

A year later, I settled my civil case with the SEC, agreeing to forfeit $25 million without admitting or denying my guilt.

If you're wondering about the fate of the rogue FBI boss David Chaves, he has not yet been charged with any wrongdoing and was allowed to quietly take early retirement in 2017. His illegal leaking was referred for investigation of criminal contempt and obstruction of justice to the FBI's Office of Professional Responsibility and the Office of Inspector General within the Department of Justice. All in all, no fewer than three governmental units were charged with investigating his *admitted* crimes. Six years later, we still don't know what, if any, action was taken. Judge Castel supposedly is overseeing the case. In an irony of ironies, Chaves, meanwhile, has embarked on a career as an expert in cybersecurity and securities fraud.

After leaving the U.S. Attorney's Office, Preet Bharara visited Las Vegas to speak at UNLV's William S. Boyd School of Law in October 2017. I was in prison at the time. In a question-and-answer session, Bharara was asked about my case. He noted that other prosecutors for years had failed to convict me, but he had brought charges and "didn't have a chance to see it through." He knew very well that the hometown audience was likely aware of the outcome of my case.

When asked about the FBI's Chaves and any lack of prosecution for his illegal leaking, Bharara said the agent "did a terrible thing, will suffer the consequences and he should, he absolutely should." He also claimed Chaves's leaking "came to light because we voluntarily brought it to the attention of the court." What gumption. The truth is that less than a year earlier Bharara had denied there was any leaking and only fessed up after we convinced the court to hold an evidentiary hearing. If we hadn't requested that hearing, the illegal behavior never would have come to light. Bharara's performance in Las Vegas was shameless.

The other crook who helped put me away, Tom Davis, stood before Judge Castel for his sentencing hearing. Prosecutors requested leniency for their star witness, acknowledging that he wasn't forthcoming about his own behavior, but assuring the court that his stories about me were all true. The judge wasn't buying the leniency request—especially after Davis admitted in court to threatening two of his ex-wives. At his sentencing on October 19, 2017, Castel said Davis "paraded through Dallas as a peacock . . . when he was a phony, a fraud and a crook" and sentenced him to two years behind bars for insider trading. Davis served less than eleven months before being released. But none of that really mattered to me. Nine days before Davis was sentenced, I had begun doing time in Federal Prison Camp, Pensacola.

26

Pensacola

Ten days before reporting to FPC Pensacola, I flew from Carlsbad to our home in Las Vegas. In a final, frenzied push to get my business affairs in order, I turned to the people I trusted most—Mike Luce, longtime president of The Walters Group; Joe Kelly, head of my golf courses; Joe Dahlstrom, my general manager of operations; and Mitch Epstein, who headed up food and beverage at Bali Hai. I gave them the latitude they needed to keep things up and running in my absence.

I felt like everything was in good hands when I left my office at Bali Hai around six o'clock on the evening of October 1. Four hours later, a friend called with horrific news: there had been a mass shooting at the Jason Aldean concert on the Vegas Strip.

I caught a few hours of uneasy sleep not knowing the devastating details: Aldean was onstage as the closing act of the three-day Route 91 Harvest country music festival. A crowd of twenty-two thousand was singing along to "When She Says Baby" when a barrage of gunfire erupted from the thirty-second floor of the Mandalay Bay hotel overlooking the concert site.

Police later identified the shooter as a sixty-four-year-old, high-rolling accountant from nearby Mesquite, Nevada. For several days, he had checked into connecting suites in the hotel tower with twenty-two suitcases packed with high-powered weapons, including AR-15 and AR-10 assault rifles. Before the massacre ended, more than a thousand rounds of armor-piercing bullets were fired into the crowd, leaving 58 people dead that night and upwards of 850 injured. The gunman was found dead of a self-inflicted gunshot to the head.

Early the next day, I negotiated my way past a series of police roadblocks to the Treasure Island Hotel & Casino for a meeting with owner Phil Ruffin as part of my last-ditch effort to secure a pardon from Phil's friend, President Donald J. Trump.

Phil and I had worked on a couple of political campaigns together with Terry Lanni. After listening to my appeal, he reminded me that the president, just ten months into office, had a lot on his plate. Phil's parting words were honest and direct. He didn't have much hope for a quick pardon.

I was officially out of options. Later that same day, I landed in Louisville to see my two sons and take care of a few more last-minute details. When I arrived at our home, the television news was dominated by coverage of the sniper shooting. Footage from the aftermath showed a gruesome scene. Las Vegas residents like to refer to their hometown as "Small City, Big Family." That description never felt more apropos than during that surreal moment of collective grief.

I felt horrible for the victims and their families. Susan and I made a $500,000 donation on one condition—it had to remain anonymous.

Two days later, the then chairman of the Clark County Commission, Steve Sisolak, called with a request. He said they had hit a wall raising money for the shooting victims and wanted to know if he could publicly announce our donation in hopes of encouraging others to come forward. I told him if he thought it might help, go ahead and do it.

The community eventually raised more than $20 million on top of the $800 million settlement from MGM Grand Resorts, owners of Mandalay Bay, awarded to families of the dead and injured. The money certainly never made up for the losses suffered by family members and loved ones, but hopefully it helped in some small way.

As I would soon learn, the FPC Pensacola population consisted mostly of drug offenders mixed with a few crooked doctors, lawyers, and financial con men.

Early on in my stay, I was introduced to an inmate destined to become my best friend on the inside—Ernesto "Flaco" Ortiz, the Pensacola version of the Morgan Freeman character Red in *The Shawshank Redemption*. He was halfway through a ten-year sentence for importing drugs from Venezuela into his native Puerto Rico.

Flaco was regarded as a leader among the Puerto Rican inmates. If you needed a better room, a certain food, or seemingly anything else, Flaco could hook you up. In my case, he produced a used pair of tennis shoes that he no longer wore. I told him I would pay for them as soon as my money was credited to my commissary account.

Flaco simply replied, "Pay me back when you can."

Cash wasn't the only everyday amenity I lacked. In the first weeks, I found myself instinctively reaching into my pocket for the ghost of my seized cell phone to check texts or emails.

To add to my misery, we were under the thumb of five head counts each day, six on weekends. The evening count began at 4:00 p.m., followed by counts at 9:00 p.m., midnight, 2:00 a.m., and 4:00 a.m. (an additional 10:00 a.m. count was done on weekends).

Occasionally, fire alarms would blare during the night, most intentionally set off between head counts by AWOL convicts returning from surreptitious shopping trips to the nearby Walmart or Burger King. Inmates playing hooky from a prison without walls was a regular occurrence given there were never enough guards to monitor the perimeter around the clock.

If those cons were running late on their forbidden missions and afraid they wouldn't make the counts, they had someone inside yank the alarm, knowing that the entire dorm population had to empty out of their bunks and stand outside until the fire department showed up and inspected the building. This gave the returning cons plenty of time to play cat and mouse with the guards. They'd discard the burgers, booze, or whatever other contraband they had bought, and then quietly meld into the milling crowd of convicts ahead of the 4:00 a.m. count.

I wasn't inside Pensacola more than a week before the infectious air and unsanitary conditions took their toll. I went to the infirmary, where another doctor, better known as Dr. Death, told me it was just the flu.

"Drink a lot of water," he advised.

I begged, but Dr. Death refused to prescribe any antibiotics or medication. He basically booted me out of his office.

During the next two days, I barely left my bed. Finally, I summoned the strength to go back to the infirmary, where the personnel there chewed me out for bothering them again. I went to the commissary and bought some aspirin, but that didn't help.

The infection knocked me down and out for another week. I honestly felt like I was going to die. Inmate Louie Duluc came to my rescue by tapping his personal prison supply chain to obtain the antibiotics I needed to knock out the bug and help me get back on my feet.

Like a lot of folks, I thought I had understood and appreciated the concept of individual freedom. But I had no clue just how much we all should treasure our liberties until I lost mine. The daily decisions I had taken for granted—what to eat, what to wear, what time to go to bed—suddenly were stripped away. The only way to survive was to adapt and adjust to the realities of life inside "the System."

One of my first challenges involved finding a way to satisfy the most basic human needs: decent food, clean water, warm clothing, a dry towel, a new toothbrush, toothpaste, soap, a hairbrush, Band-Aids, cotton swabs—the dozens of everyday items we use without thinking. Inmates weren't permitted to bring anything in, so we had to purchase those essentials from the commissary at aggressive retail prices.

I learned early on that prison is a lot like betting sports. Numbers are the name of the game. You have an inmate number, a laundry number, and other numbers that govern your daily existence—a maximum $360 a month commissary allowance; three hundred minutes (and not a second more) per month in phone calls; and visitation hours from 5:00 p.m. to 8:30 p.m. on Friday, 8:00 a.m. to 3:00 p.m. on Saturday and Sunday.

We were rousted before daylight five days a week, ready to report for work by six thirty, the beginning of an eight-hour shift that paid between thirty and eighty cents per hour. As I would soon discover, inmates with a business background were a prized commodity in departments that required keeping inventory and budgets. One of the most prized places of employment was Laundry, where I was taken under the wing of the wily Mike Meisner.

A big, booming former Boca Raton commodities trader, Mike was in his late fifties and about halfway through a fifteen-and-a-half-year sentence after pleading guilty to running a multimillion-dollar Ponzi scheme. (Mike joked that he would have gotten less time if he had shot his clients. Prison humor—you gotta love it.)

Mike became my savior when I developed terrible stomach problems from the prison food. I needed laxatives, but my commissary funds hadn't landed yet. Thank god, Dr. Mike had an old-fashioned prison remedy. He gave me a squirt bottle filled with warm soapy water to create an improvised enema to flush my pipes. It wasn't pretty, but it worked, and it beat another visit to Dr. Death.

Mike had worked his way through several stops in the federal corrections system before arriving in Pensacola in 2013. Eventually, he landed a coveted and demanding job working in Laundry. The operation consisted of washing, drying, sorting, folding, storing, and distributing prison uniforms for as many as eight hundred men. Each day, the team cleaned up to three hundred mesh bags filled with dirty clothes.

I came under Mike's care while dropping off my laundry bag a few weeks into my time. He noticed the carpal tunnel braces on my hands, the result of far too many rounds of golf and far too many hours of practice.

Mike knew that inmates with carpal tunnel had trouble dealing with the buttons on the fly of their prison pants, which had no zippers. On my next visit to the laundry, he presented me with pants that had zippers. It was my first prison perk.

Turns out, Mike had seen and heard it all after seven years in prison.

The last thing Meisner wanted to do, he said, was deal with anyone else or the daily bullshit. To that end, he could get me a job in Laundry if I wanted.

True to his word, Mike got me work in the Cage—the repository of the laundry inventory. I'd done next to no time in the laundry room at home, so Mike taught me the basics, including how to properly sort, fold, and put away clothes. Before long, I was his right-hand man, helping to order supplies, meet the budget, and account for the inventory.

The overseer of the laundry was Mr. Dwyer, who was a capable department head. If you did your job, he was on your side. If not, he held you accountable. He was No. 3 in the Pensacola pecking order. Our direct supervisor was Mr. Johnson, a great guy who treated us with respect. Mr. J., as he was known, valued the fact that we were numbers guys with business smarts, so he let us do our jobs.

The laundry staff became my family inside Pensacola. Frankly, if there had been a bunk and a bathroom at work, I would have preferred to live there instead of the rowdy dorm room.

I stayed busy for a while by working two jobs. After I paid back Flaco for the tennis shoes he gave me, he used connections to get me a job in Designated Zone 23, an area on the outskirts of camp where various forms of manual labor needed on the base were performed. My supervisor there was James Helms. Just like Mr. Dwyer and Mr. J., he was a good man to work for as long as you did your job. James also happened to be from Kentucky and lived for UK basketball.

In DZ-23, I worked in a tiny office trailer writing service orders for lawn mowers, weed whackers, tractors, and other pieces of maintenance equipment that needed to be repaired or replaced. My shift ran from 6:30 a.m. until 3:00 p.m. When work was finished for the day, about thirty-five guys packed onto a bus back to camp, where, one by one, we'd get searched before the free-for-all walk to ten shower stalls. Absolutely no running allowed. Of course, there's walking and there's Billy Walters walking. I can tell you that all the time spent speed walking the track paid dividends when it came to securing a stall. I never waited to take a shower.

After my shower I reported to my second job in the Cage for three more hours of work. I was told that I was the only inmate at FPC to work two jobs. After five months of this routine, I found myself dead on arrival in Laundry and under the supervision of the complete asshole who replaced Mr. Dwyer, who left for a better job. So I quit.

One of the worst people I encountered at Pensacola wasn't a convict; he was the man in charge of the Residential Drug Abuse Program—RDAP for short.

Dennis Profitt was a six-foot-five former college basketball player. He displayed a photo of himself in his uniform on an office wall. He also had a master's degree in clinical psychology, and he liked to play God at Pensacola. There is no other way to say it. He was in a power position because he controlled the nine-month RDAP program, which inmates sought to complete because it could reduce your sentence by a full year.

Given my history with alcohol, I certainly qualified for RDAP.

Typically, you don't apply until the last couple years of your sentence. I found it strange when, about seven months into my five-year stretch, Profitt called me in and told me I had been approved.

The timing could not have been worse. I had an appeal pending before the U.S. Second Circuit. Dean Foods had just sued me for $45 million, my son Scott was on a deep downward slide, and IRS auditors were examining my books.

I explained to Profitt that I'd only been there seven months and had a pending appeal, legal visits. and family issues. If I entered RDAP, I wanted to commit 100 percent.

No problem, he told me. Wait and reapply any time.

Seven months later, after I lost my appeal for an evidentiary hearing on my conviction, I reapplied. During the interim, I'd heard a lot of complaints from fellow inmates who viewed Profitt as very vindictive, very controlling. We were told, on good authority, that there were so many complaints about him that prison management had requested an investigation by Bureau of Prisons headquarters.

When Profitt called me in for my second RDAP interview, I found him sitting at a table surrounded by three colleagues. They began interrogating me about issues that seemed completely irrelevant to RDAP: my net worth, the cost of my attorney fees, my living plans after prison. It felt like a sham interview, and I'm convinced it was.

Profitt left the room at one point, only to return with the last words.

"You think you're privileged. Too good to accept the offer the first time around. Your request is denied."

And so was my opportunity to reduce my sentence by a year. I was especially angry because a year of my life, at age seventy-two, could have made the difference in whether I would have ever seen my son again.

Despite word leaking out that Billy Walters was in the house, I did my level best to maintain a low profile. Just being one of the guys came naturally to me. That's the way Grandmother raised me. It was "Yes sir" and "No sir" to guards and officials alike. Whatever street cred I earned on the inside was due to keeping my eyes open and my mouth shut. I waited my turn and didn't stand out. At the same time, I never backed down. In the end, I was just another con.

"Your time is your time," Mike once told me, meaning that I could choose to make the most of the hours and hours of free time with none of the distractions of everyday life. For my own sanity, I had to find ways to keep my mind and body sharp and my anger in check. I created a daily routine that rarely wavered. I worked. Then I worked out, either power-walking three miles on the track, hit the elliptical, or did squats and lifted weights. I'd call Susan between seven and eight every night on a prison phone before taking a quick shower and falling into bed, a book in hand.

I read autobiographies and history, mostly, learning about Sam Walton, Phil Knight, Andre Agassi, Howard Hughes, General Dwight D. Eisenhower, and World War I. Turning the pages wasn't easy because I had to wear gloves to keep my fingers warm in the winter.

When I wasn't reading a book or working out I spent my free time listening to music. I was able to buy an MP3 player and earbuds through the commissary and downloaded some songs. Far and away, my favorite turned out to be "Sunday Morning Sunshine" by the singer-songwriter Harry Chapin. I can't tell you how many times I listened to that song, eyes closed, thinking about growing up in Kentucky, life in Las Vegas, life inside, and my love for Susan as Harry's words and voice echoed in my ears:

I came into town with a knapsack on my shoulder
And a pocket full of stories that I just had to tell.

Louie Duluc was one of the inmates who helped me get through the brain drain of everyday prison life. As time went on, we had a series of long, reflective talks about the different stages of our lives.

When the bunk below Louie's opened up, I moved into his room with Louie and Mike Meisner, and our friendship deepened.

Louie was the consummate entrepreneur who took an interest in how people who started with nothing managed to create better lives. We discussed how bootstrappers share common traits, among them discipline, focus, and the ability to bounce back from failure.

I told Louie that anyone can tell you they were successful. But the reality is that no one can say they're successful until they have failed.

Before long, I found myself acting as mentor and sounding board to dozens of inmates. You never see yourself as the older, wiser guy, but some inmates saw me as that. I spent many hours listening to my fellow convicts tell their life stories.

Most of the men I got to know were not violent offenders or hardened criminals. They were just unlucky to be born into circumstances far worse than mine. I was surprised to learn that 60 percent of my fellow inmates never had a visitor, mostly because their families had given up on them or lacked the financial resources to travel to Pensacola.

One of them was Little Joe.

I had first met Joe Ramirez after overhearing him complain about his heartburn as he cleaned a bathroom. I offered him some Zantac, a drug that helps with acid reflux. Joe gave me one of those *I don't know you; I don't want to owe you anything* stares. But he eventually warmed up as we talked.

Little Joe was in his late forties and twenty-plus years into his sentence when we first crossed paths. He was a workout fiend and a feared fighter—only five foot eight, but 220 pounds of coiled steel.

Joe was born in Florida and raised by his grandmother in Mexico until age eight. Then he returned to Florida and settled in Wahneta, a mostly Mexican enclave a little more than an hour southwest of Disney World, but vastly different in every way.

In Wahneta, Joe said, he was drawn into the drug trade, the

dominant local business. In 2001, he was arrested and sentenced to twenty-seven years in prison for trafficking. His girlfriend was six weeks pregnant when he went in. By the time we met, Joe had spent fourteen years in a high-security penitentiary in Atlanta. He arrived in Pensacola angry, depressed, and believing he had no reason to live.

Joe was also the leader of what the BOP called a Hispanic prison gang—which Joe called a brotherhood—an affiliation that gave him power but did not make him a contented man. By his own admission, Joe didn't care if he lived or died.

He shared his greatest sorrow with me—that he had never met his daughter, Jordan Elisa Ramirez, who was seventeen years old.

They had traded phone calls twice a week when she was younger, he said, but those calls had dwindled as the years passed. Often, Joe said his calls to Jordan went unanswered.

I saw more than a bit of myself in Little Joe. He had made some bad choices that led to broken relationships with loved ones.

"Let's find out if it's possible to reach her," I said. "I'll try to help you reconnect with Jordan so she can visit you."

As it turned out, it *was* possible. Through connections on the outside, my guys tracked Jordan's mother to her job in Iowa. We then arranged to have the mother and daughter flown to Pensacola for a Friday night visit.

Susan and I were in the visitation room when they arrived. If there was a dry eye in the room, we didn't see it. Little Joe and his daughter hugged until their bodies shook from joy and gratitude.

Up until that moment, Little Joe said he'd never had a single visitor. He later told me he didn't even know what his daughter looked like. Her mother had changed as well. She had to wave her hand to let Joe know she was waiting at a table.

Jordan walked in wearing a yellow top and jeans. In prison, you're not allowed more than a quick embrace—no prolonged contact. Joe didn't care. He and Jordan just sat there and hugged and cried. One of the guards was going to break things up before I walked over and whispered, "Let him hold his daughter."

Jordan's first words to Joe were "I really needed that, Dad."

After twenty-two years in prison, Joe earned a COVID-related release from FPC Pensacola in July 2020. At age fifty-four, he now works at a Kia dealership in Florida, where he is a model employee. Joe recently told me he sees Jordan on occasion and her surprise visit was the best gift a father could ever have.

"I can die a happy man," he said.

27

Doing Time

As weeks crept into months and months turned into years, I adapted to doing time. I learned that Pensacola, like every prison, was crawling with snitches and professional con men.

One of the first snakes to slither up to me was the son of a former Arizona governor, a con artist who tried to pawn himself off as an art consultant. I found it amusing when he told me that he'd spent two weeks with none other than Steve Wynn before he came to prison.

Right.

I brushed him off and focused on building a trustworthy inner circle of fellow prisoners. My new friends included "Boz," an ex–weight lifter by way of Bosnia who was nearing the end of his fifteen-year term. Boz, who had once trained for the Olympics, could bench press four hundred pounds and snatch more than six hundred. His shoulders were so wide and his muscles so thick you had to turn sideways when he walked down the hall to avoid bumping into him. I had heard that he trained other inmates, so I asked Boz to work out with me two days a week. On Sundays we hit the weights and on Thursdays we did core exercises and squats. I became obsessed with doing as many squats as I could—adding one rep to my routine every time I did them. In my last workout, I was up to 191 squats in a row.

I first got to know Boz in a way that would only happen in prison. We met after my second dorm room was disrupted over an incident involving forbidden cell phones and something called a Pocket Pussy. Yep, a Pocket Pussy, the No. 1 Male Sex Toy in the World.

Normally, getting busted with a cell phone in a higher-security prison earned you an immediate trip to the hole. Pensacola didn't have a hole, so they sent prisoners to a different facility packed with hard-core criminals. At Pensacola, you also risked losing visitation rights or receiving a reduction in commissary and phone privileges.

Our dorm room violator was a big guy named Leon. During a random search, corrections officers found not one but two cell phones in Leon's locker, along with the aforementioned sex toy—a portable, battery-operated, vibrating self-pleasuring device. Mike Meisner called it "Leon's girlfriend." None of the other nine men had any clue that Leon kept contraband in our room.

Well, you can only imagine the ruckus that followed those discoveries. Leon was sent to Hard-Core U, and the corrections officers broke up our dorm room crowd. I was moved to the far end of the hall in a room with Boz and Carlitos, a quiet kid from Puerto Rico who had no business being in prison. After spending a good part of my life working in tobacco barns and gambling in bars and at racetracks, I had no problem fitting in with people like Flaco, Carlitos, Rock, Swag, and every other inmate at Pensacola. No gangs. No turf battles. No tests. No drama. No violence.

As one day bled into the next, I tried to serve as a low-key mediator and a voice of reason, especially when situations grew tense. After I had moved in with Mike, I befriended a guy in our dorm room named James, who stood six foot three and weighed more than three hundred pounds. James had been locked up for twenty-three years. He was well liked, but volatile.

One day, James got carried away in sharing his evangelical Christian beliefs. If there's one thing you do *not* talk about in prison, it's religion. Unless you want to stir up trouble, that is. Now, James could handle his share of physical trouble, but I worried more about his emotional well-being when he began delivering one of his hellfire-and-brimstone sermons on how the Bible condemned homosexuality.

I was minding my own business in my bunk, reading *The New York Times*, when James launched into his sermon. One of our dorm mates, Mike Berlon, abruptly cut him off. Mike, an attorney who had once served as the head of the Democratic Party in Georgia and was now serving five years for stealing more than $2 million from clients of his former law firm, felt compelled to defend LGBTQ rights by insisting the Bible never condemned homosexuality.

I tried to ignore the back-and-forth until James made a menacing move toward Mike. I popped out of my lower bunk and tried to play peacemaker.

"Now, James, hold on a second," I said. "You're leaving this place in a few short months. Don't do anything to jeopardize it. And, really, I don't need the hassle in this room. So please pipe down."

Someone in the room muttered, "I think the old man's lost his mind."

James was half a foot taller than me and twice my weight. His eyes had a crazy shine to them. But I managed to talk him down because James was one of the inmates I had been mentoring. We had formed a bond of trust and respect.

From the look of the cafeteria menu, you would have thought the Bureau of Prisons was feeding the U.S. Olympic team. That's how nutritious the food items appeared. Talk about false advertising. I don't think I ate a dozen meals in the prison chow hall during my entire time inside. I just couldn't stomach it. The prisoners who transferred into Pensacola from elsewhere said it was the worst food in the system.

Like most of my fellow inmates, I preferred the food sold in the commissary, but we paid a steep premium for it. I lived on boxes of Raisin Bran ($3.65), shredded pork ($4.40), and chorizo sausage ($2.10). We cooked our food purchases in secondhand microwaves passed down by the Navy. Chef Meisner taught me the ropes and together we made and shared many a meal.

My main source of sustenance came from three industrial-size vending machines in the visitor's area. Every week an older woman and her daughter filled the machines with wholesome food purchased from the local Publix—fresh fruit, yogurt, protein shakes, cheese chicken, Jimmy Dean sausage, and eggs.

Susan made sure that I filled up with that healthier fare every time she visited. She was my savior. Nearly every week, she flew down to Pensacola from Louisville, after enduring a layover in Atlanta's hyperactive airport. Virtually every Friday, upon my return on the bus from DZ-23, I'd see her waiting for me on the lawn near the front gate, usually at least two hours before the 5:00 p.m. visitation period began.

On many Saturdays and Sundays, she'd be out front by 5:00 a.m., three hours before visiting hours began. Come rain, sleet, snow or shine, I could count on seeing Susan's smiling face. I think she only missed maybe fifteen out of some 370 possible visitation days during my entire time behind bars.

No matter the day, Susan was usually first or second in line, ready to make a mad dash to the first-come, first-serve vending machines. She would drop as much as a hundred bucks into those machines on each visit. As inmates, we weren't allowed to touch the machines or any money. More often than not, I'd stand nearby barking out the food I wanted: *Get the chicken! Grab the yogurt!* When my son Derin first visited, I thought he was going to have a heart attack as I stood three feet away ordering him to push this button and that button, orchestrating his purchases.

Sitting with my wife on a Friday night, I rarely uttered a word for forty-five minutes, stuffing my face until my jaws hurt, barely taking a breath as I devoured bowls of fresh fruit and yogurt, pieces of chicken or pork, and slices of cake.

Depending on the weather, Susan and I would sit inside or outside at picnic tables, trying to avoid the fire ants that would leave festering red welts on our feet and ankles. We'd play dominoes or cards while catching up. It was so damned hard, especially during the first few months, when Scott's neurological condition worsened.

Without question, some of the most emotional moments came when Derin, who works in real estate in Lexington, made one of his dozen visits. We hugged more than ever and cried openly. We talked about Scott and Tonia, reminding me how much I love my family. The strong man Derin had known on the outside had changed—softened, humbled, deeply depressed at times.

My steady flow of visitors was the talk of the prison. I had at least one guest every weekend, as family members, friends, and business associates made the trip to help ease my loneliness and isolation.

Mike Luce came down twice a month. He'd leave Vegas on a 6:00 a.m. Friday flight, connect in Houston, and get to Pensacola in time to line up for the 5:00 p.m. vending machine rush with Susan. He'd join us again on Saturday before jumping on a flight back home. Our conversations focused on keeping my businesses afloat, keeping customers and team members happy, and weeding out employees who tried to take advantage of my absence.

Jim Colbert visited a half-dozen times. Former University of Pittsburgh head football coach and ESPN analyst Mike Gottfried and sports analyst Danny Sheridan made many a trip. So did former New York City police commissioner Bernie Kerik, who had been introduced to me by former *60 Minutes* correspondent Lara Logan, who also visited me several times. Before the Las Vegas Raiders played the Miami Dolphins on the road, Mark Davis stopped by to see me in prison. Rob Goldstein, the chairman and CEO of the Las Vegas Sands, also visited. So did singer-songwriter Mac Davis, one of my best friends, and his wife, Lise.

The official tally came to 1,400 visits by more than 200 different people. I was told by one prison official that those numbers set an all-time BOP record—not exactly the kind of milestone you set out to achieve in life.

FPC Pensacola served as a cruel reminder that, even in an institution without bars or walls, the inmates are penned up like cattle. The solitude could be crushing, but it also allowed for time—sitting alone in the yard or walking the track—to think back on my life.

As I sat quietly in the yard one day soaking up some sun, reflecting on my past, the name Gabe Kaplan brought a smile to my face.

For those of a certain age you may remember the name. For the uninitiated, Gabe was an actor-comedian and the co-creator and star of *Welcome Back, Kotter*. The 1970s sitcom featured Gabe as a wisecracking high school teacher who returns to his alma mater to teach a remedial class of racially diverse students known as the Sweathogs. The show was funny, especially with a very young John Travolta as Vinnie Barbarino, the head Sweathog, which proved to be his breakout role.

Gabe was equally well regarded in the professional poker ranks. He had won Amarillo Slim's first Super Bowl of Poker in 1980, and ground out several high finishes on both the World Poker Tour and World Series of Poker. Gabe and I and a bunch of the poker pros, including Chip and Doyle, were playing a private game in Beverly Hills one night when the table talk turned to golf. Gabe, who was not a golfer, started yapping about how he could break 90 on the Champions Course at La Costa if he practiced enough and got serious about the game.

Well, with that group of sharks 'round the table, he might as well have thrown some chum in the water. Wagers and challenges flew, and pretty soon there was a half million dollars on the line. That gave Gabe all the incentive he needed. He rented a place at La Costa, hired an instructor, and went to work on his game.

Now, Gabe was a good athlete who had once dreamed of playing professional baseball, so it wasn't long before word got around that he was a ball beater and closing in on shooting 90 for eighteen holes. Chip and Doyle were eager to play him for money. They knew that there was a big difference between playing with a golf instructor in your cart and playing with professional gamblers.

Professional gamblers who are just decent golfers can often beat much better golfers who aren't used to playing for high stakes. But Gabe was an experienced gambler, a smart guy. He was confident that he could come out on top in any matchup.

Still, I looked at him as a poker player who could play under pressure at the table, but maybe not on the golf course. I liked the risk relative to a seven-figure reward.

"I'll give you seven, eight, and nine a side in match play," I told him, laying out three different bets. "Along with that, I'll spot you ten shots a side in medal play. We'll play a $10,000 Nassau on each bet."

Gabe took the bet. Some of my friends thought I'd started drinking again. They worried Gabe would make a punch line out of me.

I told Chip and the rest that they didn't understand. If Gabe beat me one or two days, I was done with it.

I knew if he didn't buckle under the pressure, there was no way I could win by giving him that many shots. But I also knew that, even if I was beating him, he would keep playing because he was getting all those shots.

I was betting that Gabe, a relative newcomer to the game, wouldn't play well under the pressure. I had seen it countless times before—even on Sundays on the PGA Tour!

Sure enough, the first day at La Costa, we reached the last five or six holes on the back nine and Gabe started dogging it. He couldn't make a par, or even a bogey, suffering through a double, triple, or quad on every hole. Sometimes he'd only have to make a seven or eight to win the medal bet, but instead he'd make ten or twelve. I beat him every day for several days in a row.

As the week of golf we'd scheduled wore on, Gabe was doing exactly what I expected. He was improving every day and learning how to handle the heat. He played well until the last four holes of one match, then over the next few days, he'd play well down to the last three or two holes.

By the end of the week, Gabe was making a real game of it.

On the last day we played, Bobby Baldwin flew in from Vegas to join us and get some action. We came to the eighteenth hole, a 495-yard par-5 over water, and all Gabe needed was a nine on the hole to win every bet and take home a couple hundred grand. As we stood on the tee, Gabe was anything but cocky. I could tell he was replaying earlier meltdowns in his mind.

He was teed up and ready to hit at one point, but backed off, and then tried to pull off a classic bluff.

"What will you give me to get out of this bet?" he asked. "All I've got to do is make a nine."

"I won't give you anything," I said. "Just go and hit it."

Gabe returned to his teed-up ball, waggled his club a couple of times, but then stepped back again.

"What will you give me to settle?"

"I'm not going to give you anything to settle. Just hit it."

At which point, Bobby looked at me and said exactly what Chip Reese had said when I made the original bet.

"Billy, have you lost your mind?" Bobby asked.

"Just let him hit it," I said, giving Bobby a wink.

Had Gabe been more experienced under pressure, he would have considered playing it down the adjacent seventeenth fairway to avoid the water. Instead, he took a hard swing and flubbed his drive, hitting it just fifty yards and straight into some nasty rough.

Again, his inexperience showed. Instead of using a short iron, clearing the water, and getting back into play, Gabe pulled out a

3-wood and proceeded, if memory serves, to top another shot. Then he splashed two more shots into the drink. By the time Gabe putted out, he had a twelve or fourteen on the hole.

I'd won a lot of money, not because I was a great player, but because I knew what inexperience and pressure could do to a person on a golf course.

But, trust me, not every match with a professional poker player went so well.

By the time I met Gene Fisher, out of El Paso, he had won the first of two World Series of Poker bracelets and finished third in the 1980 WSOP Main Event. We had first crossed paths at Jack Binion's annual professional gambler's golf invitational in Vegas. I knew that Fisher was a friend of Lee Trevino, who had gained early fame in the region for beating Raymond Floyd in a big-money match when both were in their early twenties. At the PGI, Gene and I arranged to play a match at his home course of Vista Hills Country Club in El Paso.

It was 1981 and I was still living in Louisville playing some of the best golf of my life. The day before heading to El Paso, I'd shot even par at the Standard country club in Louisville. I was feeling extremely confident when Fisher agreed to give me two shots a side for a $20,000 Nassau.

I arrived in El Paso with my friends Calvin Hash and Carl De-Cesar. When we got to Vista Hills, we headed to the range. Calvin suggested we play a practice round because he'd heard the greens were tricky. I declined, figuring I was playing so well it didn't matter.

The next day, the first tee was lined with railbirds ready to bet on our match, and I obliged every last one. I had brought $200,000 with me, close to every penny I had. I hit the ball just as I'd hoped—from tee to green I was striping it.

But once I got to the putting surface, I found myself in a horizontal hall of mirrors. Not only were the greens icy fast—far faster than what I'd been playing on at home—I could not read them to save my life, especially whether the putts were running uphill or downhill.

I missed a few short putts early on and my confidence began to wither.

By the final hole, I was a beaten man. I had three-putted fourteen greens and lost a total of $280,000. I paid off the railbirds, gave Fisher what was left of my bankroll, and promised to send the rest, which I did shortly thereafter. Then I headed home, earning nothing but another knot on my head.

In prison, your heart breaks minute by minute, hour by hour, day by day. So it was when I learned that Scott was in a near catatonic state from medication needed to stabilize his constant seizures. I was in a panic, knowing he needed me and I couldn't help him from where I was sitting. I had nightmares that he may die and I would never see him again.

Finally, we arranged to fly Scott down to Pensacola on a chartered plane to see me for the first—and what I thought could well be the last—time.

I wanted to scream when I watched him wheeled into visitation. He was not the same Scott I had last seen. Instead, I fought back tears.

For all of the anger and guilt I felt about my son, the most difficult challenge during my time in Pensacola was dealing with the struggles of my daughter, Tonia.

As you might recall, my first wife, Sharon, and I were just teenagers when Tonia was born in Louisville. I was in no way prepared to be a father, our early struggles one hundred percent my fault. After our divorce, Tonia moved to Germany with Sharon and her new stepfather, who assumed the bulk of the responsibility for raising her. Tonia and I had little contact until she was twelve and Susan and I were married. Even then, what little communication we had revolved around money. When Tonia turned sixteen, I bought her a car, and I was supportive of her in her teen years.

Later, after Susan and I moved to Vegas, Tonia came to visit a couple of times. That's when Susan noticed the manipulative side of my daughter. Tonia had a habit of "losing" her purse or having it "stolen" while visiting casinos, and she would ask to borrow money from my friends.

She married in her twenties and had a son named Jimmy. She was having a hard time financially in Louisville and battling a prescription drug problem. When her marriage ended in divorce, Sharon asked me to step in to support Tonia. I arranged for Tonia and Jimmy to move to Las Vegas.

I put my daughter to work on our golf course marketing team and later in my sports-betting operation. During those years, we got to know each other better. She met a guy named Mike Snyder and they got married. The newlyweds couldn't afford a mortgage or a down payment, so I bought a house for them. I fully intended to give them the home once I became convinced that Tonia was living a clean life.

When Jimmy hit his teens, we had concerns about the environment he was living in. After a discussion with Tonia, she agreed that we could send Jimmy to Oak Hill Academy, a private boarding school in Virginia. I was so proud of my grandson for graduating that I bought him a new truck.

When he was accepted to the University of Arizona, I told him: "We're going to pay for your college, your room, and your truck. This is your chance. If you mess this up, there are no more chances."

He messed it up. We found out Jimmy was drinking and partying down in Tucson and never went to a class. He showed up one Thanksgiving at our house in Vegas and never went back to school. The next thing we knew, Jimmy was hooked on Oxy. I got him into a rehab program in Las Vegas. Not once but twice. He was fine Monday to Friday, but wanted to leave on weekends. When they told him no, Jimmy punched a wall and walked out. He's been in and out of trouble ever since.

After living and working in Vegas for a few years, Tonia—no doubt carrying some of my bad genes—got addicted to gambling and the high life. Her drug use worsened. Our worries increased when Tonia constantly complained about various stomach and neck ailments. Her prescription drug problem had escalated to Oxy as well. Like so many Oxy addicts, she was searching for drugs to treat the phantom pain. Tonia denied it. But deep down I knew she was lying.

Our suspicions and fears about Tonia's behavior escalated in 2012 when she showed up for work driving a Mercedes while decked out in designer clothes and shoes, and carrying a Louis Vuitton handbag. She was making good money, but not that much money. That's when Susan noticed a series of transfers from a bank account that didn't look right.

Susan and I met Tonia at Bali Hai with our accountant and one of our employees, Ray Coy, whose nickname was Cabbage. Ray was a down-to-earth good 'ol boy from Kentucky who got his nickname from slinging bushels of fruit and vegetables at the hay market in Louisville. He spent nine years with me in our wholesale car business in Louisville before following us to Vegas to work in our sports-betting operation. He was one of my best friends.

I'll never forget how my daughter looked when she walked into the office that day. I was clad in golf course casual. Susan was dressed in blue jeans and a sweatshirt. Tonia was all dolled up in designer clothes, carrying a Gucci bag. We went over the bank transactions one by one, asking her about the missing funds.

"Tonia," I said, "this doesn't make sense."

At that point, my daughter stood up in a huff.

"I don't like the way this conversation is going," she said.

Then she walked out.

A couple of days later, Susan, Cabbage, and I met with Tonia again, this time at a little breakfast place. By then we had calculated that my only daughter had embezzled at least $2 million from us.

"Tonia," I said, "we know you're doing this."

She tried to pin the whole thing on Cabbage, but that didn't fly. We'd known him for forty-plus years and he had never been dishonest or disloyal.

Tonia just sat there with her head down. Finally she broke down and started crying.

"Yeah," she said, "I did it."

After that meeting, Tonia no longer worked for The Walters Group. We later found out she was selling her designer clothes and handbags on eBay to support her drug habit.

Out of frustration and concern, I tried to help her. I called a dear friend, a doctor at Scripps Hospital in San Diego, and he lined up appointments with several specialists. We flew Tonia to San Diego, but she was a no-show for nearly every appointment. The doctor told me there's nothing wrong with my daughter; all she's doing is pushing doctors for more prescription drugs. She was spiraling downward, yet her doctors kept obliging. I was beside my-self, but Tonia was an adult, and there was little I could do.

Although our relationship was strained and I didn't see Tonia very often, we talked regularly. Especially when she had a problem in her life. Which was often.

Right before I went to prison, Tonia reached out and said she wanted to see me. When she showed up at my office at Bali Hai, I couldn't believe my eyes. I wish I could report that my once-beautiful baby girl had finally gotten clean. But sadly the Oxy addiction had given way to meth and crack cocaine, destroying her life just as it had countless others'.

The woman I saw was frail, walked with a cane, and looked much older than her years. I wanted to cry.

After Tonia left, I told Susan that I feared getting a call in prison informing me that my daughter had died of a heart attack.

On March 12, 2019, a corrections officer stopped me as I stepped off the bus while returning from work in DZ-23.

"Walters," he said, "they need to see you at Control."

I'll never forget what happened next. Ms. Kennedy, who oversaw Control that day, told me that Susan had made an emergency call to the prison. I called her right back to learn the news: Tonia had gotten her hands on a gun and killed herself. She was fifty-four years old.

I lost it right there. There is no greater pain than the loss of a child. Unless, that is, you learn of that loss locked away in federal prison, powerless to be where I wanted to be, needed to be— mourning my daughter with family and friends, consoling others even in my own grief. I am certain Tonia would still be alive if I was anywhere but penned up in Pensacola. She would have called me as always, and her death never would have happened.

The next morning, I was standing in the bus barn waiting to head out to DZ-23, head down, totally withdrawn, when Louie Duluc came to my side. He gave me a long hard hug. I broke down for maybe ten seconds, ten seconds that felt like a lifetime of sorrow.

"It's hard, Louie, it's hard," I told him.

We submitted a travel request to the Bureau of Prisons and probation departments in two states. Based on my clean record, nothing short of a small miracle occurred. I was awarded two days to travel back to Kentucky and bury my baby girl.

Hard to believe, but I flew to Louisville by myself on the honor system. I landed in the afternoon and headed straight to the funeral home. Yes, my relationship with Tonia was strained, but I loved her very much. Standing alone in front of her casket, all I could think about was that, if I hadn't been in prison, my daughter would still be alive.

In what seemed like an episode out of *The Twilight Zone*, I had dinner with Susan at our home and spent the night in my own bed. Talk about a torturous tease of freedom. In the morning, I attended Tonia's service before hopping on a couple of planes back to Pensacola. Later, someone asked me if I was tempted to slip out of the country on my private plane. The thought never crossed my mind. It was difficult to go back to prison, but it was something I had to do.

One year later, in March of 2020, Pensacola's federal prison camp went into lockdown in response to the rapidly spreading and increasingly deadly coronavirus. And when I say lockdown, I mean *locked down*. No visitation. No cafeteria (box meals three times a day). No microwaves. No track. No exercise. No sun. Two phone calls a week, one for fifteen minutes, the other ten.

The sinful sanitary conditions festering in the showers and bathroom multiplied by ten. Basically, you were stuck on a floor with two hundred other men twenty-four hours a day. I watched CNBC on the rare occasions when the TV room was vacant. Trust me, no one else inside wanted to watch CNBC.

And then another small miracle occurred.

On May 1, two and a half months shy of my seventy-fourth birthday, I received the gift I'd long been praying for when the Bureau of Prisons was authorized to release more than twenty-four thousand of its oldest and most vulnerable low-risk offenders out of fear that the COVID-19 pandemic would overwhelm the system. Given my age and flawless prison record, I was one of those prisoners.

The day of the announcement, I walked out of FPC Pensacola for good after serving thirty-one months of my sixty-month sentence. Before leaving, I shared hugs and tears with Flaco, Little Joe, Louie, Carlitos, and a few corrections officers I'd come to respect. Mike Meisner, who was sixty-two, had already earned an early release three months earlier.

In the movies, the freed inmate takes his first steps outside the prison gates, gazes up at the sky, throws his arms up in the air, and takes a deep, soul-cleansing breath. Not this inmate. I couldn't wait to get the hell out of there.

Marius Telehoi, my partner in a Kia dealership in St. Augustine, Florida, picked me up. It was a fitting ending, since he had dropped me off at FPC to begin my sentence. I took a flight straight to Susan in Carlsbad. That night I had my first home-cooked meal in what seemed like forever. It was nothing fancy, just a good down-home supper of meatloaf, Kentucky cornbread, sweet potatoes, green beans, kale greens and vinegar. I was essentially under house arrest, allowed to go only to work or church, but in my mind freedom never felt so good.

Since the day I was convicted in April 2017 of insider trading I'd been working with a parade of high-priced D.C. attorneys and power brokers in an attempt to receive a pardon from President Donald J. Trump. Nearly four years later, on January 19, 2021, the final full day of Trump's presidency, I was at home in California, still tethered to that insidious ankle bracelet, waiting and waiting for a telephone call from my attorney.

After dinner—a meal I could barely touch—my friend Bernie Kerik, the former New York City police commissioner, called at 9:00 p.m. with the news I'd longed to hear from the West Wing.

The final list of presidential pardons would be released within twenty minutes.

Nearly three hours later, I'd still heard nothing. It was approaching midnight on the West Coast, 3:00 a.m. in the East and already January 20. Susan was in bed downstairs, snuggled with the dogs. I was in my office chair, cell phone in hand, dozing in and out, struggling to stay awake.

Suddenly my phone screen brightened with an alert from the website WhiteHouse.gov.

The moment of truth: I slowly scrolled down the randomly organized list of bold-faced names beginning with Todd Boulanger, full pardon. Abel Holtz, full pardon. Representative Rick Renzi, full pardon.

I kept scrolling and searching, with my stomach turning, until, finally, 107 names down the list, right after Randall "Duke" Cunningham, I hit the jackpot: William T. Walters.

I did not read another word. Instead, I screamed.

"Honey, honey! We got it. *WE GOT IT!*"

I collapsed into bed exhausted, but elated. I slept soundly, con-

vinced that every twist and turn during a three-and-a-half-year political odyssey had finally been worth it. I was thankful after years of
breathless hope and broken promises that an eleventh-hour appeal
by my friend Butch Harmon—and President Trump's longtime family friend—had been successful.

My first clue something was amiss came early the next morning.
Senator Reid called with congratulations, only to call back thirty
minutes later.

"Billy," he said, "I'm not sure you got a pardon."

Another clue came when I called the probation hotline to get
my ankle monitor removed. The lady on the other end said, "Mr.
Walters, here's the number of the probation officer you need to call."

Probation officer? What?

Once the ankle bracelet was off, I reached out to my attorney
Rick Wright.

Please tell these people I received a pardon!

Rick tried my pardon attorney, John Dowd, former White House
lead counsel to the president on the Russia investigation. No answer.
He called the office of the pardon attorney. Closed. He checked their
website. Shut down. The press release announcing clemency was
nowhere to be found.

What did I expect? It was Inauguration Day.

I finally got my hands on a copy of the document signed by President Trump on January 13, 2021. Four paragraphs in, I found the
words I had been searching for:

"I commute the 60-month sentence imposed upon the said
WILLIAM T. WALTERS to time served. I leave intact and in effect
the remaining one-year term of supervised release with all its conditions, the unpaid balances, if any, of his fine, restitution, forfeiture,
and special assessment obligations, and all other components of the
sentence."

Translation: There would be no full pardon for me. Instead the
president had granted me clemency.

At that point I was pissed off, believing I'd been screwed one final time by the president's bosom buddy Steve Wynn.

It is no small irony that Wynn remains a controversial figure within the gambling and entertainment mecca he helped create. Today, he is persona non grata around town. His toxic reputation is tied to myriad allegations of sexual harassment, coercion, indecent exposure, and misconduct involving dozens of Wynn employees over the years, including one allegation of sexual assault that he reportedly paid $7.5 million to settle.

Wynn and President Trump have known each other for more than forty years. They have dined together, golfed together, sued each other, and seen the Justice Department accuse Wynn of lobbying the president on behalf of the Chinese government—which Wynn denied—as part of their complicated "frenemy" relationship. In 1996, for example, Wynn told *The Wall Street Journal* that Trump was "an incompetent . . . all hat, no cattle." Trump hit back in 1998, telling *New York* magazine: "You know, I think Steve's got a lot of psychological problems. I think he's quite disturbed."

Nonetheless, one Wynn family member had gone so far as to say that President Trump sees a lot of himself in Wynn, and perhaps, in a way, even worships him. But one thing is certain: as former finance chairman of the Republican National Committee, the political arm of the GOP, Wynn held overwhelming influence over President Trump's efforts to remain in the White House, as well as my efforts to obtain a pardon.

How do I know Steve Wynn stabbed me in the back? Because on the morning of the February 2018 pardons, Wynn broke the news at a private fundraising retreat in Sun Valley attended by a slew of heavyweight Republican donors, including several casino executives.

At the retreat, Wynn was overheard bragging about killing my chances for a pardon, his fundraising influence over the president, and the enormous pleasure he took in, essentially, screwing me over.

News of the commutation made me want to scream. But after a few hours of outrage, a strange thing happened. Strange at least for a man who has done nothing but keep score since he was six years old. As the minutes passed, so did the anger and obsession, the twin spirals of my DNA.

No, I hadn't been pardoned. Yes, I was still a convicted felon.

Even so, out of 11,611 petitions received by President Trump, mine was just one of 237 to be granted a pardon or clemency. I knew there were many others like me who had been unjustly convicted, but whose appeals, due to lack of resources and clout, would never be granted. I allowed myself to revel in the fact that the GPS anklet that tracked me like an animal day and night was gone.

The stress and strain of the three-week trial, thirty-one months in prison, eight months of home confinement, and three and a half years of playing the pardon game had drained away. Replaced by a blissful new feeling one evening as Susan and I cruised along Encinitas Boulevard looking for a place to eat.

I was out after dark for the first time since October 9, 2017.

"My God," I said aloud, "that's beautiful."

Susan said, "What do you mean?"

"All the lights," I said. "Seeing the world at night. The businesses with their lights on."

That's when it hit me: after four long years, perhaps my entire seventy-four years, my view of the world had shifted.

Pardon me, but I was finally feeling free.

28

Full Circle

Tuesday, March 23, 2021.

The butterflies in my stomach had little to do with the winds buffeting the plane during its initial descent into Las Vegas.

My sixty-day probation travel ban had officially expired, and I returned to the life of a man bent on making every moment count.

The round trip is complete, I thought.

It had been forty-two long months since I'd left Las Vegas for prison in the aftermath of the tragic Jason Aldean concert. I was anxious to see how my homecoming would be greeted, though I was not so naive as to believe a brass band would be playing on the airport tarmac.

I knew that my release from prison and subsequent clemency had stirred up a few old feuds and rivalries. A certain element believed that Billy Walters had long played by his own set of rules, lived in a gray area, and was nothing more than a cheater who got what he deserved.

I'm pleased to report that none of those people were present or accounted for at Bali Hai. A couple of dozen current and former employees—bartenders, waiters, waitresses, cooks, caddies, and golf pros—broke into applause as I entered the club, welcoming me home. I exchanged one bear hug after another, bringing back memories of all that went into building beautiful Bali Hai.

Those first few days back in Vegas remain a blur. I caught up on a backlog of business, attended a series of lunches and dinners with old friends, and saw one doctor after another in an attempt to undo the damage incurred by months of microwaved food, a COVID lockdown, and the sheer incompetence of Dr. Death.

I had heart issues that required a valve replacement. I needed surgery on both hands. Dental implants were in the offing, along with shoulder and heart valve replacements and knee surgery. It would be a long road to recovery, but at least I was on it.

Imagine yourself on your deathbed. As your life flashes before you, the tendency is to consider the most important things in life. Mine come easily to mind. I love my wife. I love my family. I love being on or near the water. I love warm weather. I love the game of golf.

After my release from Pensacola, the only thing I yearned to do was to go someplace warm, throw on a pair of shorts, play golf, breathe clean air, work out, and be with friends. For Susan and me, that special place was a villa on the beach in Maui. In December 2021, we were staying at a private resort there when a tropical storm battered the islands. Amid the high winds and heavy rain, Susan sighed and declared we were having a "bad day."

"Honey," I said, "this isn't a bad day at all. Know why? I chose what I want to eat and when I want to eat it. I went to the bathroom without six other guys and didn't have to hold my nose. I'm free to do whatever I want whenever I want."

Prison makes that course correction in your life. It puts everything in perspective, reminding you of the many things you otherwise took for granted and the things that actually matter.

I don't take *anything* for granted anymore, especially family. This was brought home to me when I went back to Kentucky in the summer of 2021 for the annual Walters family reunion. I had more fun than I'd had in years. We threw a big birthday party for Susan, and I had a hoot of a lunch with three of my oldest and best friends, Sammy Marrillia, Luther James, and Mo Moorman.

The drive down to Munfordville from Louisville was a chance to revisit some sights and to reminisce about Grandmother, Uncle Harry, pool halls, and paper routes, to visit the family cemetery and buy new headstones for my mother and father, to feel like a little boy again with Susan along for the ride and me playing tour guide. *The Dairy Queen was right there. Used to be a Standard Oil station over there. Mr. Stewart lived up that hill.*

The reunion affected me far more than I thought it would. About sixty of us from the Walters and Quesenberry sides—aunts, uncles, cousins, nieces, nephews, children, grandchildren, and great-grandchildren—came together on a Saturday for a scrumptious potluck spread at a local church.

I reminisced with cousin Timmy Quesenberry and old friends like Junior Puryear. It was a kick to see my cousin Gayle calling various family members up to say a few words, honoring at least three couples who'd been married sixty years or more.

After that trip, Susan and I decided to come full circle and make Kentucky a permanent part of our lives. We're building a new home in Louisville and plan to spend more quality time with Scott, who continues to fight a courageous battle every day.

Meanwhile, my servant's heart had found new callings. Susan and I are supporting Kentucky's equivalents of Opportunity Village: the Guthrie Opportunity Center in Bardstown, and Cedar Lake Lodge in La Grange. Both serve those with developmental and intellectual disabilities.

And finally, my newest and greatest challenge: finding ways to fix a broken prison system.

First, there's something I want to make clear about my encounter with the justice system. I know I was mistreated, but I also know that I'm one of the lucky ones. I had money; I could afford lawyers. There are a lot of people who can't, and end up with inexperienced public defenders.

I'm white and I have terrific friends. I know that legions of people who don't look like me have been absolutely screwed by our so-called system of justice. I don't want to sound like I'm whining because I'm not. Writing this book provides me an opportunity to give you a glimpse inside the system and I want you to know that I'm fully aware of the grave injustices that have been done to people, particularly minorities, in this country.

It is no exaggeration to say that a single year in prison takes five years off your life. After many prisoners are released, they are depressed, angry, and totally unprepared to become contributing members of society. As a result, far too many people wind up right back behind bars.

We can and must do better as a society. Words are one thing; actions are quite another. To that end, I've resolved to become an action man for prison reform.

My idea, which I am prepared to support financially, is to create vocational schools inside select prisons. Inmates would have to qualify and earn the right to attend these schools by proving that they are completely committed. The schools will be operated by private entities outside the Bureau of Prisons. They will be run like charter schools, offering courses and training in automotive, electrical, construction, and plumbing trades, and other fields in desperate need of workers.

Under my plan, every person who successfully completes vocational training will have a job waiting upon release from prison. The schools will have career counselors on the inside and outside to ensure that inmates have a job and the skills they need to become contributing members of society.

As it stands today, prisons are breeding grounds for generations of criminals. Fathers and mothers who come out of prison with no hope cannot offer hope to their children. But those who learn trades and support their families are far more likely to raise children who have a greater vision for their lives.

I have an important new ally in this endeavor. His name is Jon

Ponder. My introduction to Jon came courtesy of Bill Young, the former sheriff of Clark County. Jon is a former inmate who founded the nonprofit Hope for Prisoners in Las Vegas in 2010. His programs for helping inmates reenter society with better life, financial, and trade skills have won the support of law enforcement officials, including the FBI, whose agents put Jon in prison for bank robbery in 2004.

In all, 450 people go through Jon's program every year and nearly three-quarters enter the workforce. Jon and I share the same vision and are working together to bring it to reality. In fact, I was so impressed with Hope for Prisoners that, in February 2022, Susan and I funded the creation of a new Las Vegas facility called the Billy Walters Center for Second Chances. The new location will offer in-house vocational training, higher-education opportunities, substance abuse and mental health counseling, access to parole and probation officers, a family reunification center, and Department of Motor Vehicles and Social Security resources.

"There was only one positive thing that happened to me while I was in prison," I said that day. "I had the opportunity and pleasure of mentoring more than two dozen men over the thirty-one months I was in Pensacola. What I learned from those men is that not a one of them wanted to go back to prison. But they felt like they had no hope. Hope for Prisoners bridges the desire, the opportunity, and the tools for you to achieve what you have sought out to achieve. But at the end of the day, you can get all the support in the world, but if you're not totally committed to this, don't BS yourself, this isn't going to work. And if you are not totally committed to this, don't take up the space for someone else who is committed to it."

In April 2023, we committed an additional $2 million, with a matching donation from Las Vegas's Engelstad Foundation, to create a vocational school at Southern Desert Correctional Center in Indian Springs, Nevada. The school will be operated by Hope for Prisoners and the Nevada Department of Corrections and will provide job training for a range of skills, including commercial truck driving, construction trades, hospitality, and warehouse logistics.

In addition to my work on prison reform, I'm proud of the small role I played in the effort to rename McCarran International Airport in honor of former Senate Majority Leader Harry Reid (now Harry Reid International Airport). And rightly so, given Harry's tireless efforts to open Las Vegas to the international market and modernize a facility that welcomes 40 million visitors a year.

The senator's battle against pancreatic cancer kept him from attending the official renaming ceremony in December 2021, but in a statement he called it "one of the greatest honors of my life."

Two weeks later, Harry Mason Reid Jr., who grew up in tiny Searchlight, Nevada, the son of an alcoholic miner who committed suicide and a mother who made ends meet washing laundry from local whorehouses, lost his four-year battle to cancer at the age of eighty-two.

The pain of losing Senator Reid was compounded by the unexpected death, that very same day, of Jbird, the former head of my Panama betting operation, who died of a massive heart attack at the age of fifty-two.

Jbird was like a son to me, and I was devastated by the news.

As I conclude this account of my wild and crazy life, I take comfort in a few absolutes: I'll work until the day I die. That said, having spent my entire life under the gun, I no longer feel driven by the burning desire to press the accelerator straight to the floor.

Truth be told, I'm a deal junkie and I'll take risks until I'm six feet under. In case you were wondering, yes, the gambler in me is still alive and doing quite well, thank you. I recently hired a brilliant new lead programmer from a field of eighty candidates, still calculating every factor and angle to retain that elusive edge in sports wagering.

Like most men and women my age, I've thought a great deal about how I'll be judged when I meet my maker. You come into this world with nothing and leave with nothing except your reputation.

Was I a good man or not? In weighing those words, I find myself reflecting on a life at risk. In doing so, I'm invariably drawn to the dozens of letters written on my behalf prior to my sentencing in New York because they remind me, on page after page, of the positive effect Susan and I have had on the lives of others.

With that and more in mind, I'd like to be remembered for helping all sorts of people. I've tried to give something back. My word is my bond. In the end, I've concluded that the rewards of a singular life have far outweighed the risks.

In sum, there are those who look at the Kentucky kid turned near octogenarian and wonder if ol' Billy Walters has one more card to play. Naysayers predict that I'm about to ride off into the sunset. To which I say what I've always said to those who have doubted me, demeaned me, or otherwise tried to destroy me:

Don't bet on it.

Acknowledgments

This book would not be possible without the support, input, and patience of Susan B. Walters, my partner in life for going on fifty years. She was with me every step of the way on this journey. Her advice and influence appear on each page.

I started working on this book in 2005 with author Jack Sheehan. His early contributions were instrumental in helping shape the manuscript. Author Kevin Cook also worked with me for a brief period while I was in prison. I want to extend a special thank-you to Armen Keteyian, my journalist-friend-companion on this lengthy trip. Armen and I met in the summer of 2020. We spent hundreds of hours together in person and on the phone sorting through the ebbs and flows of my life in painstaking detail. Armen's award-winning reporting and storytelling skills were essential in telling my life story the way I wanted to tell it.

In that same vein, I want to acknowledge the efforts of Glenn F. Bunting and his team at the strategic communications firm G.F.Bunting+CO for their expertise and guidance in overseeing this project. Glenn offered trenchant editorial advice and counsel throughout. Dave Satterfield stepped in at a critical juncture to help with several of the more complex chapters. Miranda Jilka kept this speeding train from running off the tracks. Jenny Coyne provided crucial assistance from start to finish.

Writer Wes Smith and researcher Caroline Borge Keenan also provided indispensable support.

At Simon & Schuster, I can't say enough about Jofie Ferrari-

Adler, vice president and publisher of Avid Reader Press. His careful and concise editing lifted *Gambler* to another level. Along with Jofie, I would like to thank the team at S&S, including president Jon Karp; David Kass, head of publicity; Carolyn Kelly, assistant editor; and Rob Sternitzky, copyeditor.

On the literary side, I want to thank my agent, David Vigliano, for his belief in and stewardship of the book from his first reading to last. My longtime attorney, Richard Wright, deserves a standing ovation for standing by my side in one legal battle after another for more than forty years. A round of applause goes to entertainment attorney Ken Ziffren and his team at Ziffren Brittenham for having my back at all times.

I am truly blessed to have so many loyal and unwavering relatives, friends, and supporters and I would have to write another book to list them all. That said, I do want to acknowledge some of the special people in my life.

The list begins with cherished family members—my father, Thurman Walters; my mother, Aileen "Dale" Quesenberry Walters; and most of all, my grandmother Lucy Quesenberry. I am thankful to grandfathers, aunts, uncles, nieces, nephews, cousins, grandchildren, great-grandchildren, and especially my daughter, Tonia, for all their love and understanding throughout the years. The same love and affection that I have for my sons, Scott and Derin.

My closest friends include Jim Colbert, Ray "Cabbage" Coy, Mac Davis, Dr. Hugh Greenway, Calvin Hash, Johnny Humphries, Luther James, Sammy Marrillia, Mo Moorman, Randy Peterson, Brent Rice, J. T. Sims, Herb Vine, Garland "Big Maverick" Walters, and Bob Ward.

A shout-out goes to the cast and crew at The Walters Companies, led by Mike Luce, Jeff Colton, Joe Dahlstrom, and Mitchell Epstein.

Heartfelt thanks go to my gambling buddies present and past

who have put up with my shenanigans. They include Bobby Baldwin, Billy Baxter, Jack Binion, Carl Boblitt, Nick Bogdanovich, Doyle Brunson, Alan "Red" Dvorkis, Sarge Ferris, John Kent, Mike Kent, Jay Kornegay, Jack Newton, Gene McCarlie, Puggy Pearson, Chip Reese, Mark Thayer, Dewey Tomko, John Trijonis, and Stu Unger.

My golf mentors and friends deserve special mention: Jimmy Ballard, Scotty Cameron, Roger Cleveland, David Feherty, Jason Finley, Mark Ford, Hank George, Billy Harmon, Butch Harmon, Dick Helmstetter, Peter Jacobson, Joe Kelly, David Leadbetter, Jim "Bones" Mackay, Roger Maxwell, Gary McCord, Eddie Merrins, Mike Nuich, John Redman, Jerry Roberts, Greg Trias, Terry Turigliatti, Paul Vizanko, and Bob Vokey.

And, finally, a big thank-you to my partners in the automobile industry: Bob Bayer, Sam Brnovich, Jared Gaiennie, Nathan Stahl, Marius Telehoi, and Dave Zuchowski.

Index

About the Author

WILLIAM T. "BILLY" WALTERS is a living legend among gamblers and sports bettors worldwide. An adopted son of Las Vegas, Walters has had great success in business, real estate, investing, and gambling. He also has been flat broke many times. Born into poverty in rural Kentucky, Walters has battled personal addictions, mob figures, and overzealous federal agents. He is also one of the top philanthropists in Las Vegas.